From Children's Services to Children's Spaces

More than ever before, children are apparently being recognised as social actors and citizens. Yet public policy often involves increased control and surveillance of children. This book explores the contradiction. It shows how different ways of thinking about children produce different childhoods, different public provisions for children (including schools) and different ways of working with children. It argues that how we understand children and make public provision for them involves political and ethical choices.

Through case studies and the analysis of policy and practice drawn from a number of countries, the authors describe an approach to public provision for children which they term 'children's services'. They then propose an alternative approach named 'children's spaces', and go on to consider an alternative theory, practice and profession of work with children: pedagogy and the pedagogue.

This ground breaking book will be essential reading for tutors and students on higher education or in-service courses in early childhood, education, play, social work and social policy, as well as practitioners and policy makers in these areas.

Peter Moss is Professor of Early Childhood Provision and **Pat Petrie** is Reader in Education, at the Thomas Coram Research Unit, Institute of Education University of London.

From Children's Services to Children's Spaces

Public Policy, Children and Childhood

Peter Moss and Pat Petrie

London and New York

First published 2002 by RoutledgeFalmer
11 New Fetter Lane, London EC4P 4EE

Simultaneously published in the USA and Canada
by RoutledgeFalmer
29 West 35th Street, New York, NY 10001

RoutledgeFalmer is an imprint of the Taylor & Francis Group

© 2002 Peter Moss and Pat Petrie

Typeset in Sabon by BC Typesetting, Bristol
Printed and bound in Great Britain by
St Edmundsbury Press, Bury St Edmunds, Suffolk

British Library Cataloguing in Publication Data
A catalogue record for this book is available from the British Library

Library of Congress Cataloging in Publication Data
A catalog record for this book has been requested

ISBN 0–415–24781–0 (hbk)
ISBN 0–415–24782–9 (pbk)

Contents

Acknowledgements

This book has been developed over several years, and draws on ideas, experience and information made available to us by many people and many organisations. It has also been made possible by the generosity of several different funders, in particular the Paul Hamlyn Foundation. We are grateful to all of these and hope that we have acknowledged them, by name, in earlier publications that arose from specific projects. It is difficult, if not impossible at this stage, to mention by name all who have contributed to our thinking; however there are some individuals who we would especially like to thank. They are the people who read and commented on the early discussion paper that was to lead to this book. They include Lisbeth Flising, Tim Gill, Linda Kinney, Barbara Martin Korpi, Marion Kozak, Melian Mansfield, Sandra Mellville, Ann Phoenix and Shelagh Webb, all of whom made stimulating and productive comments on what we had written. We thank, too, our colleagues at Thomas Corm Research Unit for the support they have provided over the years.

1   In praise of many possibilities

A children's space

The *Venture* is an adventure playground, in a town in North Wales. It occupies a large area of ground, perhaps 2 acres, enclosed with a wooden stockade. In addition to being a playground for a wide age range of children, *Venture* includes a playgroup, motor bike club, homework club and reading club, all of which are very popular with children, many of whom have not been succeeding at school. Activities are seen as a means for forming relationships with and between children and this is an important part of the work.

The terrain is varied in many ways. There are open spaces for ball games, an enclosed camp fire area with its own graffiti board (when one of us visited, there were no other graffiti on the site), ramps, tyre swings, aerial runways, platforms and towers built of logs and a tree house area. It has been in existence for more than twenty years and the manager says that this is 'children's own space'. They use it for their purposes and their friendship groups. Older children may ride and repair their bikes, younger children play in the sand, while parents can come and sit with their toddlers.

In the course of using the playground, children gradually come to take responsibility for it. They rake sand, make a cup of tea, take over from staff in games with younger children and get involved in the staff group activities in other ways. The manager says it would be impossible to operate with so few staff without the children's consent: 'staff respect children for what they are, not for what they want them to become. This is a refuge where they can be themselves.' Staff must explain and negotiate with the children, rather than take an authoritarian stand. There are only a few rules, which are based on health and safety considerations. For their part, children have the expectation that staff will respect them. They take part in staff selection, meeting candidates and giving their opinions.

The manager says that children are aware of child abuse, 'but if there is no sign of physical affection between child and adult, then something has been cut off. If a child likes an adult, they'll touch them'. He comments that respecting children's rights is the biggest safeguard against abuse, because children who are listened to and respected will be assertive in their dealings with adults, reject unwelcome advances and discuss any problems with those adults who they can trust to take their concerns seriously.

What we are about

This book is about the possibility of rethinking public provisions[1] for children – or rather, it is about *one* possibility out of the many possibilities that might exist. It is about how public provisions for children might be reconceptualised as ethical and political endeavours that require explicit choices about who we think children are, what is a good childhood and the purposes of public provisions for children. This reconceptualisation is in place of an image of provisions as primarily technical and disciplinary undertakings, concerned with regulation, surveillance and normalisation, instrumental in rationality and purpose. It is about how public provisions for children are inextricably linked with how we understand childhood and our image of the child, which are taken to be contestable constructions produced in the social arena rather than essential truths revealed through science. It is about situating public provision for children within an analysis of a changing world and the implications of that world for such provision. But it is also about how this provision, through being a site for democratic and ethical practice involving critical thinking, might contribute to the political project of influencing the direction change takes – how children and their provisions may come to shape an uncertain future rather than being shaped for a predictable and predetermined future.

The book is about the possibility of public provisions for children being envisioned as spaces for children and for the childhoods children are living here and now, as well as for creating relationships and solidarities between children, between adults and between adults and children. In taking this standpoint, we want to question a number of ways in which public provisions for children are commonly justified, for example: the rescue and protection of children who are needy, weak and poor; the protection of society from children who represent a threat to order and progress; the child viewed as futurity, as a becoming adult, as a redemptive agent, epitomised by what has been termed the 'myth of infant determinism' (Kagan 1998) – 'that early experience . . . leaves an indelible, irreversible mark on the mind–brain–psyche for life' (Bruer 1999: 29) – and the belief that powerful human technologies applied to children below a certain age (the current favourite is under 3 years) will cure our social and economic ills.

Of course, some children do need protection, others can pose threats. But we question the consequences of a discourse about childhood dominated by such constructs and their accompanying images. Of course, there are connections between the child's present and the child's future. The present leaves traces on the future. The future has been reached through the present.

But we doubt the linearity and inevitability of the relationship; question the critical importance and irrevocable consequences of early experience; and have serious reservations about the devaluation of childhood *per se*, the ethics of instrumentality and the abrogation of adult responsibility that follow from a belief in the child, and her normalisation, as a cure for society's ills.

We are also led to ask why so much attention is given just now, at least in the English-language world, to interventions with children, especially young children. Or rather, taking a more historical perspective, why now appears to be an interventionist high point in the cycles of intervention going back at least to the nineteenth century, whose rationale has been a concern for the conditions and practices of the poor and anxiety about their consequences for social stability and national performance, military, colonial or economic (see, for example, Rose (1990) for a critical historical analysis of attempts to 'govern the soul' of children and their families). Is it because services, initiatives and programmes, targeted at children, seem to offer promising technical solutions to the social damage caused by a neo-liberal market capitalism that has gained a prominent position in parts of the English-language world (in the USA, New Zealand, Australia, as well as the UK) over the last twenty years (Gray 1999) – solutions which require neither questioning of the values nor regulation of the processes embedded in this form of capitalism? Is 'social engineering' of children's lives the way to give the modern nation state a competitive edge in the global rat race? Can it provide a means of reconciling the promotion of an 'enterprise economy' with aspirations to social cohesion and social justice? Does the practice of free markets and individual choice need greater discipline and control, so that more economic deregulation requires greater social regulation?

Finally, it could perhaps be said that this book is about 'modernisation' of public provision for children. If the reader detects a certain hesitancy to use this term, she would be right. For 'modernisation' is one of those words much used and beloved of government (at least in Britain), offered as an unarguable justification for change – but which on closer scrutiny reminds us that we live in 'a civilisation of clichés' (Rajchman 2000). Like all clichés, 'modernisation' is used as if it had one self-evident, shared and uncontestable meaning. Its use is intended to limit discussion (for who can be against 'modernisation'?) rather than to open up many possibilities. Yet there are many possible ways of 'modernising', and 'modern' societies come in many forms (Gray 1999). Rather than there being only one true way to be followed of necessity, there are choices to be made about how we understand the modern world and the past through which it has emerged, about what needs changing and about what changes to make. In this book we offer one of those choices.

We shall return to these themes and questions. But first we want to explain how we have come to write this book.

Children's services: time for a new approach

> Before we can arrive at the right answer, we have to decide the right question. . . . [P]resent-day children's services are too often answers to the wrong questions. What are the right questions to be asking? There are many, but we would suggest five are of pre-eminent importance:
>
> - What do we want for our children?
> - What is a good childhood?
> - What is the place of children and childhood in our society?
> - What should be the relationship between children, parents and society?
> - What is the quality of relationship we wish to promote between children and adults at home, in children's services and in society at large?
>
> We have long neglected these fundamental questions and the issues they raise. As a result we have not developed services, policies and government structures that adequately meet the needs and interests of children as a social group.
>
> A public debate about these important questions is overdue. It is time to develop a new discourse about children, childhood and the relationship between children, parents and society. It is time for a new approach to services, policies and government structures informed by this new discourse. It is time to welcome children, with all their diversity, as young citizens, equal stakeholders with adults in a common social enterprise.
>
> (Moss and Petrie 1997: 15–16)

These were the concluding words of a discussion paper we wrote in early 1997, *Children's Services: Time for a New Approach*. After many years of following our own specialist interests (one of us in the 'early years' field, the other in the 'school age' field, symptomatic of the fragmented and atomising approach we shall question later), we thought it would be interesting to collaborate in taking a broader view of services for children, from birth through to the end of school. The discussion paper was the first result of this collaboration.

In the discussion paper, and focusing our attention on Britain, we produced a critique of existing children's services. We argued that services were:

- fragmented, compartmentalised and 'uni-functional', both the concept and the purposes of services being too narrowly conceived;

- that consequently resources were often wasted, citing in particular the potential of the school which 'has been too little recognised and even less exploited';
- that new developments were the product of piecemeal initiatives often originating from different agencies with different values, cultures, policies, concepts and objectives;
- that the pay and other employment conditions of staff who worked with children are often poor, their training limited, their work devalued; and
- that in most children's services, children are excluded in a variety of ways.

Overall 'the broader social and cultural roles of services and their contribution to childhood and the lives of children are often overlooked. . . . [Instead] the image that springs to mind is of factories processing children on behalf of adults, in order to produce "better" adults for the future' (ibid.: 9).

But we tried to go beyond a list of problems. We tried to understand *how* this situation had come about. We sought some answers in what we called a dominant discourse about children and their relationships with parents and society, suggesting that this dominant discourse had been very productive of policy and provision. In particular, we saw three ideas lying at the heart of this dominant discourse: that children are the *private* responsibility of parents; that children are *passive* dependants; and that parents are *consumers* of marketised services for children. These ideas 'construct children as *poor* and *weak*'.

We touched on how a different discourse about children and childhood, which foregrounded the child as a citizen, a member of a social group with rights, might construct children as 'rich in potential, strong, powerful and competent'. It might also produce a new approach to children's services, with services conceptualised differently and with broader purposes:

> [as a means] for enriching childhood, promoting children's culture and enabling children to participate in an essential world of relationships and activities. . . . Children's services should be a means for fostering the visibility, inclusion and active participation of all children in society. . . . Children's services should be conceptualised as community institutions, public spaces where children and adults engage together on a variety of projects of social, cultural, political and economic significance.
>
> (Ibid.: 12–13)

This new approach would have implications for the organisation of services, for example the possibility that a new type of profession would be needed to work across a wide range of services, more effective government structures for children and stronger consultation with children. We paid particular attention to the place of the school, which from the start we viewed as a children's service:

> Despite their dominant position, schools for the most part stand as a perfect example of the narrow, compartmentalised and uni-functional nature of most modern children's services. . . . This narrow vision represents a lost opportunity and a wasteful use of resources. . . . There is potential here: for community building, for social inclusion and participation and for making a major contribution to the development of a new approach to children's services. . . . The school is not, and should not be, the only institutional basis for a new approach to children's services – but it could play an important part. The position of the school – and our construction of 'schooling' – needs reconsideration in any proposals for new models for children's services.
>
> (Ibid.: 14–15)

Finally, we were concerned that the discourse of children as citizens and as being 'rich in potential, strong, powerful and competent' should apply to children across the board. Children should not, in any way, be excluded from full participation in services by reason of socially divisive understandings of gender, race, disability and social class.

Rethinking schools

> In our view, rethinking the relationship between school, family and community also means rethinking schools and other services for children – their purposes, their administration and legislation, and the structure of staffing. And this in turn requires rethinking children and childhood. . . . [For] concepts and practices are produced from particular discourses about, and constructions of, children and childhood.
>
> (Moss *et al.* 1999: 38–39)

Two pieces of funding enabled us to take these initial ideas further. First, we were commissioned by a British foundation to look at evidence from other countries of 'ways in which, and in what circumstances, the involvement of school beyond the conventional boundaries of formal education (as understood in Britain) can generate benefits (however defined) for children/ young people, their families and local communities'. We decided to conduct case studies of relations and collaborations between school, family and community in three countries – France, Sweden and the USA – and these formed the basis of our report, *Rethinking School: Some International Perspectives* (Moss *et al.* 1999). This comparative approach proved very revealing.

American initiatives (which, it seemed to us, had much in common with those in Britain) were mainly targeted at particular 'high risk' areas or groups with the intention of reversing economic inequality and social dislocation, and were driven by alarm at the conditions of children. We further noted that:

> while much of the discussion [in the USA] is about children, and in particular their poor structural position, there is no discussion about who children might be nor about childhood or the possibility of its social construction. . . . As Baker (1998) observes, in relation to the American public school, 'much educational work flows around assumptions about children and their development – but what is meant by being a child is not debated' (118). . . . There is an implicitly individualistic approach to children, with no recognition in the discourse that children might be understood as a social group and no reference to concepts such as children's culture or children's rights or indeed the possibility of children themselves having agency. . . . [C]hildhood emerges as a state of adulthood in waiting. Children as becoming adults are valued (or feared) for what they will be when 'fully developed' (the discourse of 'development' producing adulthood as a completed state of being).
>
> (Ibid.: 25–26)

Swedish developments, by contrast, were not targeted. They were concerned instead to reform and extend a system of services with a strong tradition of universal provision and within a strong discourse of democracy, participation and children's rights: 'issues of social exclusion [were] not prominent, perhaps because other policies have prevented or mitigated processes of inequality and dislocation' (ibid.: 37). Within this context, new understandings of the child were emerging, the child

> as an active and creative actor, as a subject and citizen with potentials, rights and responsibility. A child worth listening to and having a dialogue with and who has the courage to think and act by himself. . . . This child is seen as having power over his own learning processes and having the right to interpret the world.
>
> (Dahlberg 1997: 22)

France came somewhere in between, with both extensive and long established universal services and programmes targeted at disadvantaged areas, all within a framework of strong republican values emphasising citizenship, equality, secularity and culture. Less individualistic than the American child, but also less autonomous than the Swedish child, the construction given to the French child is as

> a future adult citizen of France, who will, through effective education and induction into French culture, be the equal of their peers. A focus

on school achievement promotes future equality and secures the child's
future civic status.

(Moss *et al.* 1999: 13)

What was particularly apparent, as these excerpts show, was how
national differences of policy and provision in our subject of study –
relationships between schools, families and communities – were produced
not only from different political and economic contexts, but from particular
discourses about, and constructions of, children and childhood.

> For example, Sweden and the US have quite different policy agendas,
> not just because their economic and social conditions are different, but
> because as societies they understand children and childhood differently.
> That is why we have emphasised from the beginning the need to com-
> bine a legitimate concern with effectiveness (management and measure-
> ment) with an equally legitimate concern with values, in particular the
> ethical issues involved in how we choose to understand childhood and
> the relationship between children, family, local community and wider
> society.
>
> (Ibid.: 39)

This work added to our interest in the relationship between understandings of children and the public provisions that are made for them. It made
concrete the idea of different possibilities. It suggested that though there
were many social and economic constraints, some degree of choice existed
which implied scope for agency, and the importance of political and ethical
considerations in applying that agency. It also added to earlier indications
that structural reforms to public provisions for children in Sweden in the
late 1990s (including schools, out of school provision and early years
services) were one part of an important national experience also involving
a process of rethinking – not only of the child, and indeed of work with
children, but also of concepts such as 'learning' and 'knowledge'.

After the publication of our discussion paper, we received funding from
another British foundation to explore the approach outlined in that paper
and its implications in more detail – what it might mean in practice to transform children's services. This enabled us to visit a variety of locations both
in the UK and in Scandinavia, in particular in Sweden, selected because
they seemed to be working in innovative and interesting ways and had
something in common with the approach to children's services we had
proposed. It also gave us time to write this book.

From children's services to children's spaces

> Our experience [of pre-school services in Reggio Emilia] is only one
> possibility out of many. Behind every solution and organisation is a

choice, a choice of values and ethics, a social and political choice, and a responsibility for that choice. The identity of our schools is based on concepts and values. We do not offer a recipe, nor a method, our work is not to be copied because values can only be lived not copied.
(Carlina Rinaldi, director of pre-school services in Reggio-Emilia[2] 1999a)

We initially envisaged writing a book called 'Transforming Children's Services', taking a broad view, across a wide age range from birth to adolescence and across a wide range of children's services, including schools. But as time went on, we came to a different conclusion: that a different understanding of children and their place in society and of the purposes of public policy in relation to children leads not to a new approach to, or transformation of, 'children's services'. It leads instead to the possibility of a quite different concept, a rethinking of public provisions for children. It has become our purpose to construct and explore this different concept, which we have termed 'children's spaces'.

Both concepts – 'children's services' and 'children's spaces' – can be applied to a wide range of institutions, including schools, nurseries and centres providing for school-age children outside school hours. What distinguishes these concepts are different understandings of children and the purposes of these institutions, from which other things flow: the two concepts produce different practices, different relationships, different ethics and different forms of evaluation. The concept of 'children's services', so it seems to us, is bound up in a particular understanding of public provisions for children: a very instrumental and atomising notion, in which provisions are technologies for acting upon children, or parts of children, to produce specific, predetermined and adult-defined outcomes. The concept of 'children's spaces' understands provisions as environments of many possibilities – cultural and social, but also economic, political, ethical, aesthetic, physical – some predetermined, others not, some initiated by adults, others by children: it presumes unknown resources, possibilities and potentials. These environments are understood as more public places for children to live their childhoods, alongside the more private domain of the home.

The concept of 'children's space' does not just imply a *physical* space, a setting for groups of children. It also carries the meaning of being a *social* space, 'a domain of social practices and relationships' (Knowles 1999: 241); a *cultural* space, where values, rights and cultures are created; and a *discursive* space for differing perspectives and forms of expression, where there is room for dialogue, confrontation (in the sense of exchanging differing experience and views), deliberation and critical thinking, where children and others can speak and be heard. In this sense, the concept of 'children's space' implies possibilities for children and adults to contest understandings, values, practices and knowledges. The concept of 'children's space' is linked to an ethos, constituted by certain understandings of children, a certain type of relationship between children and adults and certain ethical perspectives. It requires a theory and practice of working with children, and a worker able to work with children in a wide range of settings. We discuss the concept of 'children's spaces', and these physical, social, discursive and ethical components of meaning, in more detail later in the book. We also consider pedagogy as an approach – theoretical and practical – to working with children in 'children's spaces', and the pedagogue as a worker able to use this approach.

Making narratives stutter

Rather than 'transforming children's services', we want to suggest that the concept of 'children's services' (however formed, reformed or transformed) is, as Carlina Rinaldi puts it, one possibility for social policy out of many – and to put forward instead another possibility. We do not claim it as *the* possibility. It relates to a value system which we have developed – and continue to develop – as a result of different personal, professional and political experiences and through dialogue together and with others. Furthermore, as two writers we do not claim to hold one view and speak with one voice: on occasion we might each choose a somewhat different emphasis, viewing the landscape of childhood and children's provisions from rather different perspectives. Our readers, too, will have their own perspectives, their own experiences, political positions, practical concerns and value bases.

This book is, therefore, work in progress for both of us, part of a process of developing a different perspective on public policy and children, and exploring a possibility produced through that perspective. We talk about a *perspective* and a *possibility*, here and elsewhere, because there are many ways of seeing and understanding children and the provisions that we, as a society, make for children through the agency of public policy. To support and illustrate this assertion, we offer some examples in the book of texts and places – individual institutions, local communities, countries – which understand children and public provision for children in different ways.

We offer such examples not as models or programmes to be replicated or generalised, a concept with which we are uneasy, but more as lenses through which we may view ways of doing things and the assumptions that underpin them. We argue in the next chapter that working with different theories offers another set of lenses. This exercise of looking through different lenses can make the invisible visible, the familiar strange. It enables us to see better the values that permeate how we think, to ask questions about practice and the assumptions that underlie what we do, and to think critically.

The process of critical thinking involves, in Michel Foucault's words, 'stepping back from a way of acting or reacting to present it to oneself as an object of thought', 'the development of a given into a question' and, thus, 'showing things are not as self-evident as one believed' (Foucault

1988: 155). Nikolas Rose, influenced by the ideas of Foucault as well as his compatriot Gilles Deleuze, describes critical thought in his recent analysis of political power as

> partly a matter of introducing a critical attitude towards those things that are given to our present experience as if they were timeless, natural, unquestionable: to stand against the maxims of one's time, against the spirit of one's age, against the current of received wisdom. It is a matter of introducing a kind of awkwardness into the fabric of one's experience, of interrupting the fluency of the narratives that encode that experience and making them stutter.
>
> (Rose 1999: 20)

Critical thinking enables us to speak of questions and possibilities rather than givens and necessities. It shows us there are choices to be made between possibilities, that the usual way of proceeding is not self-evident, that there is no one 'best practice' or 'standard of quality' to be found (since such concepts are always value-laden and relative), that there may be more than one possible answer to any question. Moreover, these choices are not just between different methods or solutions, seeking an answer to the *zeitgeist* question of 'what works?' The choices are more fundamental, and require us first to formulate questions: 'what do we want for our children?', 'what is a good childhood?', 'what is the place of children in society?', 'who do we think children are?', 'what are the purposes of institutions/services/spaces for children?', 'what is education for?', 'what do we mean by care?' – and so on. The answers to these questions – even 'what works?' – cannot be reduced to the technical and managerial. They require choices to be made that are ethical and political in nature, and a recognition and acceptance of the responsibility that goes with making such choices.

We have come to share the view of the Italian historian Carlo Ginsberg (1989) that we live in a culture where we are constantly being offered solutions before we have asked the critical questions. Carlina Rinaldi (1999a) expresses a similar view when she observes that industrial culture has the idea that we can always find a solution for everything, rather than needing to understand, and is full of techniques to provide solutions just by pressing a button. As we shall discuss later, behind this cultural belief lies the powerful Enlightenment urge to master and manage the world and all that lives thereon, for the attainment of certain universal and predetermined goals; and the increasing dominance of a certain sort of economic or business ethic whose overriding and universal value is return on investment. In contemporary Britain, and perhaps in some other countries too, it seems all of us who work with children are increasingly expected to concentrate on universal, predetermined outcomes and methods for achieving these outcomes, pressing the right button, crowding out possibilities to think, question, understand, discuss, contest and reflect. Children are products to be efficiently processed by a workforce of technicians, applying technologies of specialisation each focused on a particular bit of the child: the 'atomisation' of the child in the structures, practices and theories of 'children's services' will be another recurring theme in this book.

To suggest the need for critical questions and to deepen understanding, for time to think and discuss, is not, however, a recipe for inaction and navel gazing. Carlina Rinaldi has headed a system of nurseries and nursery schools whose work with young children over many years has achieved world-wide recognition and admiration. Rather it is to question the consequences of action without thought, of technology and management divorced from contested ethics and politics, and of solutions offered without understandings – of opting for 'vulgar pragmatism' rather than a more 'critical pragmatism':

> *Vulgar pragmatism* holds that a conception is to be tested by its practical effects ... what is true and valued is what works in terms of what exists. This is another face of instrumentalism in pursuit of production and efficiency. . . . This form of pragmatism is unreflective and dangerous. . . . Vulgar pragmatism tests ideas and practices by comparing them to traditional and conventional norms with little or no sense of crisis or criticism. . . . [Vulgar pragmatists] promote local ideologies as global and past ideologies as those of the present and future. . . . *Critical pragmatism* continually involves making epistemological, ethical and aesthetic choices and translating them into discourses–practices. Criticisms and judgements about good and bad, beautiful and ugly and truth and falsity are made in the context of our communities and our attempts to build them anew. They are not decided by reference to universal norms that produce 'definitive' and 'objective' decisions.
>
> (Cherryholmes 1988: 178–179: emphasis added)

So, by using the language of perspectives and possibilities, we want to reflect a particular understanding of the task in hand – thinking critically about the provisions that we, as a society acting through public policy, make for children, putting a stutter into the narratives which speak as if they were the only possible version of events. We want to confront and question the 'modernist tendency in social science and management practice to convert what are essentially moral and ethical problems to technical and administrative ones' (Schwandt 1996a: 3). We also use this language to avoid implying that we (or indeed anyone else) have, or could have, *the* plan, *the* map, *the* blueprint, offering a final solution based on true knowledge. Instead, we see work on policy, provision and practice as always provisional and always contestable, because values differ, times change and new understandings emerge – the world of 2001 is very different to that of 1971, and it is a brave person who would claim to know how things will be – or even how we will think about things – in 2011 let alone 2071. Moreover (as we have said), this book is part of a work in progress – we cannot claim to have reached the end of a complex and wide-ranging undertaking, nor do we expect (or even hope) to do so, preferring provisionality to foreclosure.

The language of perspectives and possibilities also denotes the value we attach to dissensus, difference and 'keeping the question of meaning open as a locus for debate' (Readings 1997). Again, we do not see this as a recipe for inaction and apathy: positions have to be taken, measures defined and acted upon. However, we would argue the need to understand these positions and measures as choices made in relation to particular conditions and values, choices for which we must take responsibility, rather than context- and value-free technologically determined 'best practice'. By raising this we confront a large and difficult issue: how to work with diversity and complexity, uncertainty and plurality, democratically and ethically, in a society like Britain which has a strong tradition of centralisation (which expects standardisation and control), high levels of inequality (which provide a rationale for prescriptive practices in the interests of equity and the hope of eradicating inequality), a great need of certainty, and is in thrall to what the Scottish Council Foundation calls 'a culture of number' and the belief that 'scientific objectivity will explain all' (1999: 10).

Our intention, therefore, is not oppositional, although it is critical. We believe there are different perspectives and possibilities, each of which needs to be both respected and problematised. Nor do different perspectives mean necessarily 'either/or'. For example, we may problematise concepts such as 'the child in need' or 'learning outcomes', but that does not mean that we wish to ignore child protection, deny some children require additional support or reject the acquisition of certain skills. Similarly, we take a somewhat sceptical view of the current dominance of managerialism, viewing it as a historically specific form of authority, with a 'globalising and imperialistic logic which proclaims itself as the universally applicable solution to the problems of inefficiency, incompetence, and chaos in the old ways of providing public services' (Clarke 1998: 174). But we would still recognise the need for management skills as one of a range of conditions needed to support the provision of 'children's spaces'.

The rest of the book

In Chapter 2 we explore some of the main influences on our thinking about children and public policy, including theories we find useful. Then, in Chapter 3, we outline a discourse about childhood which we argue is very influential in Britain, and also perhaps in some other countries, and consider its consequences for how childhood and public provisions for children are understood, in particular the image of the 'poor child' and the concept of 'children's services'. We also examine why, in some respects, this discourse is becoming more influential at this particular moment.

In Chapter 4 we offer some examples of this discourse in contemporary Britain, through a reading of some recent policy documents.

We then change tack, to explore another possibility. In Chapters 5 and 6 we proffer another discourse, which produces another understanding of childhood and another concept of public provision, as 'children's spaces'. We consider what some of the possibilities of 'children's spaces' might be, including learning, children's culture and a politics of childhood. In Chapter 7, we explore pedagogy, a theory and practice of working with children, widely established in continental Europe, but less well known in Britain and other English-language countries. Pedagogy, we suggest, provides one possible approach to working with children in public provisions understood as 'children's spaces'.

Chapter 8 offers a case taken at a particular point in time – Sweden around the year 2000 – which illustrates a country which seems to be working, to some degree at least, with the discourse about children and childhood we outline in Chapter 5. Sweden provides an example of a society which now works with an explicit recognition that there are different ways of understanding the child, each bringing in train its own major consequences. Sweden as a case is not a clear cut and exact example of the discourse we outline in Chapter 5, but it still serves to illustrate our argument about the connections between understandings of childhood and public provisions for children.

In the final chapter, 9, we talk about our work contributing to a crisis of thinking about children and the provisions we, as a society, make for them. We also admit to some of the risks and contradictions that we see in our line of argument – just as there are in any line of argument. While eschewing a prescription – 'a ten point Children's Spaces plan' – we offer some thoughts on conditions that might encourage local innovation along the lines we have discussed. For we think that local efforts to ask critical questions and seek satisfying answers provide an important possibility for thinking differently, creating new practice and producing children's spaces.

As a final point by way of introduction, we wish to situate ourselves as authors. First, we acknowledge that we are speaking as adults about children, begging the question of what children might themselves contribute to the discussion. We believe that children, if they wish, should themselves engage in any discussion of children and childhood. They, after all, are experts in their own lives and experiences. To this extent, our position is paradoxical. We are engaging in a cultural form and a cultural arena – academic writing – that is unlikely to be accessible or appealing to children (or to many adults for that fact), while at the same time we shall argue for children's social participation and citizenship. Not to have included children themselves in our deliberations means that the perspective we take is certainly not theirs, although there may be some echoes of, and direct references to, what some children have told us in the course of various research projects.

The representation of children within this discussion, if we had made that choice, would have presented considerable methodological difficulties. While children in this society share some characteristics in common, any particular child, or group of children, occupies a social position that derives from, for example, gender, age, ethnicity, skin colour, disability status, poverty and wealth: social and physical characteristics that relate to powerful systems of control. Discussing children in the abstract by means of the term 'childhood', or speaking of 'the child' as though this is a universal position, blinds us to important social facts about actual children and their lives.

Any particular child has a specific social identity. Like adults, different children have different perspectives on childhood, connected to this identity, the specific social contexts in which they live their lives and the matters that concern them immediately. A sample of children from all of these contexts would be required to properly represent children in this discussion. Our intention in writing is, however, more limited. In this book, we offer one set of perspectives, our own, and choose to engage with a limited sector of other adults, rather than with children or, indeed, with adults across the social board, while recognising that for adults to engage in this discussion is to do so from a position of relative power *vis-à-vis* children.

We want to recognise one other aspect of our situation. Our lives, including our research, are situated in Britain – or, to be more specific, in England, one part of Britain, appreciating that recent decentralisation policies in Britain, which have devolved powers to Scotland and Wales, have led to increasing diversity between the constituent parts of Britain.[3] We understand and try to make sense of the world through a lens of English experience and the medium of English language (the dominance of which in many aspects of communication is a superficial benefit to us, but also deeply disturbing for its effects on power and knowledge, diversity and complexity).

However, we have tried to write with a non-English reader in mind, avoiding parochial detail and offering a modicum of contextual information. Our hope is that much of what we write about, although England-based, will interest a wider audience. One reason for such presumption is that much discourse and practice in England relates to a powerful Anglo-American[4] narrative about children and children's services, spoken in the English language. Located in a liberal political and economic context, and dominated by certain disciplinary perspectives, the narrative is inscribed with Enlightenment assumptions about objectivity, mastery and universality, and with particular understandings of childhood, learning, evaluation and so on. It offers a particular construction of childhood, and generates particular problems, questions and methods. It is a regime of truth about children's services as a technology for social stability and economic progress, the child as a redemptive vehicle to be programmed to become a solution to certain problems. It is instrumental in rationality, universalist in ethics, technical in its approach. It produces a public policy which, as Alan Prout (2000) observes, emphasises control, regulation and surveillance.

This forceful narrative insists on being heard throughout the world, amplified by the cultural, economic and scientific influence of the USA and the emergence of English as a *lingua franca*. It threatens to drown out other, quieter narratives: it expects to be heard but is reluctant to listen to and understand others. Coming from the Anglo-American world and being native English speakers enables us to question the dominating narrative from a particular 'insider' perspective, as well as to voice some of the other, quieter narratives being spoken in our world and in our language. By trying to put a stutter in the dominating narrative, we may encourage others to get a word in edgeways.

2 The need for some theory

The British pride themselves on being a pragmatic people, with a practical turn of mind. Problems are stated and solutions found. Theory is suspect, an excuse for unwarranted and distorting prejudice. This view is expressed by a senior British politician when speaking about a new programme – Sure Start – focused on young children and their families living in economically disadvantaged areas: '[Sure Start] is based on evidence and experience, not on theory and dogma' (Sure Start Unit 1999: 22). Other charges laid against theory include incomprehensibility and distracting irrelevance. So we approach this chapter with some trepidation, for we must admit that it seems to us that theories are important and inescapable.

We do not believe there is a choice between 'theory' and 'no theory', or indeed between 'theory' and 'practice'. Nor that somehow 'evidence' or 'experience' can be neutrally produced and interpreted, and that actions self-evidently and inevitably follow. Theories – whether in the form of academic, political or professional ideas, or offered in the guise of 'common sense' – shape our understandings and govern our actions, whether we recognise this or not, through the concepts and explanations they provide us with to make sense of the world and our experience.

One way of thinking about theories is as filters, with which we construct an understanding of the world from what these filters let in and retain. Or they can be thought of as lenses. They 'tell' us what 'things' are to be seen and interpreted from an infinite number of events and actions: they 'orient the observer to the empirical world' (Popkewitz 1998: 15).

Great importance is attached to theory in the pedagogical work in Reggio Emilia, for the part it plays in the search for meaning, as a way of interpreting life:

> For adults and children alike, understanding means being able to develop an interpretative 'theory', a narrative that gives meaning to the events and things of the world. These theories are provisional, offering a satisfactory explanation that can be continuously reworked, but which is something more than simply an idea or a group of ideas. It has to please us and convince us, to be useful, and able to satisfy

our intellectual, affective and aesthetic needs. . . . In representing the world, our theories represent us.

(Rinaldi 2001: 79–80)

Nor are practice and theory in opposition. In Reggio they say that there is no practice without theory, and that theories come from practice.

To be apparently untouched by theory, to take the position of 'no theory', means there is theory – but that it is hidden away and rendered implicit. This gives a misleading impression of self-evident and value-free issues and problems, with attention focused once again on answers, and on the one question 'what works?' But theory *produces* particular questions as well as possible answers, it influences what we constitute as problems as well as what we think might be suitable solutions, what evidence we seek and how we seek it, how we make sense of evidence and experience, the objects of policy and practice, and how we conceptualise, organise and name the interventions of public policy.

The British politician quoted above is speaking in support of a major government initiative and wants his listeners to believe that he speaks some 'evidence-based' truth, unsullied by theory *or* dogma (note theory's guilt by association with dogma). In fact, he relies heavily on theories. Theory offers an explanation, satisfying to the politician, about the cause of poverty, what has been called the 'cycle of deprivation' theory, the idea that disadvantage is passed on from one generation to another. This theory is spelt out by two Ministers in a Foreword to a recent Sure Start publication, when they say that this programme aims 'to break the cycle of disadvantage for this generation of young children' (Morris and Cooper 2001: 2). Yet, it might be asked, how does this theory explain a trebling in the number of children in Britain living in poverty in just twenty years? Why was the increase in child poverty in Britain over this period greater than in other European countries (Department of Social Security 2000; UNICEF 2000)? Why, if most countries managed to stabilise or reduce their child poverty rates in the face of the economic and social changes of the last two decades or so, has Britain 'had one of the fastest-growing child poverty rates – an annual increase between 1974 and 1995 of twice the rate of the United States, for example' (Bradshaw 2001: 15)?

Theory also underpins a policy strategy, to which the politician has committed large sums of public money, which assumes the unique benefits of early intervention. Yet others have argued that this theory of 'infant determinism', with its belief in the overriding importance of the first few years, is a myth. The distinguished American psychologist Jerome Kagan, for example, observes that 'the doctrine of infant determinism ignores the many powerful influences that affect the profile of adolescents and young adults after the second birthday' (1998: 130). Bruer, in his sceptical look at the current American vogue for brain research, also questions what he calls the myth that the first three years of life constitute a unique window of opportunity:

> there is also a substantial body of research that supports the claim that experiences throughout life have a profound effect on personality, character and mental health and that these effects swamp the impact of early childhood experience. ... [L]ooking through the prism of the first three years tends to distort rather then enhance our view of children, brains and social problems.
>
> (Bruer 1999: 53, 209)

The point we are making here is not whether or not the politician's theories prove convincing or useful. But that by assuming a supremely pragmatic approach, he makes his theories invisible, perhaps even to himself, and therefore uncontestable, a practice lacking both rigour and democracy.

In this chapter, we explore some of the theories that we have found important in thinking about childhood and public provision for children, the lenses that we have found to provide us with 'interpretations of life' and 'explanations' that we find satisfying, or at least useful. We hope to make clear where we are coming from and where we are hoping to go. So that in subsequent chapters, when we get down to problematising certain concepts and ideas about childhood and provision for children and offering other concepts and ideas, the reader can understand some of the influences on our particular perspectives. By so doing, by pleading guilty in open court to theory, we want to make what we write more subject to contestation and critical judgement.

Social construction

> The immaturity of children is a biological fact of life but the way in which this immaturity is understood and made meaningful is a fact of culture. It is these 'facts of culture' which may vary and which can be said to make of childhood a social institution. ... [In the emerging new paradigm for the study of childhood] childhood is understood as a social construction. As such it provides an interpretive frame for contextualising the early years of human life. Childhood, as distinct from biological immaturity, is neither a natural nor universal feature of human groups but appears as a specific structural and cultural component of many societies.
>
> (Prout and James 1997: 7, 8)

Social constructionist theory starts from the premise that the world and our knowledge are socially constructed and that all of us, as human beings, are active participants in this process, engaged in meaning making relationship with others.

> In a social constructionist perspective, phenomena in the world around
> are seen as socially constructed phenomena and man as an active and
> creative subject. This way of thinking contains the emancipatory
> potential which means that we as human beings, as actors in our own
> lives, can change ourselves through our actions and in the power of
> the result of our actions.
>
> (Dahlberg 1997: 21)

Social construction therefore is a social process, and can in no way exist
apart from our own involvement in the world. The world is always our
world, understood and constructed by ourselves, not in isolation but as
part of a community of human agents, and through our active interaction
and participation with other people in that community (Berger and
Luckman 1966; Gergen and Gergen 1991; Maturana 1991).

As James and Prout (1997) observe, social constructionism has had a
major impact over the last ten to fifteen years in the field of childhood
studies: 'certainly writers or researchers who do not acknowledge the construction of childhood within socially and historically situated discourse
and who fail to give weight to its variability and relativity are more or
less guaranteed a much more critical reception than was once the case'
(ibid.: x). Rather than 'the child' or 'childhood', an essential and universal
being and state waiting to be discovered, defined and realised, a social constructionist approach has foregrounded plurality and stimulated a growing
interest in the idea of many and diverse childhoods, related to particular
temporal and spatial contexts, and constructed by adults and children themselves through discourse. Social constructionism 'prises the child free of
biological determinism' (James *et al.* 1998: 28).

For while childhood may be a biological fact, the way in which it is
understood and lived is socially determined, within an actively negotiated
set of social relations: 'our images of what a child is, can be and should be,
must be seen as the social construction of a community of human agents,
originating through our active interaction with other people and with
society' (Dahlberg *et al.* 1999: 62). Or, in the words of Carlina Rinaldi
(1999b), 'childhood does not exist, we create it as a society, as a public
subject. It is a social, political and historical construction'. Social constructions, however, do not differ only at the general level of community or
society. Particular disciplines, professions, agencies, settings and policy
areas each create or construct particular versions of childhood and images
of the child shaped by their own theories, understandings and perspectives:
'there is no child, as object-of-study, in a school until discursive strategies
are applied to enable one to "see," think, talk and feel about the object of
study in school' (Popkewitz 1998: 9). Just as there is a 'school' child, or
the child of education, so too there is the child of child development, of
psychoanalysis, of medicine, of play, of social work and so on.

We recognise that the very constructs 'child' and 'childhood' have been questioned. Canella proposes that they require, at the very least, continual critique:

> childhood can be interpreted as a positivist construction that has dis-empowered younger human beings by creating them as incompetent and dependent on adults for care, knowledge, and even bodily control. The discourses of childhood have fostered regulation of a particular group of human beings by another group (described as adults) and generated multiple sites of power for these adults.
>
> (Canella 1997: 44)

We also appreciate that the social constructionist approach is open to criticism for its emphasis on difference rather than identifying common features of childhood. This represents a major problem for those who take a more structural approach which identifies children as an exploited and inferior social group (Wyness 1999).

Both of these critiques raise important issues around power and the position of children/young humans in relation to adults/older humans. Not only is the way childhood is understood and lived a social construction: but so, too, is the very idea of childhood itself, with its marking out and naming of a certain part of the life course as separate, a construction, an invention of thought, which 'emerged with the bourgeoisie society and especially with the division between public and private space that relocated the child and segregated him or her from the worldly affairs of the adults' (Hultqvist and Dahlberg 2001: 2). Childhood, as Hultqvist comments, is not 'the natural space of the child . . . [but] a technology that fabricates the child in the "mirror" of the imaginaries, theories and ways of reasoning that delineates such a space for the child' (2001: 143). Similarly, the idea of social constructionism, and the possibility that identities can be not only constructed but also plural, complex and shifting introduces an important tension of the modern day: between flexible individualism and group identity, between self-realisation and solidaristic relations and action.

We shall return to both of these issues throughout the book. We shall, however, choose to work with the concepts of 'childhood' (i.e. the early stage of the life course) and 'child' (i.e. the human being living through that stage), not least because our subject is the institutions for childhood produced through public policy. We also choose to adopt social construc-tionism as a theory we find both useful and satisfying. Doing so has major consequences. We are no longer seeking the essential child, some unitary truth, looking to objective science to assist us in the process of revelation. Instead, we face a myriad of different children, created from different dis-courses: the 'schoolchild', the 'child in need', the 'looked after child', 'the child of child development' and so on. The child we create, our 'object of study', has enormous implications for policy, provision and practice, since our constructions shape social and political life. Above all, if there is no essential, 'real' child, but many possibilities, then we have choices to make about how we understand the child, with all its implications. We have to decide what is *our* image of the child, not hide behind the constructions of others, and take responsibility for the consequences of our choice, not claim there is no alternative. If there are many possibilities, and we have to choose, then childhood becomes contestable.

We refer to the pedagogical work in Reggio Emilia throughout the book: indeed, Reggio offers a powerful example of the possibility of thinking differently about children, and the profound consequences of this for policy, provision and practice. But for the moment we want to flag up its explicit social constructionist approach, an example of an open relationship between theory and practice. The starting point for all those working with young children in Reggio is a question which assumes the constructed nature of children – 'what is our image of the child?' Their answer to this question was expressed by Loris Malaguzzi, the first head of the early childhood provisions in Reggio, when he wrote that 'our image of the child is rich in potential, strong, powerful, competent and, most of all, connected to adults and other children' (1993a: 10). Being explicit in their approach, the early childhood workers in Reggio are self aware of what they are doing, their own implication in the act of construction (subjectivity), and their responsibility for the consequences, both for children themselves and for the public provisions that are made for them:

> When we choose the image of the child, we make a pedagogical and political choice. Who is the child? What image do we have? An image is an interpretation, what kind of child do we want to see. To see is a subjective activity. What expectation do we have of him or her.... Many images take something away from children, children are seen as weak, poor, needy.... [And the] poor image of the child supports an image of the preschool or social services.... Each choice means to take a responsibility. Choosing means having the courage to risk.
>
> (Rinaldi 1999b)

We should add one other qualification before leaving social constructionism. We have referred to different understandings of the state of childhood and of the child. But we need to take diversity at least one step further, recognising that the 'child' is not homogeneously constructed, that 'child' is only one part of the plural identity of a younger human being. Multiple social constructions attach to any particular child, and are in interaction with each other:

> Within the minority group known as 'children' there are differentiated positions and further minorities. Children hold different social class

positions, they differ as to age, gender, ethnicity – and there are inter-actions between these. . . . an individual disabled child is not an abstrac-tion whose life is to be seen purely within the context of disability. Each disabled child has a complex social identity. A disabled child may be Black or White, male or female, with parents employed or unemployed. . . .

(Petrie *et al.* 2000: 3, 5)

Furthermore, 'the exploration of these positionings . . . can develop our understanding of how social disadvantage and exclusion operate as well as provide insights into the operation and development of social policy towards all children' (ibid.: 3). For just as the socially constructed category 'children' can be viewed as disadvantaged in some respects in relation to another category – 'adults', so too do other socially constructed categories – relating, for example, to gender, sexuality, social class, ethnicity and dis-ability – affect children's experience of life and are means through which social control operates, differentially and with unequal outcomes. To give just three broad examples: dominant social constructions of masculinity have implications for young men's use of alcohol and their willingness to participate in juvenile crime; constructions of femininity may influence girls' eating and smoking habits and their compliance with school work; and young people from minority ethnic groups, or those who are gay or lesbian, may experience childhoods marked by implicit and explicit discrimination and by real or threatened violence.

When we consider a construction of public provisions for children which we will call children's spaces, we must consider what they might offer any child who uses them and how they can operate in such a way that they pro-vide social space for *all* children, not advantaging and including certain groups and disadvantaging and excluding others. We will choose to apply the image of the child as 'rich in potential, strong, powerful, competent and, most of all, connected to adults and other children' to *all* children, call-ing into question current constructions not only of the 'universal' child, but also of the child whose social position is undermined by differentiating constructs of race, gender, sexuality, class, disability.

Modernity and postmodernity

At the heart of the postmodern culture is an acceptance of the pluralistic character of social experiences, identities and standards of truth, moral rightness and beauty. In place of the abstract, universal self, a post-modern culture asserts selves that are differentiated and individuated by class, gender, race, sexuality, ethnicity, nationality, physical and psychological ableness, and on and on. In place of a unitary concept of reason and uniform cultural standards, in a postmodern culture we speak of traditions of reason and a plurality of cultural standards that express different traditions and communities. If modernity is organized round a series of neat divisions (family/economy, science/ideology, politics/morality) and hierarchies (e.g. reason, science, individualism, the subject, progress, the West, the identity of humanity), post-modernity underscores a process of differentiation or the blurring of these boundaries, the disruption of hierarchies and the questioning of modern foundations.

(Siedman 1998: 347)

We cannot leave social construction on that note. We should acknowledge that this theory emerges from what has variously been termed post-modern conditions, postmodern culture, postmodern sensibility, a poststructural turn. What these variations on a theme are getting at is the idea of moving beyond a mind set, a system of beliefs, a way of viewing the world, which has had a powerful hold over Europe and North America for several centuries – modernity and Enlightenment thinking. 'Modernity' is both a historical period and a project that has held sway during that period. Bauman (1993) defines the historical period of modernity as beginning in western Europe in the seventeenth century, with a series of profound social and intellectual transformations. It achieved its maturity as a socio-cultural project in the eighteenth-century Enlightenment, and as a 'socially accomplished form of life' with the growth of industrial society. What has been the project of modernity and Enlightenment?

Central to that project has been a cluster of assumptions and beliefs: an ordered world, certain, controllable and predictable, built on foundations of universal, knowable and decontextualised essences, properties, laws and explanations; knowledge as an objective, non-perspectival mirror of the world, separate from values and politics, and uniquely revealed by science, occupying a value-free and universal standpoint, and the exercise of autonomous reason; the separation of reason and emotion, one of a number of important dualisms (others include spirit/body; self/other; culture/nature; freedom/necessity; public/private); linear progress to a universal civilisation, without cultural differences, and founded on universal morality; the superiority of the West, whose institutions and values would be the basis for this universal civilisation; and one true, reason-dictated solution for every problem.

But during the last century, disenchantment set in: many aspects of Enlightenment and modernity began to lose credibility. The possibility of finding foundations for universal claims has receded: the existence of a 'theoretically neutral, pretheoretical ground from which the adjudication of competing claims can proceed' (Gray 1995: 151) has come to seem implausible. For some modernity has become discredited by its perceived implication in the Holocaust, the Gulags and other horrors of authoritarian rule, legitimate offspring of the modern age – of that optimistic view, that scientific and industrial progress in principle removed all restrictions on the possible application of planning, education and social reform in everyday life, of that belief that social problems can be finally solved.

(Bauman, 1991: 29)

Modernity has been further implicated in a global process of environmental degradation, the product some claim of a belief in the possibility and desirability of one species controlling and mastering the natural world, turning nature into an object of human will:

the conception of the natural world as an object of human exploitation and of humankind as the master of nature is one of the most vital and enduring elements of the modern world-view and the one which Westernization has most lastingly and destructively transmitted to non-Western cultures.

(Gray 1995: 158)

Faced by such events, the notion of human progress becomes increasingly hard to swallow, at least without a strong dose of qualifications.

There is also a growing incredulity about the very assumptions and beliefs of modernity, which have lost some of their appeal and conviction. They fail to capture the world that many people experience today or indeed the world in which they want to live:

Looking back at the intellectually challenging years between 1650 and 1950, from a position of lesser confidence but greater modesty, we can appreciate why the projects of Modernity carried the conviction they did. Not the least of these charms was an oversimplification that, in retrospect, was unrealistic. . . . The seduction of High Modernity lay in its abstract neatness and theoretical simplicity: both of these features blinded the successors of Descartes to the unavoidable complexities of concrete human experience.

(Toulmin 1990: 200–201)

What has emerged during the later part of the twentieth century has been another set of ideas and views about the world we inhabit, sometimes referred to as postmodern. Gray refers to postmodernity as our historical fate, a 'condition of plural and provisional perspectives, lacking any rational or transcendental ground or unifying world-view' (1995: 153). As this suggests, postmodernity, like modernity, has its own assumptions and beliefs: 'postmodernity reverses the signs of the values central to modernity, such as uniformity and universalism . . . liberty, equality, brotherhood was the war cry of modernity. Liberty, diversity and tolerance is the armistice formula of postmodernity' (Bauman 1991: 98). Postmodernity foregrounds diversity, complexity and the 'ineradicable plurality of the world' (ibid.), viewing the 'dualisms which continue to dominate Western thought [as] inadequate for understanding a world of multiple causes and effects inter-acting in complex and non-linear ways, all rooted in a limitless array of historical and cultural specificities' (Lather 1991: 21). It recognises the inevitability of contingency, ambivalence and uncertainty, and recognises no essences or universal foundations existing outside history and culture.

From a postmodern perspective, there can be no absolute knowledge, no absolute reality waiting 'out there' to be discovered: instead, as we proposed at the beginning of this section, the world and our knowledge of it are seen as socially constructed. Knowledge and its construction is always context-specific and value laden, challenging the modernist belief in universal truth, scientific neutrality and an absolute reality waiting to be discovered and accurately represented. Similarly, there is no 'essential' human nature or identity, independent of context and relationships, struggling to be realised and described. From a postmodern perspective, the self is constituted and reconstituted relationally and historically, in the jargon 'decentred', 'a shift-ing self in contrast to the static and essentialised self inherent in the [modernist] concept of free and self-determining individuals' (Lather 1991: 118). We are back to the complex and plural identities with which we ended the last section.

The passing of modernity (and there are still arguments about where that process has got to: are we in the era of late modernity? On the brink of, or in, the postmodern epoch?) and the dimming of the Enlightenment project represent major transformations and the drawing to a close of an important episode in Western culture. But while we may mourn, we can also look forward to new possibilities:

> once we cease to be captivated by the Enlightenment project of a universal civilization animated by a unified world view, we may come to think of the plural inheritance of incommensurable perspectives which is our unalterable condition in Western cultures as an historical gift to be enjoyed rather than merely as a fate to be accepted or endured.
>
> (Gray 1995: 157)

Siedman also finds cause for hope:

> postmodernity may renounce the dream of one reason and one humanity marching forward along one path towards absolute freedom, but it offers its own ideal of a society that tolerates human differences, accepts ambiguity and uncertainty, and values choice, diversity and democratization.
>
> (1998: 347)

Nor can we, nor need we, ignore modernity and the Enlightenment. Post-modernity does not stand in total opposition to the Enlightenment, nor are the values completely different. Siedman distinguishes between the values and the assumptions of Enlightenment:

> most critics are looking to preserve the Enlightenment values of auton-omy, tolerance, equality, and democracy. . . . I see new paradigms of human studies developing in the postwar West. They have to varying degrees broken away from key Enlightenment assumptions without surrendering many of its values and social hopes.
>
> (Ibid.: 347–348)

We have introduced, even if in very condensed form, this discussion of modernity and postmoderrnity, to locate our discussion of social con-struction, which plays such a large part in our thinking about childhood and provision for children. But it is also relevant to all discussions about childhood and public provision for children. Much current public policy and political discussion about these subjects, in Britain at least, is located within a framework made up from the assumptions and values of modernity. Many of the disciplines which influence training, practice and research have their origins deep in the project of modernity, for example developmental psychology ('a paradigmatically modern discipline arising at a time of commitment to narratives of truth, objectivity, science and reason' (Burman 1994: 18)) and managerialism (with its promise 'of coping with the complexities and uncertainties of the modern world' (Clarke 1998: 178)).

Michael King has argued that one of the main approaches to improv-ing the world of children, what he calls 'demythologising', is an Enlightenment-inspired endeavour, premised on abiding beliefs in man-kind's capacity to control and master to predetermined ends:

> Once we know how people or society really work, proponents of this approach claim, we shall be able to identify those controls, buttons and levers that will enable social workers, judges and policy makers to steer people or society in one specified way rather than another. . . . [O]pening our eyes to the misconceptions and ephemeral nature of much we accept as truth and reality is a very useful exercise. It is also, however, a misleading enterprise. It suggests that somewhere beyond the myths lies a universe called 'objective reality' or 'people as they really are' and that myth-destruction will provide us with a clear route to this world and these people.
>
> (King 1997: 188)

Yet this partiality that arises from being located within a particular way of thinking and seeing, this perspectivism, is not acknowledged in the policies or provisions we make for children, or in the practices or research conducted with or on children. Rather than being a contestable position, the perspective of modernity is treated as a matter of fact, a taken for granted truth. Our problem is not with people choosing a particular perspective, approach or framework. It is with not acknowledging the choice that is made and the implications of that choice. Once again, what is contestable is offered as if it were self evident.

The discussion of modernity and postmodernity is important for another reason. Much policy, provision and practice involving children claims to be based on knowledge. Within modernity and postmodernity, knowledge is understood in very different ways. In the former case, knowledge is conceptualised as an objective and demonstrable entity. It is the revelation through science and reason of reality, the non-perspectival representation of things as they really are: the issue is correspondence of knowledge to objective truth, the world as it really is. In the latter case, knowledge is perspectival, 'socially constituted, historically embedded and valuationally based' (Lather 1991: 52) – and inextricably linked to power: the issue is its inherent contestability.

Power and knowledge

> I interpret poststructuralism, at least Lyotard and Foucault in their most hopeful moments, as saying that, if we wish to realise Enlightenment social hopes, we need to translate them into a different social vocabulary and vision of knowledge, power and society. The poststructural vision is that of socially produced selves whose identities are multiple and unstable, an awareness of the coupling of power and knowledge, a new moral responsibility attached to the production of knowledge, and an image of society as fragmented, pluralistic and productive of heterogeneous local struggles.
>
> (Siedman 1998: 250)

At one level, it is obvious that power is an issue when we consider children in relation to the adult world. Adults, after all, are physically stronger; children are economically and politically dependent on adults. But discussion of power needs to move beyond this rather simple relationship, in which one group has power and another has none. It takes no account of the social agency of children, who are not simply acted upon. And it takes no account of the important writings of Michel Foucault concerning power: in particular the ability of power to shape and form both the population as a collectivity and individual subjectivity, through claims to knowledge and truth and by the application of a range of techniques, or disciplines, including surveillance, normalisation, exclusion, classification and regulation (Gore 1998).

Foucault describes the emergence of 'disciplinary power' from the seventeenth century onwards. This new kind of power was not about asserting and maintaining sovereignty through overt coercion of people. Rather, it was about governance without overt coercion to productive ends. It was concerned with the management, organisation, orchestration and shaping of population, with steering people in the desired direction, with the determination of conduct, and with 'shaping the human material at one's disposal' (Ransom 1997: 29).

> For all systems of power in the west since the eighteenth century, the population has appeared as the terrain of government par excellence. Not the exercise of sovereignty – though this still plays a part . . . but the regulation of the processes proper to the population, the laws that modulate its wealth, health, longevity, and its capacity to wage wars and to engage in labour and so forth. . . . The actions and calculations of authorities are directed towards new tasks: how to maximize the forces of the population and each individual within it, how to minimize their troubles, how to organize them in the most efficacious manner.
> (Rose 1990: 5)

Central to this form of power has been the ability to order and normalise, in particular through classification and categorisation:

> By defining groups in particular ways and maintaining records that gave material qualities to the construction of groups, populational reasoning 'normalized' certain characteristics. What were socially constructed criteria appeared in time as 'natural attributes' (e.g. 'racial' characteristics). . . . The construction of groups and specific group characteristics emerged at a very specific historical moment. The art of governing required a kind of 'governmentality' related to the role of the state as a definer, watcher and manager of difference.
> (Baker 1998: 129–130)

Foucault emphasises that power relations are local and diffuse. He pays particular attention to the operation of power in local settings and institutions, highlighting the importance of smaller discrete social units such as hospitals, mental asylums, schools, the military, prisons and universities. 'He shifted our attention to heterogeneous local social dynamics precisely because they are important sites of social conflict today' (Siedman 1998: 247).

He also views power as a productive, rather than a repressive, force, productive in the shaping of the social world (Ransom 1997): 'power is embedded in the governing systems of order, appropriation and exclusion by which *subjectivities are constructed and social life is formed.* . . . [A]vailable systems of ideas discipline individuals as they act, think and see themselves in the world' (Popkewitz and Brennan 1998: 19; emphasis added). Power, in Foucault's words, 'produces things, it induces pleasure, forms knowledge, produces discourse' (Foucault 1984: 61). More specifically, power also produces practices in many fields, including education and social work, shaping not only how problems are understood and how people are classified as having such problems, but also what are considered appropriate ways to steer and shape behaviour. The power of competing discourses is well understood in certain fields, for example that of disability, but has been less explored in relation to childhood.

Language plays a critical role in power relations. The language we use shapes and directs our way of looking at and understanding the world, and the way we name different phenomena and objects becomes a form of convention. Foucault calls such conventions – our way of naming things and talking about them – *discourses*, and those discourses that exercise a decisive influence on a specific practice can, in his view, be seen as *dominant discursive regimes*, or *regimes of truth*.

> Truth isn't outside power, or lacking in power. . . . Truth is a thing of this world: it is produced only by virtue of multiple forms of constraint. And it induces regular effects of power. Each society has its regime of truth, its 'general politics' of truth: that is the type of discourse which it accepts and makes function as true; the mechanisms and instances which enable one to distinguish true and false statements, the means by which each is sanctioned; the techniques and procedures accorded value in the acquisition of truth; the status of those who are charged with saying what counts as true. . . . [Truth] is linked in a circular relationship with systems of power which produce and sustain it.
>
> (Foucault 1980: 131)

Discourses provide the mechanism for rendering reality amenable to certain kinds of actions (Miller and Rose 1993). By the same token, they also exclude alternative ways of understanding and interpreting the world. In short, regimes of truth make assumptions and values invisible, turn subjective perspectives and understandings into apparently objective truths, and determine some things are self-evident and realistic while others are dubious and impractical.

Such dominant discursive regimes or regimes of truth serve a disciplinary or regulatory function: 'discourses that carry public authority shape identities and regulate bodies, desires, selves and populations' (Siedman 1998: 235). Through the concepts, classifications, norms and categories that we use to represent reality, they provide means by which we govern others, for they are about 'who can speak, when, where and with what authority . . . (so that) certain possibilities for thought are constructed' (Ball 1994: 21–22). But we also govern ourselves through these regimes, for they order or organise our everyday experience of the world, influencing our ideas, thoughts and actions. They exercise power over our thought by governing what we see as the 'truth', what we accept as rational and how we construct the world – and hence our acting and doing. Or rather, since we are ourselves inscribed in dominant discourses, we govern ourselves through dominant discourses, acting upon ourselves rather than being directly acted upon: 'we do not speak a discourse, it speaks us. We are the subjectivities, the voices, the knowledge, the power relations that a discourse constructs and allows' (ibid.: 22).

Self-governing in this way, through the production of self-managing subjects who are responsible for managing their own conduct in accordance with prized goals and activities, involves a particular idea of the exercise of power: governmentality. Relating this analysis of power more specifically to children, and work with children, Fendler argues that the child is governed through the normalising effects of psychological classifications and categorisations:

'Developmentally appropriate curricula' [is] a widely applied curriculum theory that correlates lesson plans with a sequence of capabilities. . . . It appeals to developmental psychology for its scientific base, it inscribes assumptions of progressive efficiency, and it assumes a behaviourist approach to establish educational objectives. . . . [This] interweaving of developmental psychology, efficiency, and behaviourism in educational curricula becomes a technology of normalization. I call this technology *developmentality* as a way of alluding to Foucault's governmentality, and focusing on the self-governing effects of developmental discourse in curriculum debates. Developmentality, like governmentality, describes a current pattern of power in which the self disciplines the self.

(Fendler 2001: 120)

For Foucault, therefore, language is the effect or product of power, as well as a means for reproducing power. So, to take an example from the USA related to the subject of this book, 'talking of "children at risk" is not merely the words of a teacher but [is] part of historically constructed ways of reasoning that are the effects of power . . . embodying a range of historically constructed values, priorities, dispositions towards how one should see and act towards the world' (Popkewitz and Brennan 1998: 9). The 'child in need', a central concept in British welfare legislation, has been similarly problematised as the effect of historically constructed ways of reasoning (Moss *et al.* 2000).

Power and knowledge are also inextricably linked. Foucault paid particular attention to the human sciences (which include sociology, psychology, psychiatry, demography, economics and criminology), and to the social effects of these knowledges. By so doing, he examined a relationship between power and knowledge unrecognised in the Enlightenment vision of objective, value-free science. Foucault argued that power produces knowledge, what is taken to be true or false, and knowledge sustains power, lending it authority and justification as well as the means to discipline and control. He claimed

> that discourses that aim to reveal the truth of the abnormal personality or human sexuality or the criminal help to create and control the very objects they claim to know. Scientific knowledge functions as a major social power: through the state, the family, hospital, and therapeutic institutions, the scientific disciplines shape the dominant cultural ideas about who we are, what is permissible and unacceptable, what can be said, by whom, when, and in what form.
>
> (Siedman 1998: 236)

Influenced by Foucault, in his study of teaching in America, Popkewitz (1998) observes 'much of modern life is ordered through expert systems of knowledge that discipline how people participate and act' (5). He describes power as 'the effects of the systems of knowledge through which reason is formed and the objects of reflection are constructed' (17). He goes on to take the relationship between power and knowledge as the basis for his study:

> Rather than focus on power as a question of who rules (or who is ruled – the sovereignty concept of power), my concern is with how the different pedagogical knowledges 'make' (construct) the teacher who administers the child. I argue that knowledge of pedagogy is a constitutive, material element of the contemporary world. Not only do the rules of 'reasoning' about teaching and childhood 'tell us' what to notice (and not to notice), what things belong together, and what things are not 'thinkable' within the rules and standards of the thinking applied: the knowledge systems of teaching also embody a continuum of values whose consequence is to compare children discursively through the distinctions, norms, and divisions linguistically produced in pedagogy.
>
> (Popkewitz 1998: 17)

So knowledge is not a process of representing the real world, but rather the means by which we construct particular understandings about it – more of a lens than a mirror. Gaining knowledge is a process of construction, not of revelation, of saying 'this is how I see it' rather than 'this is how it is'. It is a

> selecting out among the many readings and possibilities present in a concrete instance, of those characteristics and aspects that will promote

the goals of the individual or group doing the selecting . . . [so that] by picking out what to emphasize and what to present positively or negatively, knowledge shapes the world it describes.

(Ransom 1997: 19)

Facts and knowledge should not be confused. Facts by themselves are meaningless; knowledge is the process of constructing meaning involving the connecting and interpretation of certain facts from a particular perspective.

To summarise. Power operates through relationships. It is not a case that some have power, but most are without. All exercise and all are affected by power, although we should add the rider 'to a lesser or greater extent' in recognition of there being major inequalities of power (and we should also recognise one critique of Foucault, that he goes too far in stressing the dispersion of power and that he downplays too much the importance of sovereign or juridical power and the interpenetration of different forms of power (Sousa Santos 1995)). Nor is power to be seen simply as a constraint and a bad thing. It is an inescapable part of life and relationships, as well as being a productive force – producing, for example, policies and practices the value and benefits of which may be widely agreed. Power, language, discourse and knowledge are closely connected: language and discourse are agents of knowledge, power produces knowledge, knowledge sustains power.

In what way are these theories about power relevant to our discussion in this book about children and public provision for children? We would suggest in at least three ways. First, the two sets of theories – social construction and Foucault's analysis of power – are related. As Rose points out, although

it is now a commonplace to refer to the objects of the scientific imagination as 'socially constructed' . . . it is not very enlightening to be told repeatedly that something claimed as 'objective' is in fact 'socially constructed'. . . . [T]*he interesting questions concern the ways in which they are constructed.*

(Rose 1999: x; emphasis added)

Foucault's analysis suggests how constructions of children and childhood are constituted, through power relations and dominant discursive regimes: 'dominant knowledges shape human life by naturalizing and normalizing the construction of personal and social identities' (Siedman 1998: 235). These constructions become embodied into professional thinking and are productive of public policy and professional practice – and without necessarily engendering self-awareness of this process, since power is not only pervasive but also often invisible (Gore 1993), while knowledge is 'assumed innocent of power, [because] we believe that knowledge is disinterested'

(Ransom 1997: 19). Indeed, a climate, as now in much of the English-speaking world, which prioritises technical and managerial discourses and values is, arguably, particularly unsympathetic to the type of critical thinking that brings self-awareness. It favours 'vulgar pragmatism' over 'critical pragmatism': 'the language and assumptions inscribed in current discourses are conducive to the development and improvement of ever more effective techniques of meeting objectives and at the same time inhibit thinking outside the parameters of the stipulated objectives' (Fendler 1998: 59).

These two sets of related ideas – social constructionism and the Foucauldian analysis of power relations – speak of a childhood that can no longer be perceived 'as a natural phenomenon with natural laws guiding its natural unfolding'. Instead the child

> seems to be a product of categories, techniques and reasonings through which we perceive things as being 'natural'. . . . [C]hildhood is not an objective concept. . . . New kinds of children are being produced through new categories of assessment – categories such as 'ready to learn' and 'at risk' suggest the limits of normal childhood. Such categories of deficit owe less to nature, more to culturally specific practices – practices which privilege concepts of intelligence, orderliness etc.
> (Baker 1998: 138)

Second, we are all actively involved in power relations. We are not just servants or instruments of some centralised and monolithic concentration of power, such as the State. If we are governed by power, we also exercise power. Those of us, for example, who are researchers or practitioners exercise authority 'through a whole variety of technical innovations and practical mechanisms' backed by truth claims.

> The exercise of government has become enmeshed with regimes of truth concerning the objects, processes and persons governed – economy, society, morality, psychology, pathology. Government has both fostered and depended upon the vocation of 'experts of truth' and the functioning of their concepts of normality and pathology, danger and risk, social order and social control, and the judgements and devices which such concepts have inhabited.
> (Rose 1999: 30)

The power that results from a combination of government and experts, knowledges and procedures is considerable, making 'childhood the most intensively governed sector of human existence' (Rose 1990: 121). More generally,

> Our personalities, subjectivities, and relationships are not private matters, if this implies they are not the objects of power. On the

contrary they are intensively governed. . . . Government and parties of all political complexions have formulated policies, set up machinery, established bureaucracies, and promoted initiatives to regulate the conduct of citizens by acting upon their mental capacities and propensities. The most obvious manifestation has been the complex apparatus targeted upon the child: the child welfare system, the school, the juvenile justice system and the education and surveillance of parents.

(Ibid.: 1–2)

Third, the issue is not to do away with power, which is impossible. Nor can any of us – policy makers or practitioners, researchers or other experts, parents or other relatives – stand outside power, occupying some objective position from which we can discern the truth. Instead we can become aware, through critical thinking, of how power operates and to what effects, for example through determining what will be considered truth and knowledge. It then becomes possible to unmask assumptions and question them, offer alternative possibilities, find ways of doing things differently and being governed less. This, rather than revolutionary politics, was the purpose of Foucault's work: 'all my analyses are against the idea of universal necessities in human existence. They show the arbitrariness of institutions and show what space of freedom we can still enjoy and how many changes can still be made.'

Foucault attaches great importance to critique as a means of unmasking the working of power relations, 'to show that things are not as self-evident as one believed, to see that which is accepted as self-evident will no longer be accepted as such' (Foucault 1988: 155) and making visible 'the workings of institutions which appear to be both neutral and independent' (Foucault, 1974: 71). He also argues that while dominant discourses, concepts and institutions are the product of historical forces, these forces and their effects are neither inevitable nor immutable.

> What reason perceives as its necessity, or rather, what different forms of rationality offer as their necessary being, can perfectly well be shown to have a history; and the network of contingencies from which it emerges can be traced. Which is not to say, however, that these forms of rationality were irrational. It means that they reside on a base of human practice and human history; and that since these things have been made, they can be unmade, as long as we know how it was that they were made.
>
> (Foucault 1988: 36–37)

The Foucauldian analysis of power therefore points to the importance of problematising commonplace assumptions – as expressed, for example, in constructed concepts such as 'the child in need', 'child development' or 'quality' – and the rationalities that sustain these assumptions, and by doing so to make the familiar strange (Fendler 1998). This carries the potential for change since 'as soon as one can no longer think things as one formerly thought them, transformation becomes both very urgent, very difficult and quite possible' (Foucault 1988: 155). In relation to public provision for children, therefore, this suggests the need to treat all concepts, theories, knowledges, assumptions, methods and 'truth claims' as never neutral and independent, self-evident or obvious, and always contingent and contestable.

But how? And where? Foucault's analysis points to the need for critique to be local and specific, related to specific institutions and practices. Later we will discuss the possibility of public provisions for children practising, as one of their potential possibilities, a politics of childhood. By 'politics of childhood' we mean making childhood itself and public provisions for children the subject of public deliberation and contestation, both to critique what there is and to make choices about what should be. This involves questioning dominant discourses and their associated concepts, theories, knowledges, ethics, assumptions, methods and 'truth claims'. It requires that practices are made visible and questionable. It provokes the identification and debate of critical questions of the sort: What do we want for our children? What is a good childhood? What is the place of children and childhood in our society? What are the purposes of institutions for children? How do we evaluate good practice in these institutions? What values and what relationships do we seek for these institutions?

But this implies that childhood, and related issues concerning, for example, care and parenthood, are important political subjects, and that what we call children's spaces might be capable in some cases at least of being sites for democratic critique and dialogue about such subjects. This brings us to our next area of theory: democratic politics in a fast changing world.

New forms of democratic politics

> The measure of any society that calls itself liberal is its capacity for critique, for encouraging citizens, through the education process and the to and fro of cultural and public life, to take up the standpoint of reflective critique towards their social and political processes.
>
> (Critchley 1999: 114)

Recent years have witnessed the increasing dominance of a particular form of capitalism – neo-liberal or market capitalism. This has had major consequences – economic, social and political. For example, economic deregulation of capital flows has led to vast sums of money passing round the world (the daily turnover in foreign exchange markets increased from a mere $10–20 billion in the 1970s to $1.5 trillion in 1998 (United Nations 1999)). Companies become increasingly detached from any loyalty or other ties to a particular country, becoming more and more demanding of national governments if they are to bestow their investment bounty. Maximising shareholder value becomes the overriding business objective, flexibility the overwhelming business demand.

Such economic developments, in turn, contribute to what has been termed the hollowing-out of the nation state, a loss of economic control in the face of deregulated global capital seeking profit without regard to national boundaries. This has led to a redefining of the role of the nation state:

> Money scours the world for the highest return and, in doing so, it generates colossal instability. The role of government is to maintain order in their territories . . . and package their populations into skilled, docile workforces with the correct attitudes in the hope that international finance may offer jobs through inward investment.
>
> (Atkinson and Elliott 1998)

As neo-liberal capitalism becomes more dominant, the nation state 'does not disappear, but becomes more and more managerial' (Readings 1996: 47), a sort of glorified economic development agency. Power and politics become separated, as politics remains local and territorial, left behind by capital in the form of financial and commodity markets and flows, non-political forces no longer bound by space or distance yet with an increasingly coercive and indoctrinating impact (Bauman 1999). The weakened nation state responds by reducing economic regulation and increasing social regulation, focused ever more narrowly on the direct rule of certain social categories, not least by applying ever more powerful 'human technologies'. Rose defines 'human technologies' as acting upon human capacities, and consisting of

> an assemblage of forms of practical knowledge, with modes of perception, practices of calculation, vocabularies, types of authority, forms of judgement, architectural forms, human capacities, non-human objects and devices, inscription techniques and so forth, traversed and transected by aspirations to achieve certain outcomes in terms of the conduct of the governed.
>
> (Rose 1999: 52)

The welfare state contracts, while at the same time becoming a more powerful means of regulation in those areas where it retains an interest.

The weakening of the nation state coincides with what Crouch terms 'post democracy', what he describes as an almost inevitable falling off from moments of more vibrant democracy which tend to occur in the early years of achieving democracy or after great crises, such as wars:

elections certainly exist and can change governments, [but] public electoral debate is a tightly controlled spectacle, managed by rival teams of professionals, experts in the techniques of persuasion and considering a small range of issues selected by those teams. The mass of citizens plays a passive, quiescent, even apathetic part, responding only to the signals given them. Behind this spectacle of the electoral game politics is really shaped in private by interaction between elected governments and elites which overwhelmingly represent business interests.

(Crouch 2001: 2)

There is, Crouch argues, an increasing blurring of public and business interests and ethics. Far from clarifying the boundary between government and business, 'neo-liberalism has linked them in manifold new ways – but all within the former territory reserved to government' (ibid.: 61).

These changes in the nation state and democracy occur alongside (the exact relationship need not detain us here) an increasing alienation of the population from traditional forms of democratic participation (mainly through voting and party membership) and political institutions (assemblies, politicians and governments). Fewer and fewer people vote – only 59 per cent in the 2001 British general election, around half for the President of the United States – and mainstream politics and politicians are held in increasingly low esteem.

Once the state recognizes the priority and superiority of the laws of the market over the laws of the polis, the citizen is transmuted into the consumer, and a consumer demands more and more protection while accepting less and less the need to participate in the running of the state. The overall result is the present fluid conditions of generalized anomie and rejection of the rules in all their versions. . . . As things stand at the moment, the laws of the strong triumph at the expense of the weak; the really existing version of liberal democracy seems to gestate a society of two gears, a two tier nation.

(Bauman 1999: 156–157)

Beck (1998) points to other failings. Politics as it is lacks fun. Politics is populated by older people who have nothing to offer young people, because they have not experienced the conditions and problems confronted by the young and do not take them seriously. Political parties (but other collective institutions also) cannot deal with increased diversity: 'those in charge must ... stop demonizing individualism, which has already become a reality, and instead acknowledge it as a desirable and inevitable product of democratic revolution' (ibid.: 7).

There are already a number of responses to this situation. One is to create more local forms of traditional politics, through decentralisation and devolution. But form is only part of the problem. Equally, if not more, important is the content of politics. It fails to address the most pressing concerns and desires of individuals, families and communities, it offers nothing for the future except more (paid) work, more productivity and more consumption – none of which, past a certain point, seems to add to the sum of things that make life worth living. Despite our immense power and resources, our endless quest for efficiency and improvement, the words of the philosopher John McMurray from the 1930s still strike a chord: 'we do not know how to live finely' (1935: 76). As one newspaper columnist points out, 'depending on which research you plump for, we're either getting more miserable or staying the same: either could throw some light on our political culture of declining voter turnouts and party membership, and its profound cynicism' (Bunting 2001). Or in the words of an educational researcher, troubled by the direction of educational policy in Britain:

> We are operating in the wrong frame of reference and as a consequence our lives will continue to become more busy, more exhausting, less humanly productive or satisfying and increasingly devoid of meaning. Alternative frameworks exist that are likely to serve our human needs more profoundly and more engagingly: it would be foolish to ignore them.
>
> (Fielding 2001: 13)

Into this gap has entered a wide range of new social movements, often focusing on particular issues or areas that individuals or groups feel are neglected by elected politicians or beyond their ability to influence (for a useful overview of research on new social movements, see Martin 2000). Feminist movements are one example, environmental movements another. Such movements, offering what Crouch terms 'new disruptive creativity', provide hope for a democratic future including the reining in of the growing political power of the global firm, a renaissance of politics led by civil society and a rebalancing of economic and social needs and interests.

Ulrich Beck proposes a new framework for politics in these changed circumstances, what he calls 'cosmopolitan republicanism'. This has five main principles:

> First is the new significance of the individual. . . . Second is the centrality of cosmopolitan agents, identities, networks and institutions. . . . Third is the new significance of the local, the magic of place in world society. . . . Fourth, there is the crucial significance of political freedom, that is, an active civil society, for the cohesion and self responsibility of democracy beyond labour society, as well as for how it might become possible to respond to ecological crisis. . . . [Fifth is] the necessity for deep-seated institutional reforms, indeed a reformation of primary

industrial modernity that would affirm diversity and 'cultivated' conflict.

(Beck 1998: 14–15)

Beck adds three more points that are very relevant to our enquiry into public provisions for children. Solidarity and community cannot be recreated from the top, 'but must be freed up by questioning and brought about in struggle through individual and biographical problems, it must be agreed on, negotiated, justified and experienced' (35). There is a need to create a new focus of activity and identity that will revitalise the democratic way of life, public work:

> How do the values and goals of an earnings-based society relate to the grass-roots organization of civic society? The relationship is one not of mutual exclusion but of complementarity. In the future what will probably win out is a blending of formal work and voluntary organization, the dismantling of legal and mobility barriers between the two sectors, the creation of opportunities for leaving or changing one's principal occupation.... Two things would thus become possible. First, the equation of public activity with remunerated employment would be broken. Second, public work would create new foci of political action and identity formation.... The material and cultural foundations for 'individualism coupled with solidarity' would be established.
>
> (Ibid.: 60)

Beck goes on to explore various ways of paying for 'public work', to take the 'invisible practice of social self-help and grass roots political organization and make it visible: give it economic, organizational and political weight' (64). In this way, social and political participation – including, for example, by parents and others in provision for children – becomes more valued, both literally and metaphorically, and therefore possibly more likely.

Finally, Beck seeks for a value to sustain a reinvigorated critical democracy, and proposes scepticism:

> Scepticism, contrary to widespread error, makes everything possible again: ethics, morality, knowledge, faith, society and criticism, but differently, a few sizes smaller, more tentative, more revisable and more capable of learning and thus more curious, more open to the unsuspected and the incommensurate, with a tolerance based on and rooted in the ultimate final certainty of error.... Perhaps the political programme of radicalized modernity is scepticism? Established doubt, after all, requires a different distribution of power, a different architecture of institutions, a different technology and technological develop-

ment, a different science, different groups in which to learn, and decisions that can be revised.

(Ibid.: 113–114)

In addressing the general context of democratic decline, Beck offers a vision of a new democratic politics – which seems to us to connect with our concept of 'children's spaces' as a place for the conduct of local politics around issues of childhood (and other matters) – undertaken with a scepticism which opens up important social practices, such as work with children, to questioning and debate, but also to public commitment and support. There is something of the same idea in Critchley's call for citizens to take up a reflective critique of social and political practices; or in Bauman's search for an *agora* or space that is public and private and where private worries can connect and be translated into public issues. Bauman explicitly links the critical reflection reminiscent of Foucault with the search for democracy:

Critical reflection is guided by the need to scrutinize the de jure validity of human institutions and significations. . . . [It] is the essence of genuine politics as distinct from the merely 'political' – that is related to the exercise of power. Politics is an effective and practical effort to subject institutions that boast de facto validity to the test of de jure validity. And democracy is a site of critical reflection, which derives its distinctive identity from that reflection.

(Bauman 1999: 84)

Nikolas Rose offers a similar idea of democracy which he terms 'minor' politics. He again locates his formulation as a response to the decline in 'old forms of political mobilization' and the emergence of new less 'arrogant' and more 'modest' forms and issues, which relate to people's everyday lives and concerns:

If one were trying to characterize the creativity of what one might term . . . a 'minor' or 'minority' politics, one would not seek to identify particular agents of a radical party – be they classes, races or genders – or to distinguish once and for all the forces of reaction from those of progression in terms of fixed identities. Rather, one would examine the ways in which creativity arises out of the situation of human beings engaged in particular relations of force and meaning, and what is made of the possibilities of that location. These minor engagements do not have the arrogance of programmatic politics – perhaps even refuse their designation as politics at all. They are cautious, modest, pragmatic, experimental, stuttering, tentative. They are concerned with the here and now, not with some fantasized future, with small concerns, petty details, the everyday and not the transcendental. They frequently arise in 'cramped spaces' – within a set of relations which are intolerable, where movement is impossible, where change is blocked and voice is strangulated. And in relation to these little territories of the everyday, they seek to engender a small reworking of their own spaces of action. But the feminist politics that was conducted under the slogan of 'the personal is political' is the most obvious example from our recent past of the ways in which such a molecular and minor engagement with cramped space can connect up with a whole series of other circuits and cause them to fluctuate, waver and reconfigure in wholly unexpected ways.

(Rose 1999: 279–280)

We started this section with globalisation and have now ended up with a discussion of a local and specific politics. This is not surprising when we look in more detail at the complex processes currently underway, which link the global with the local. Beck distinguishes between three concepts:

- Globalism: 'the view that the world market eliminates or supplants political action – that is the ideology of rule by the world market, the ideology of neoliberalism'.
- Globality: 'means that we have been living for a long time in a world society, in the sense that the notion of closed spaces has become illusory. No country or group can shut itself off from others. . . . [It is] the totality of social relationships which are not integrated into or determined (or determinable) by national-state politics'.
- Globalization: 'denotes the processes through which sovereign national states are criss-crossed and undermined by transnational actors with varying prospects of power, orientations, identities and networks. . . . What is new is not only the everyday life and interaction across national frontiers, in dense networks with a high degree of mutual dependence and obligation . . . [but] the self-perception of this transnationality'.

(Beck 2000: 9–11)

What these have in common is the nation state's hollowing-out and the end therefore of its centrality, though not its relevance:

one constant feature is the overturning of the first modernity: namely the idea that we live and act in self-enclosed spaces of national states and their respective national societies. . . . Borders become markedly less relevant to everyday behaviour in the various dimensions of economics, information, ecology, technology, cross-cultural conflict and civil society.

(Ibid.: 20)

But Beck also points to the complexity of these processes and how they are not necessarily to be equated with uniformity. 'World society', as discussed in relation to *globality*, 'means difference or multiplicity'. Furthermore, questioning fears of 'McDonaldisation' of the world, Beck argues that

> The widespread view of linear convergence of content and information driven by world market concentration fails to appreciate the paradoxes and ambivalences . . . of globalization. . . . [G]lobalization also involves a process of localization. . . . Analyses that base themselves on the G-word are everywhere giving rise to a new emphasis on the local. . . . Local cultures can no longer be justified, shaped and renewed in seclusion from the rest of the world. In place of that knee-jerk defence of tradition by traditional means (which Anthony Giddens calls 'fundamentalism'), there is a compulsion to relocate detraditionalized traditions within a global context of exchange, dialogue and conflict. In short, a non-traditionalist renaissance of the local occurs when local specificities are globally relocated and there conflictually renewed.
>
> (Ibid.: 44–46)

This idea – of how a world horizon opens up the production of new meanings, symbols and identities, new cultures, a reinvention of the local within a global context – is captured in the term 'glocalisation'. Politically, this points to the need for new democratic institutions at both global *and* local levels, the former to regulate matters beyond national control but of cross-national effect (e.g. speculative capital flows, pollution), the latter struggling locally to resist power and to produce just, democratic forms of life through addressing issues of everyday life and the concerns of all citizens, including children. We shall argue that these institutions might include *inter alia* public provision for children understood as children's spaces, and that these institutions might also provide one means for a process of localisation within a global context, local areas constructing new identities, values and cultures in relationship with other parts of the world, forming new networks that cross borders.

We shall argue in a later chapter that Reggio Emilia offers an important case of a community that has invested its public provision for children with these political and social projects. In the process it has become a locus of dissensus and diversity, not only in thought about children and public provision for them but also in actual practice. As such it challenges dominant regimes, proclaims the possibility of thinking and doing other, and problematises normalising concepts such as 'best practice', 'excellence' or 'quality'.

A final concern. We need to remind the reader, and ourselves, that this discussion of power, critical thinking and new forms of, and issues for, democracy involves children as much as adults or even more so if, as Rose suggests, 'childhood [is] the most intensively governed sector of human existence'. This can easily be lost sight of given that none of the (all male) authors quoted here have anything to say about the place of children in politics and democracy. Indeed, one of the main challenges is to find ways and means for children's participation in critical democratic practice, in both the provisions they use and in the wider world they inhabit. The discourses and practices surrounding 'children's rights' and 'children's participation' have a role to play, but are far from sufficient. Writing about Danish examples of how to take even young children's views and opinions about their own lives seriously, Langsted downplays procedures and structures: he foregrounds instead 'the cultural climate which shapes the ideas that the adults in a particular society hold about children' (1994: 41), since the wish to listen to and involve children originates in this cultural climate. It is an understanding of the child and practices in provisions for children which together assume children's participation as a normal part of democratic life and their ability for critical thought that will make children's rights and participation a taken for granted part of everyday life.

Ethics and politics

Some examples of inequality and injustice from the UN *Human Development Report 1999*:

- In 1960, 20 per cent of the world's people in the richest countries had thirty times the income of the poorest 20 per cent – in 1997, seventy-four times as much.
- The richest 20 per cent of the world's population have 86 per cent of world GNP, the poorest 20 per cent just 1 per cent.
- The net worth of the world's 200 richest people more than doubled in four years – from $440 billion to more than $1 trillion between 1994 and 1998, more than the combined income of the world's people. The assets of the three richest people were more than the combined GNP of the forty-eight least developed countries.
- A yearly contribution of 1 per cent of the wealth of the world's 200 richest people could provide universal access to primary education for all.
- Among the seventeen wealthiest industrialised countries, the highest levels of poverty are in the USA, Ireland and the UK. Income inequality increased in most OECD countries in the 1980s and early 1990s.

We have referred already on several occasions to the ethical and political nature of our subjects: childhood and public provisions for children. It is our recurring theme that these subjects involve making choices that are not primarily technical – does this technology do the job more effectively than that one? – but are primarily judgements of value – do we judge this to be better than that, and why? Yet as many have argued, ethical and political problems are at risk of being sidelined by, or translated into, technical and scientific matters. Indeed, it has been a feature of modernity to transform ethical and political problems into scientific and technical problems, which can be handed over to experts to be solved by the application of science and technology, the great engines of progress.

The ethical might be said to be the continuous process of making judgements, of trying to determine what is right or wrong, a process which cannot be avoided but which is full of uncertainty and ultimately undecidable. Politics, by contrast, involves making choices. Yet political decisions are inevitably compromises: 'in politics, it is always a question of the least bad . . . there can never be a wholly just decision, and this is why all decisions are political' (Critchley 1999: 108).

Why is ethics a matter of continuous uncertainty? Living in postmodern conditions means there are no universal foundations, no common rule book, which can provide certainty in determining ethical decisions. But that does not mean, as some suggest, that there is no ethics and that we face only an infinite number of positions of equal value. Bauman (1993) argues that in postmodern conditions ethics (or morality as he prefers to term what we are talking about) exists but without a universal, infallible code to tell us what to think and do. We – ordinary people – are our own moral agents. We have to make choices between good and bad without seeking shelter in a universal code, and we must take responsibility for the choices that we make. This, he says, is uncomfortable. Human reality is messy and ambiguous, so decisions are uncertain and ambivalent:

> Confronting the choice between good and evil means finding oneself in a situation of ambivalence. . . . Dilemmas have no ready-made solutions; the necessity to choose comes without a foolproof recipe for proper choice; the attempt to do good is undertaken without guarantee of goodness of either the intention or the results.
>
> (Bauman 1995: 2)

Yet far from being pessimistic, Bauman is hopeful. Without universal foundations or study of moral philosophy, ordinary people make moral decisions and show moral competence – indeed, society is made possible by this competence. He welcomes a repersonalising of morality, and the release of morality from constructed ethical codes: 'personal responsibility is morality's last hope' (Bauman 1993: 34).

Taking responsibility for ethical decisions, rather than relying on universal rules or codes, is also an important feature of what has come to be called 'an ethics of care'. Joan Tronto (1993) describes an ethics of care as 'a practice rather than a set of rules or principles. . . . It involves particular acts of caring and a "general habit of mind" to care that should inform all aspects of moral life' (127). She defines caring as 'a species activity that includes everything that we do to maintain, continue and repair our "world" so we can live in it as well as possible' (103).

Care itself consists of four elements – caring about, taking care of, care giving and care receiving. The ethics of care has a further four elements – responsibility, competence, integrity and responsiveness.

The ethics of care has been linked by Tronto to a tradition of 'contextual morality' going back through the Scottish Enlightenment thinkers such as Hume as far back as Aristotle. It differs in many important ways from what can be termed a universalist or Kantian ethics, which sees ethics as a universal code, 'a totality of rules, norms, principles equally applicable to everyone and acceptable to every rational thinking person'. The ethical subject in the ethics of care is different to the ethical subject of universalist ethics:

> the moral agent in the ethics of care stands with both feet in the real world. While the universalist ethicist will see this as a threat to his independence and impartiality, or as an obstacle to creating in his moral imaginary, the care ethicist sees this precisely as a crucial condition for being able to judge well. . . . The ethics of care demands reflection on the best course of action in specific circumstances and the best way to express and interpret moral problems. Situatedness in concrete social practices is not seen as a threat to independent judgement. On the contrary it is assumed that this is exactly what will raise the quality of judgement. . . . Rather than an atomistic view of human nature, an ethics of care posits the image of a relational self, a moral agent embedded in concrete relationships with others.
>
> (Sevenhuijsen 1999a: 59)

Sevenhuijsen goes on to distinguish the ethics of care from a universalistic ethics, or ethics of rights, in three main respects: the ethics of care is concerned with responsibilities and relationships rather than rules and rights; it is bound to concrete situations, rather than being formal and abstract; and it is a moral activity rather than a set of principles to be followed.

How can we make childhood and public provision for children the conscious subjects of ethics? Rose (1999) notes the injection of ethics into many spheres of activity in Britain, for example 'ethical business' or 'ethical foreign policy'. He welcomes this as an antidote to attempts to translate ethical judgements into more objective and scientific language. But he also notes the danger that ethics can become yet another method of control, a means to manage through establishing yet more codes of universal good behaviour. This is an ethico-politics that 'attempts to technically manage the way in which each individual should conduct herself and her relations to others to produce politically desired ends . . . it seeks to inculcate a fixed and uncontestable code of conduct . . . to govern better'.

Rose proposes another idea of ethico-politics, one

> which attempts to make forms of life open to explicit political debate . . .
> a politics whose ethos is a reluctance to govern too much, that mini-
> mizes codification and maximizes debate, that seeks to increase the
> opportunities for each individual to construct and transform his or her
> own life forms, that validates diverse ethical criteria and encourages all
> to develop and refine their practical and experimental arts of existence.
>
> (Rose 1999: 193)

What Rose is emphasising is the importance of an ethics that enables individuals and groups to think critically, to question commonplace assumptions and to contest dominant discourses and constructions – and by doing
so to make the invisible visible, the familiar strange. This raises the question
of means, and leads us back to the issues we raised in the previous section of
finding sites for the conduct of related practices – a minor politics and an
ethico-politics – both of which address *inter alia* childhood.

We have talked about a repersonalised ethics, an ethics of uncertainty,
ambivalence and responsibility. We have also referred to an ethics of relationships, in the sense that ethical positions are better taken in relation
with others. But ethics also involves relationships in another way, the
concept of an ethical relationship. Emmanuel Levinas writes of 'the ethics
of an encounter', which addresses the issue of how we relate to the Other.
This concept struggles with issues of difference and alterity. How might we
relate to the Other without trying to make the Other into the same as us?
How can we move from grasping and absorbing the Other to respecting
the Other? This is a major challenge since as Robert Young says

> the concept of Totality has dominated Western philosophy in its long
> history of desire for unity and the One. In Western philosophy, when
> knowledge or theory comprehends the Other, the alterity of the Other
> vanishes as it becomes part of the same.
>
> (Young 1990: 13)

Similarly, in her discussion of an 'ethics of care', Tronto (1993) both
acknowledges that 'questions of otherness are at the heart of contemporary
theory' and discusses the importance of 'responsiveness' in an ethics of care,
as a way to try and understand the needs of the other: 'responsiveness
suggests a different way to understand the needs of others rather than to
put ourselves into their position. . . . [O]ne is engaged from the standpoint
of the other, but not simply by presuming that the other is exactly like the
self' (135). She also observes that current moral frameworks inadequately
address questions of otherness because they 'presume people are inter-
changeable' (ibid.).

How to establish forms of knowledge and types of relationship that do not simply grasp and turn the Other into the same, which recognise the Other as unique and unexchangeable, a relationship to a 'concrete Other'? How to escape a relationship with the Other imbued with instrumentality, which assumes expectation of exchange or recompense and that ultimately all relationships can be expressed in cash terms (the language of costs and benefits)? These questions pose great ethical challenges for public provisions for children which are concerned mainly or exclusively with producing pre-determined outcomes (an expectation that the child will make a return defined and required by the adult investor), and which work with totalising theories of how children are or should be, ordering and categorising children according to an adult schema and rendering the alterity of child-hood into the sameness of adulthood in waiting.

Gunilla Dahlberg has explored some possible implications of work with children which starts with ethics, in particular an ethical relationship between adult worker and child which does not seek to grasp or master the child but to respect his or her radical otherness. She talks of the impor-tance of opening up, of welcome and hospitality, and of attentiveness to singularity:

> One can view it as a relation, but not as a harmonious relation and encounter . . . (rather much) more characterized by inevitable and end-less uncertainty, dissensus, dissymmetry, ambiguity, interruptions. . . . How to open up for radical difference – for alterity – and to 'hear' what children are saying and doing? We can vitalize and intensify ethics and get a new possibility by opening ourselves for alterity, for the stranger, and assume that there is a reality outside the reality which gives the teacher possibilities to possess and comprehend the child. We then need spaces where children can speak and be heard. Spaces where we as adults also can become surprised and where we as pedagogues and researchers are being able to see the possibilities of uncertainty and doubt.
>
> (Dahlberg 2001: 8)

This ethical relationship to the Other is also related to a concept of justice. Influenced by Levinas, Critchley defines justice as 'a relation to the other, a response to suffering or an attempt to limit cruelty and humiliation: a relation which might be described with the adjective ethical' (1999: 106). Moreover that relation is marked by an 'infinite responsibility', for in the words of Derrida:

> I believe that we cannot give up on the concept of infinite respons-ibility. . . . I would say for Levinas and myself, that if you give up the infinitude of responsibility, there is no responsibility. It is because we act and live in infinitude that the responsibility with regard to the

other is irreducible. . . . I owe myself infinitely to each and every singularity. If responsibility was not infinite, you could not have moral and
political problems. There are only moral and political problems, and
everything that follows from this, from the moment when responsibility
is not limitable.

(Derrida 1996: 86)

Nor does this broad idea of justice conflict with other more specific
concepts, for example economic, cultural and associational justice (Frazer
1997; Gerwitz 2000) – all of which involve a responsibility to the other
and a response to suffering in its many forms. Conversely, the examples of
economic injustice at the start of this section illustrate an absence of responsibility and an unresponsiveness to suffering and humiliation.

We have been making some sketch plans of an approach to ethics and
politics, which frames our thinking about childhood and provisions for
children. That sketch reveals the value we place: on personal responsibility
for ethical and political decisions; on recognition of uncertainty, ambivalence and messiness as an irreducible part of life and of making these
decisions; on the importance of making those decisions in relation with
others, with the assistance of critical thinking and scepticism, as well as
new sites for solidarity – in short through a rigorous and local form of
democratic practice; on ethical relationships based on respect for the
Other, for his or her alterity and singularity, and on struggling to assume
infinite responsibility; on interdependence, mutuality and commitment; on
Enlightenment values of tolerance, equality, and democracy; and on justice.

But childhood and provision for children are subject to other and more
dominant values, which frame a rather different ethics to the one we
are seeking to construct. At one level, as we have argued throughout
this chapter, there is a tendency to remove ethics and politics altogether
(as well as theory!). Important matters – knowledges, understandings,
purposes – are treated as essential, and therefore self-evident rather than
contestable. Contradictions and conflicts in the political, economic and
social realms, issues that are essentially ethical, are transformed into technical issues, 'problems to be managed', which managerialism offers to fix:
we shall return to this technology in the next chapter.

But despite this attempt to air-brush them out, values still abound, even
if they are not always immediately apparent. Take, for example, the emergence of advanced liberalism in the last quarter of the twentieth century as
a dominant principle of government. This has been described as a reaction
to the 'social state' which itself emerged as a governing principle at the end
of the nineteenth century as a reaction to laissez-faire liberalism and its
adverse social consequences (Rose 1999).

In liberal political thought family represents the private sphere, both outside the authority of the state and the scope of market relations: there is a
presumption that children and their care are private matters unless proven

otherwise (Randall 2001). Advanced liberalism is 'a more general and pervasive reactivation of earlier liberal scepticism over political government which will govern without governing "society"' (Rose 1999: xxiii) through the independent and self-regulating subject. This subject is a detached individual whose aim is autonomous and separate behaviour (Deacon 2000), who needs nobody and recognises dependence and vulnerability only in others, and who assumes individual responsibility for the management of risks, both his or her own and those of his or her family. The role of the advanced liberal state is not social security or service provision (as in the old social state), but the construction of a particular citizen: an autonomous subject, able to exercise choice, assume responsibilities and practise freedom. But the state must also control those who are unable or unwilling to conform to this ideal (for a fuller discussion of advanced liberalism, see Rose 1996, 1999).

So, value is attached to: promoting independence; privatisation or demutualisation of risk management; markets for all sorts of services, from schools to pensions; consumer choice (except, as Bauman points out, the choice of not wishing choice); social inclusion, meaning to bring people into this new form of citizenship. Great social and moral importance is placed on paid work: 'labour alone is the means by which the poor can acquire the status of citizen, a status increasingly a matter of consumption rights'. Other forms of human activity – such as care and play – are devalued and unrecognised, relegated to the private sphere (for a critique, see Sevenhuijsen 1999b).

Rose argues that as advanced liberalism develops, the relation of the social and economic is rethought: 'all aspects of *social* behaviour are now reconceptualised along economic lines – as calculative actions undertaken through the universal faculty of choice' (1999: 141). Rather than striving for infinite responsibility, the individual reckons the price of everything and holds it in the balance as a contracted obligation. The ideal is enterprise and the entrepreneur – the entrepreneur in business, but also becoming an entrepreneur of oneself, conducting your life and your family as a kind of enterprise: 'the powers of the state are donated to empowering entrepreneurial subjects of choice in their quest for self-realisation' (ibid.: 142). The economic reverse side of advanced liberalism as a form of political thought is neo-liberalism as a form of capitalism (also called 'free-market' or 'Anglo-Saxon' capitalism) (for a fuller discussion of different forms of capitalism, see Hutton 1995 and Gray 1999). This form of capitalism has become increasingly dominant, especially in the English-language world, since the 1970s.

What is distinctive about neo-liberal capitalism? It places great value on markets and competition; economic deregulation and contractual regulation – the rule of the lawyers over the rule of politicians; individualisation and choice; 'flexibility' (i.e. the removal of all limits on the market operator's freedom of choice) and short-termism; incentive and inequality, as forces for greater efficiency and wealth; the commodification of all activities and relationships – everything can be financially valued and traded, there is nothing that cannot be reduced to a number; and accountability solely to owners – shareholder value as the paramount value.

These particular values overlay a more general level of what might be called 'business values'. Bauman argues that business has its own rationality and its own ethics:

> The instrumental rationality is what makes business tick. . . . Means are to be used to the greatest possible effect. . . . How much the available means may bring in is the only question one can ask about their available use. Other questions – moral questions prominent among them – are given short shrift.
>
> Business has its own special kind of morality, sometimes called 'business ethics'. The paramount value of that ethics is honesty – which is mostly concerned with keeping promises and abiding by contractual obligations. . . . The code spells out how far honesty must reach and when one can say that s/he was 'honest enough'. Everything stretching beyond this boundary is no concern for business ethics.
>
> (Bauman 1995: 262)

It is not our intention to set up a simple opposition, between our ethical framework and that of advanced liberalism and Anglo-Saxon capitalism, or more broadly business. We do not deny a place for business values in a society which must find some meeting point between economic and social concerns and purposes. The problem, it seems to us, is that the relationship between the economic and social is out of kilter, with the former in unhealthy dominance over the latter, as has happened from time to time over the last 200 years of capitalist development. Rather than abolishing capitalism, which no longer faces any competition as an economic system, the challenge seems to be how to get things back to a better balance, a process which must include stronger governance of global capital, and which will have made some progress when we no longer have to justify everything in terms of the calculative instrumentality of a 'business case'.

Yet having admitted room for manoeuvre, we see some major areas of difference and contestation between our ethical and values framework and the one that seems to us to be dominant at present and which shapes ideas about childhood and produces public provision for childhood, at least in Britain and some other English-language countries. The emphasis on calculation and instrumentality, on complete autonomy and self-responsibility, on self-containment and self-centredness, is at odds with the value we place on relationships, new forms of solidarity and responsibility for the Other. There is a difference between consumer choice (what is the right product for your needs) and ethical choice (what is the right thing to do). The managerial nation state values internal strength through regulation, surveillance and normalisation, more standard and predictable outcomes, in sum an instrumental striving for order and certainty to be delivered through better human technologies. But these do not sit easily with the ethics of an encounter and of care, which seek to respect the Other, and a critical local democracy willing and able to contest truth claims, shape its own particular solutions and place in the world, and take responsibility for making its own evaluations. The production of 'children's services' through markets for sale to individual consumers, with calculated returns for investors and guaranteed outcomes for customers, seems incompatible with an ideal of public provision for children as a potential space for democratic practice and other possibilities, by children and adults, and open to all. Nor do we see how an economic system that produces, requires and justifies inequality – to the extent so vividly shown in the examples at the start of this section – can be readily reconciled with a search for justice which includes an infinite responsibility for the Other.

How these differences might shape different understandings of childhood and public provisions for children is the subject of our next four chapters.

Tying some of the ends together

Our discussion has linked social, political, economic and ethical theories and ideas to form a framework – connected, but not perfectly joined and finished – within which we situate our thinking about childhood and public provision for children. We have argued that ways of understanding the world, including ourselves, are in a state of flux, requiring a certain self-awareness that we are choosing particular positions and perspectives – which in turn are permeated by certain values, beliefs and assumptions. We have suggested that, from our perspective, childhood is socially constructed, and as such there may be many different understandings of childhood and images of the child which, in their turn, shape policy, provision and practice. Power relations are implicated in these processes of construction: understandings and images, and the knowledges used to legitimate them, do not drop out of the sky. We have examined claims that democracy, or rather established democratic institutions and practices, are not in good health, while we (or at least those of us living in the English-language world) are increasingly subjected to political and economic forms of liberalism – advanced liberalism and neo-liberalism – which bear their own particular set of highly instrumental values. The final part of our framework is ethics: like any other field of public policy, provision and practice, there is an inescapable ethical dimension to the field of childhood, which requires us to struggle with difficult issues concerning the good life and good relationships, and the values and purposes of our policies, provisions and practices.

We have offered a daunting assemblage of structural and other forces, and could have added more (not least, the environment, and the serious consequences for ourselves and future generations of its degradation through mankind's activities and belief in mastery). Our emphasis on these forces, however, is not meant to dismiss possibilities for agency, rather to question how agency can be effected. As we shall argue in the next chapter, there is a strong tendency to see children and public provisions for children, understood as children's services, as a means to resolve the problems that we, as adults, have either inherited or compounded: adults seek to achieve agency through children. Moreover, we often do so without fully confronting the nature and source of these problems, seeing children as offering a short cut or quick fix which avoids asking too many awkward questions. We hope that 'early interventions' can put right the social havoc wrought by neo-liberalism or that school teaching can make good declining democratic participation. We expect that children and children's services will enable us, as a nation, to survive riding the juggernaut of change, which individually and collectively we feel increasingly powerless to steer or rein in. To stay on board requires more flexibility, more productivity, more competition, more work, more consumption, more independence. But the final destination of the juggernaut we can no longer envisage: all we can do is stay on board for fear of falling off.

Perhaps, though, agency could lie in other directions. Rather than wishing power away or hoping to step outside power relations, neither of which is possible, we need to be aware, sceptical and critical about power, and the discourses and truth claims through which it operates, including our own part in these relations. Sevenhuijsen captures this complex relationship to power in her discussion of what she terms a 'politically formulated ethics of power', which she argues

> should not make its objective the elimination of power. Rather it should work with a multi-faceted understanding of power, which can capture both its restraining and enabling, creative and generative dimensions, and which can also differentiate between power and domination. Such an understanding should make sure that power is recognisable and manageable, and that unfair differences in treatment or arbitrariness cannot take hold of public decision-making. It can also contribute to exposing oppression, repression and systematic forms of dominance and assist in ways of reversing them.
>
> (Sevenhuijsen 1999a: 66)

Treating childhood, and provision for and practice with children, as contestable issues of value involving relationships of power implies the reassertion of ethical and political dimensions in childhood – not in place of technical dimensions, but preceding them. Based on critique, deliberation and, above all, the necessity for judgement, these ethical and political dimensions can play an important part in a revival of democracy. So too might public provisions for children if they can realise their potential as public spaces for the practice of ethics and democratic politics, as sites for a politics of childhood.

A politics of childhood is partly about making narratives stutter, questioning what is taken for granted, making the familiar strange, seeking new possibilities. We can extend this idea of agency – thinking differently as a prelude to change – more widely, to the task of envisioning what a good life would look like, including a good childhood. Perhaps, we, as adults, need to struggle to live that life not through our children's future but through our own present. Perhaps, we need to place less emphasis on provisions for children as the means to achieve a good life through the future returns they will bring, and pay more attention to these provisions as a part of that good life, here and now, as a sign of a good childhood and a civilised society – if they bring long-term benefits, so much the better! Perhaps, we need to turn away from an ethics of instrumentality and mastery that underlies so much of our discussion of children and the provisions we make for them, to find new understandings that express, and make space to flourish, an other ethics. Perhaps we need a turn from 'children's services' to 'children's spaces'.

3 Children – who do we think they are?

We have argued so far that, in the words of Carlina Rinaldi quoted earlier, 'childhood does not exist, we create it as a society, as a public subject'. Our construction of childhood and our images of the child represent ethical and political choices, made within larger frameworks of ideas, values and rationalities. In this chapter we want to explore what we believe to be a dominant discursive regime about children, a discourse which creates particular linked understandings of childhood in British society, and images of the child to match. Rinaldi, again, puts the matter succinctly: 'Many images take something away from children, children are seen as weak, poor, needy.' That, it seems to us, sums up the most powerful images of the child in Britain today. In some other parts of the world, other images are as powerful, or more so; while in yet other places, perhaps particularly in the English-language world, this image of the 'weak, poor and needy' child will resonate.

We shall explore how this image of the weak, poor and needy child is productive of a particular understanding of public provision for children, what we shall term 'children's services'. We will conclude by discussing some of the reasons why Britain, and perhaps some other countries, have created this particular understanding of childhood as a public subject, and an understanding of public provision for children to match. Having set out our argument, in the next chapter we shall offer our readings of a number of recent public policy statements and initiatives involving children, to illustrate our case that public provision has the image of the 'weak, poor and needy' child.

But before laying out our case, we should make two things very clear, lest the reader misunderstand our case from the start. First, to problematise – question – a dominant image of the child as 'weak, poor, needy' is not to deny that children are, in many respects, at a disadvantage compared to adults; it is not to deny that many children are living in material poverty; it is not to deny that children have needs. Nor are we saying that public provision for children should ignore issues such as child protection or the need of some children for more support than others by reason, for example, of a disability.

Nor, if we suggest that the dominant image emphasises children's dependence on their parents, do we imply that children should be regarded as independent and autonomous. Rather, we would question the dependence/independence dichotomy, with its assumption of the desirability and feasibility of becoming a detached, independent human being. Like Sevenhuijsen (1999b), in her critique of Giddens' book on *The Third Way* (1998), we think there is a 'need to deconstruct the normative image of the independent wage-earning citizen which is at the heart of contemporary notions of social participation and citizenship' (31). Like her, too, we would prefer to 'acknowledge everybody is dependent on care' and talk instead about our dependences on, and interdependence with, others – both children and adults.

Instead, our questioning is partly about proportionality and perspective. Why, as a society, do we in Britain choose mainly to talk about and portray children in such predominantly negative ways? Once again Rinaldi throws the issue into sharp relief when she asks 'why talk more about the needs of the child, than the possibilities or rights of the child?'. In Reggio, she says, while recognising that children have needs, they choose to focus on rights, moving from 'the child as the subject of needs to the child as the subject of rights'. Rather than weak, they choose to speak about the child as strong, rich in resources and competent, the meaning of which language we shall explore later.

Second, to speak of a 'dominant discursive regime' can give the misleading idea that we, as authors, think all people in Britain (or, more broadly, in the Anglo-American world) speak about and act towards children in only one way, share the same image, and that this way is the realisation of some general and coherent philosophy. This is not our position at all. We are not painting some Orwellian picture of a post-1984 society. We see in Britain a variety of ways of thinking and talking about childhood, and many and various images, not all by any means the image of the weak, poor and needy child. We could give many examples but will confine ourselves to four. At a national level, we can point to the increasing attention being paid in Britain to children's rights (Wales, for example, has appointed a Children's Commissioner), to children's participation, and to what has been called a new sociology of childhood or new childhood studies. Or at the level of a particular provision for children, we began this book with a description of the *Venture* in Wrexham, Wales: this seems to us to provide an example of what we call a 'children's space', a space that was psychologically available for children, and a space that supported social interaction and processes. Many play service providers would share the *Venture*'s aims.

Such examples assume very different understandings of the child compared to those found in the dominant discourse, and can support an image of the child as rich, competent and powerful.

Indeed, we would agree with Wyness when he proposes that there are contradictory developments within policy in Britain: 'whilst the trends are still towards strengthening the subordinate roles of children, there is now some recognition that children are socially competent actors' (Wyness 1999: 30). Broadly speaking, Wyness argues that educational reform has headed off in one direction, emphasising children's subordinate position to adults and especially parents as consumers of education, subjecting children to a highly centralised curriculum and not treating them as social agents with rights and responsibilities. While social welfare policy has tended to move more in the other direction. The shift in Britain towards responsibility for most policy and provisions for children being located within the education system raises important questions about whether and how this system can adopt new constructions of childhood.

If there is a dominant discourse, as we suggest, it is not the result of applying some grand design or philosophy, nothing so deterministic as this. Rather it emerges from a process of assembling together some ways of thinking, talking and acting, what Rose calls 'contingent lash-ups of thought and action' (1999: 27). This process of assembly is guided, we shall argue later in the chapter, by a mixture of forces: modernity, advanced liberalism and the business values of a neo-liberal market economy. The resulting assemblage – the dominant discourse of childhood – has a certain coherence of logic, a kind of rationality, yet is not without contradictions. We are not describing some monolithic and stylistically coherent structure, constructed in a short space of time to a master plan by a tightly controlled army of workmen, but rather an edifice erected over many years, influenced by different styles and built by many different architects and builders.

Finally, by way of introduction, we think that this dominant discursive regime operates in many ways. We will concentrate on one field: public provision for children, including policy and the practice of policy. We will provide some examples from this field. But we do not wish to suggest that discourses work only through public policies and their consequences. For example, the starting point for our earlier discussion paper was the representation of children in the British media, in particular as victims or perpetrators, with an emphasis on bad things being done to children or children doing bad things: 'their stories produce moral outrage, their scholastic achievements and failures make lead headlines' (Moss and Petrie 1997: 3).

During the period of writing this book (the last six months of 2000 and the first nine months of 2001), such stories have abounded. Children as victims has been a recurring media theme. Front-page and sustained prominence has been given to the murders of two children, to a campaign initiated by a newspaper to 'name and shame' paedophiles, and to a British couple's attempt to adopt baby twins, born in America, over the internet. At the end of this period, the murder eight years ago of a 3-year-old child by two 10-year-old children, and their release on parole, has dominated newspapers, radio and TV offering representations of children both as defenceless victims and wicked perpetrators of crime.

Not only are children a source of news in the media, but they are also portrayed in the advertisements and other promotional activities of multinational and other corporations. At the same time, large private child welfare organisations – whose fund raising strategies rely heavily on convincing the public of the need for their services to protect, to save, to prevent – offer striking visual images and narratives of children in the media: as weak, poor and needy.

The dominant discourse: constructions and images

We can discern three related constructions of the child that carry particular influence in Britain: the child as incomplete adult or futurity; the child as innocent and vulnerable; the child as redemptive vehicle. In Chapter 4, we shall take some examples from British government policies which illustrate these constructions. But first, we need to unpack them to see the ideas and understandings that they contain.

The child as incomplete adult or futurity is the child as empty vessel or *tabula rasa*, starting life with nothing, but requiring to be filled with socially sanctioned knowledge and culture, and growing into a predetermined identity. This child is passive, or perhaps pre-programmed, and so the subject of technologies which ensure an efficient process of reproduction or transmission of knowledge, skills and dominant social values which, successfully installed, ensure the best rate of return on the investment made by parents or government. A related idea is the child as nature, an essential being of universal properties and inherent capabilities whose development is viewed as an innate process – biologically determined, following general laws: 'the dominant developmental approach to childhood, provided by psychology, is based on the idea of natural growth. . . . [Childhood therefore is] a biologically determined stage on the path to full human status i.e. adulthood' (Prout and James, 1997: 10).

What both have in common is the idea of adulthood as a state of completion, maturity and full human status, epitomised by the economically productive and independent worker (before the inevitable decline from this peak to old age and the dependence of 'second childhood'). The child is in the process of becoming an adult, and represents potential human capital awaiting realisation and exploitation: he or she is that which is yet to be, a 'structured becoming' (Jenks 1982). This process of becoming entails linear progress, as the child passes through successive, orderly and predicted 'developmental' or 'key' stages. The metaphor is climbing a ladder, or building an edifice on foundations. Each stage of childhood is preparation, or readying, for the next and more important, with early childhood devalued for its immaturity yet recognised as a necessary foundation for successful progress through later life. This child therefore is defined as lacking, deficient, passive, incomplete, under-developed – and the more so the younger the child is. It is in this sense, rather than that of material disadvantage, that we say the image is of the 'poor' child, the 'weak' child, the 'needy' child.

But the child is also *an innocent, in the golden age of life*, even 'primitive', an idea that has been intriguing for many centuries. It is a construction to be found from Rousseau to Golding, which contains both fear of the unknown – the unruly, the uncontrollable – and a form of sentimentalisation, almost a utopian vision, where childhood is seen as a golden age. This image of the child generates in adults a desire to shelter children from the corruption of the world, by finding the means to offer children protection, continuity and security. Yet despite these best efforts, there is the inevitable loss of a quality with which children are born – an innocence, a naivety, an innate goodness.

Where does the child find protection, continuity and security? First and foremost in the immediate family, in particular with parents. Indeed, throughout the dominant discourse, the child's primary relationship is understood to be with her/his parents, especially the mother, and parents are presumed to have the most powerful influence on children. Other relationships may exist, but appear as secondary, even marginal to the parent–child relationship at the centre. This is expressed in the 'notion that "mothering" is the paradigmatic act of caring' (Tronto 1993: 109), with its concomitant assumption that caring is dyadic or individualistic.

> Too often, care is described and defined as a necessary relationship between two individuals, most often a mother and child. As others have noted such a dyadic understanding often leads to a romanticization of mother and child, so that they become like a romantic couple in contemporary Western discourse. The dyadic understanding also presumes that caring is naturally individualistic, though in fact few societies in the world have ever conceived of child rearing . . . as the responsibility of the birth mother.
>
> (Ibid.: 103)

There is a binary distinction here between 'hearth and home' and 'the wicked world', the private and the public sphere. Despite the evidence that child abuse is far more likely to happen in the family than outside, the family is still viewed as a haven of caring and warmth, a place of safety, the location of (gendered) care, in contrast to an instrumental, uncaring and often dangerous outside world. Indeed, it is almost as if, in Britain at least, there are no ways of talking about children being located in a network of relationships, stretching both within and outwith the home, a discourse which emphasises connectedness rather than the exclusivity of the parent/mother–child relationship.

These ideas of 'parent-centredness' have been given academic support from many sources. For example 'what was called the "socialisation process", primarily by parents in the family, was seen as a fundamental determinant of the character and personality of children as they grew up' (Prout 1999: 2). Socialisation theory not only gave parents centre stage. The other side of this coin constructs a 'poor' child:

> Socialisation theory depicts children as passively being given beliefs, knowledge, norms and attitudes, for example, rather than actively appropriating, selecting, interpreting and transforming them. It sees the process as a one-way transmission, from adults (assumed to be rational and competent) to children (assumed to be irrational and incompetent).
>
> (Ibid.)

Unlike the previous understanding, this understanding of the child as innocent assumes some loss in achieving adulthood: it is not a matter of unalloyed progress. Yet it also offers a child who is essentially weak, not only needing protection but also dependent. The child is isolated and decontextualised, except for her position in the family and her relationships with her parents, her relationship with the rest of society uncertain and full of potential danger.

Both understandings merge in the idea of the *child as redemptive vehicle*, the 'Christ child' or the socially engineered child. Here is the child as innocent who can save the world as s/he grows into adulthood – but who, to do so, will need to be shaped or filled or inscribed by adults who are themselves part of the corrupt world. What adults hope to find are effective technologies which, applied to children at early enough ages, can ensure a 'head start' or 'sure start'.

This theme of the redemptive potential of children, and the image of the child as redemptive agent or vehicle goes back a long way. Hatch refers to the rising expectations of science and technology in the nineteenth century which,

> coupled with a romantic view of the purity and perfectibility of the child, led to the perception that children are appropriate vehicles for solving problems in society. The notion was that if we can somehow intervene in the lives of children, then poverty, racism, crime, drug abuse and any number of social ills can be erased. Children become instruments of society's need to improve itself, and childhood became a time during which social problems were either solved or determined to be unsolvable.
>
> (Hatch 1995: 119)

But it is not just a matter of the child redeeming. The child also needs to be redeemed. There is a recurring theme in education and other children's services of rescuing children from their economic, social and cultural conditions through planned intervention: 'the notion of rescuing [combined] religious views of salvation with secular notions about the effects of poverty, class and social/racial discrimination' (Popkewitz 1998: 21).

Once again, we have before us a child who is weak, poor and needy – until subject to effective intervention, a sort of process of conversion (to the true path) or inoculation (from the infectious bacilli of the child's social milieu). Popkewitz, writing about the strong 'culture of redemption' in American education, comments that while 'the redemptive theme is rhetorically positioned in the name of democratic principles, the concrete strategies are concerned with governing the soul'.[5] In other words, if the child is to achieve her mission, then she must be acted upon so as to embody the right or appropriate sort of ideas, values, subjectivities, ambitions and practices. Discourses of redemption and salvation 'make the child an individual who is not reasonable, capable and competent but who – with the proper care and nurturing – can be saved' (Popkewitz 1998: 25).

These understandings of the child as futurity, as innocent and as redemptive agent are closely linked. It is the incompleteness of the child, the lack of corruption, the ability to inscribe the *tabula rasa* and to govern the soul that makes the child such a promising agent of redemption.

> The child may act as a repository for nostalgic longings for stability and certainty or as a figure of redemptive possibility, but a primary significance of this, I suggest, is that in a world seen as increasingly shifting, complex and uncertain, children, precisely because they are seen as especially unfinished, appear as a good target for controlling the future.
>
> (Prout 2000: 306)

Constructing 'children's services'

> From a social constructionist perspective [early childhood institutions], as well as our images of what a child is, can be and should be, must be seen as the social construction of a community of human agents, originating through our active interaction with other people and with society. . . . [Early childhood] institutions and pedagogical practices for children are constituted by dominant discourses in our society and embody thoughts, conceptions and ethics which prevail at a given moment in a given society.
>
> (Dahlberg *et al.* 1999: 62)

Dahlberg makes the connection between our image of the child and our understanding and image of public provision for children. So too does

Carlina Rinaldi: 'the poor image of the child supports an image of pre-schools and social services'. Speaking of Britain, Prout also connects: 'despite the recognition of children as persons in their own right, public policy and practice is marked by an intensification of control, regulation and surveillance around children' (2000: 304). He relates this tendency in public policy and practice to a widespread understanding of the child as futurity and redemptive agent, and an increasingly intense search for means to control the future through children.

Given this context, how do we understand or construct public provisions for children in Britain? It seems to us that they are constructed as instruments or technologies for producing child outputs or outcomes. The child is poor, weak and needy. She needs to be made less so through becoming the subject of processes and methods which will regulate, protect, normalise, shape, develop, prevent, supervise – and which do so to ends that must always be predetermined and calculable, and which entail controlling the present for the sake of determining the future.

This understanding of public provision we refer to as 'children's services'. Of course, the word 'services' has many meanings. Some will object to our association of it with this particular understanding or construction of public provision. 'Service' can have the sense of offering yourself to the other, the performance of a duty or obligation, being of service. A 'service ethic' has been an important motivation for many people working with children, and embodies values that have much in common with the ethical part of our framework.

Our use of 'services' links to other meanings, in particular dictionary definitions of 'service' such as 'performance of a function' and 'the checking and (if necessary) repairing and/or replacing of parts . . . to ensure efficient operation' (*Chambers Dictionary* 1998). It is our contention that the use of the term 'services' is often (though not invariably) associated with this sense. In any case, by questioning the term 'children's services', by suggesting it is problematic, we intend to show that it cannot be taken as neutral nor can its meaning be assumed to be self-evident: instead, the meaning of 'children's services' is contestable.

One metaphor for this construction of children's services is the factory or processing plant, vividly used by Lilian Katz when she speaks of early childhood provision (in the USA) while relating it to the compulsory school system:

> It seems to me that early childhood programmes are increasingly in danger of being modeled on the corporate/industrial or factory model so pervasive in elementary and secondary levels of education. . . . [F]actories are designed to transform raw material into prespecified products by treating it to a sequence of prespecified standard processes.
> (Katz 1993: 33–34)

It may be that 'metaphor' is the wrong word, as indeed is 'model'. Another way of viewing 'children's services' and 'factories' is as forms of organisation that both share certain understandings, purposes and practices, and are the product of a particular stage of modernity, what Foucault calls 'disciplinary societies'. We shall return to this theme later in the chapter.

An important component of this construction of children's services is instrumentality. Provision is made for a specified purpose, in the name of which the child is acted upon to produce outcomes, which are both predetermined and normative. Moreover, the 'customers' for these services are first and foremost adults. Purposes, functions, objectives and outcomes are usually defined by adults, and legitimated in relation to the needs of adults and the state of adulthood, i.e. producing the required adult, in particular a competitive and flexible member of the workforce and an autonomous subject who will assume responsibility for his or her own risks; protecting children from risks posed by adults; preventing future problems of adolescence or adulthood, such as delinquency and drug abuse; compensating children for parental difficulties and disadvantages; promoting gender equality between adult women and men; and so on.

Thus, provisions for children understood as children's services are not provided as places for children to live their childhoods and to develop their culture – although in practice they may become such places through the subversive competences of children. Nor do they treat childhood and the technologies applied to children as political, ethical and therefore contestable issues. The important question is 'what works?', ensuring the highest return on investment, not 'what is our image of the child?' Indeed, as public provisions for children, as well as private provisions (such as childcare services and private schools which offer to sell their product, for example, 'childcare', to adult consumers, for example, 'working parents') are increasingly viewed as businesses, competing to sell services to parents in the market place, to compete successfully brings even stronger demands for a guaranteed product, proven by league tables and other indicators that evidence success.

One consequence of this construction of children's services is a prominence given to what was described in Chapter 2 as a business ethics valuing return on investment. Another consequence is a continuous process of atomisation of the child in public policy. A particular need or problem, located in a particular part or facet of the child, is defined, by a particular discipline, profession or branch of government – and a service, with its attendant technologies and particular group of technicians, is then put in place to deal with that need or problem. Or else an existing service is redefined to take on board a new problem which adds a new outcome: for example, early childhood services are now seen as a vehicle for reducing juvenile and adult crime and, as such, brought into programmes intended to prevent future offending. The output of the service is not only pre-determined, but also ever more particular and specialised, produced by specialist staff and specialist techniques.

This process of atomisation – both of the child and 'children's services' – is no accident. It represents a particular way of understanding the world with its roots deep in modernity and modernity's search for order out of complexity. Modern (Newtonian) science, for example, as it emerged in the seventeenth century, viewed nature as passive, an object to be known, and hence dominated and controlled, and as a mechanism 'whose elements can be disassembled and then put together again in the form of laws' (Sousa Santos 1995: 13).[6] The factory, an archetypal modern economic organisation, is also based on principles of atomisation, the efficient pro-duction of particular outcomes achieved through breaking down the production process into component parts.

Fink makes the connection between modernity, ways of working with children in schools and their similarities with other forms of economic and social organisation:

> When Cartesian rationalism is combined with the Newtonian mechani-cal school of physics that suggested that we live in an orderly universe that was knowable through rational scientific methods, we have the basis for much of Western thought. Within this intellectual paradigm the world is knowable through logical, linear, cause–effect techniques. If we can just take things apart and then put them together again the object of study, be it the universe, the human body, or the child's learn-ing needs, is knowable. . . . Our businesses, schools and other social organisations reflect this way of thinking. For example, a pupil who attends virtually any secondary school is looked upon not as a whole living, breathing, feeling person, but in terms of his or her parts – the history part, the science part, the maths part, and so on. . . . The pupil then progresses in assembly-line fashion from year to year until he or she leaves school.
>
> (Fink 2001: 229)

The process of atomisation is sustained and reflected by the ever-growing numbers of government departments and other public agencies which find an interest in the child as a means to pursue their particular goals. Currently in England, and confining ourselves to government departments, there are: the Department for Education and Skills; the Department of Health; the Department of Culture, the Media and Sport; the Home Office; the Depart-ment for Work and Pensions; the Treasury; the Cabinet Office; the Lord Chancellor's Office; and the Department for Trade and Industry (which has responsibility for maternity and parental leave). Furthermore, within several of these departments there exist a number of units and divisions each with different interests involving the child. Divisions and sub-divisions occur, too, within the workforce, with an ever expanding typology of prac-titioners – nursery workers, childminders, playgroup workers, teachers of various kinds, residential and field social workers, various youth and play workers and so on.

Because of their functionality and purposiveness, services, together with the practitioners who staff them and the departments who have oversight for them, target certain groups of children, see certain parts of the child, bring certain understandings of the child, want certain outcomes from the child, have certain rationalities which shape how they think about and legitimate intervention with children. To take one example, different services or programmes in England define different age groups as the subject of their particular interventions, for example: 3- and 4-year-olds for early education; 4- to 11-year-olds for primary schooling; 0 to 3-year-olds for Sure Start; 0 to 14-year-olds for the National Childcare Strategy; 4 to 12 for 'On Track', an initiative to prevent crime; and so on. Or to take another example, the process of atomisation has been described in relation to what in Britain are called 'out of school' or 'school-age childcare' services, which in recent years have attracted the attention of an increasing number of government departments:

> These interests in school-age child care services are, in practice, separate. They are seen by the different departments as means towards their own distinct ends so that, at the level of central government, different stakeholders focus on the child in different ways, each in the light of their different value systems. For each department, a slightly different 'child' comes into the frame: the child who needs protection or, by contrast, the child from whom society needs protection; the child as the customer of leisure and recreation; the child as the offspring of employees, who needs child care in the interests of the employer, the labour market and female equality; the child as a member of society with a claim on its recreational resources.
>
> (Petrie 1994a: 84)

The process of atomisation does not however go unremarked: or at least its symptoms are noted. Compartmentalisation and poor inter-departmental or inter-agency coordination are increasingly seen as causes of inefficiency and inadequate outcomes. The response is increasing calls for coordination, partnership and 'joined-up' government, and initiatives to promote these new alignments: bringing the atoms into a new and closer relationship with each other. Yet this presents its own problems. One concerns the intrinsic difficulty of bringing different systems (and those who work within them) into closer working relationships. The term 'social autopoiesis' refers to the way social systems continually refer back to themselves for authority and to make sense of the external world: 'each [system] is closed to its external world in the sense that information from the world cannot penetrate the system in a direct manner . . . [but] has to be reproduced in the system's own terms' (King 1997: 26). In other words each system sees the world through its own lens, and each system formulates problems in terms of its own agenda and perceived competence: direct communication between systems is an impossibility, since 'these systems are able to relate to one another only by attempting to impose their own self-generated evaluations and criteria for success upon the other' (ibid.: 205).

This discussion of incoherence, fragmentation and compartmentalisation takes us into difficult territory, with no obvious way out. The road to greater coherence, integration and unity may lead to somewhere worth going: we shall indulge in writing some directions later in the book about how a less atomised approach to the child might be produced through a more encompassing theory and practice of work with children, pedagogy, which adopts a more holistic perspective. But as King's analysis suggests, there is no perfect solution since different social systems will always exist within society, even if some degree of reconfiguration takes place over time: pedagogy will not encompass all of the systems involved with children (for example, health, law). To a greater or lesser extent we are fated to live in and with a multiplicity of systems: 'this phenomenon of system non-communication provides the language for a description of society which acknowledges the existence of different perspectives, different codes of interpretation, different bodies of knowledge and different criteria for evaluation' (ibid.: 207).

The worker in children's services

The construction of public provision as 'children's services' constructs particular understandings of people who work in children's services. The workforce is, first and foremost, atomised. There are, as we have noted, many different types of worker in children's services, and particular understandings have adhered to individual groups, for example, the 'nursery nurse' and 'childminder' as substitute mothers, the teacher as a professional.

But across this diverse field, it seems to us that there is a convergence under way: towards the worker in 'children's services' being viewed and related to as a technician whose task is to follow clearly laid down procedures to produce prescribed outcomes (Fink 2001). Ball describes the process for teachers:

> In general terms there is an increase in the technical elements of teachers' work and a reduction in the professional. . . . The spaces for professional autonomy and judgement are (further) reduced. A standardisation and normalisation of classroom practice is being attempted. . . . The market is a disciplinary system and within it education is reconstructed as a consumption good. Children and their 'performances' are traded and exchanged as commodities. . . . Teachers' work is thus

increasingly viewed and evaluated solely in terms of output measures . . .
set against cost.

(Ball 1994: 49, 51)

The emphasis is on governing the actions (and souls) of workers, seeing
them as problems to be managed. Teachers and others working with
children are now judged, like many working in the commercial sector, by
the extent to which they produce outcomes that conform to externally
specified standards (Gewirtz 2000). This leaves little space for thought or
critical reflection about practice. Indeed, there is no obvious need for such
space if the worker is understood to be applying an agreed and tested
technology, which results in measurable and predictable outcomes.

Evaluation of children's services

In truth there is little that is merely measurable. . . . Drawing analogies
from the 'new science', Margaret Wheatley argues that we have been
deeply misled by the belief in scientific objectivity and a reduction into
parts that obscures our vision of the whole. The challenge, she says, is
to see beyond the separate fragments to the whole, stepping back far
enough to appreciate how things move and change as a coherent
entity. It is hard, especially in a climate obsessed with measurement, to
resist our well-trained desire to analyse the parts to death. Possibly
there is an inverse relationship between importance and what can be
easily measured. The deeper we venture beneath the surface, the more
profound the moral and spiritual character of learning and the more
elusive of measurement it becomes.

(Scottish Council Foundation 1999: 12)

In Britain, current research and evaluation of public provision for children,
including schools, foregrounds the quantification and measurement of predetermined outcomes and the workings of particular aspects of the technology: frequent terms used in addition to outcomes are indicators, targets,
goals. This approach incorporates a private sector strategy that has been
described as a 'compliance model of quality control':

Compliance models define quality as 'fitness for purpose'. They involve
the specification of standards and the institution of formal systems of
quality control to ensure that products conform to these standards.
Compliance models . . . are characterised by routinisation and
standardisation.

(Gewirtz 2000: 354)

This approach to evaluation is clearly related to a particular understanding of public provision for children – the construct of 'children's services'

as sites for technologies to produce predetermined results. As the quotation starting this section suggests, it adopts a partial and, once again, atomised approach, focused on the readily quantified and unable to pick up the unexpected and complex. David Boyle develops this theme:

> The problem is not so much trying to measure – sometimes you have to try. . . . The danger is when people or institutions think they have succeeded. That's when the damage is done and the spirit dies. Every 'bottom line' firmly held, is a generalization that fails to do justice to the individual moment or the individual person. . . . It is time we looked at those areas of human nature where computers can't follow – the world of the non-measurable, non-calculable. Love, intuition, imagination, creativity. . . . Over-reliance on numbers sweeps away your intuition along with ideology. It leaves policy-makers staring at screeds of figures, completely flummoxed by them.
>
> (Boyle 2001: 223)

Evaluation of children's services in this approach also foregrounds objectivity, resisting subjectivity and interpretation. Processes of observation, however, can never be objective and neutral, the observer never being able to stand outside the world in which he or she is situated so as to 'know' what is really going on. Moreover, the insertion of the evaluation process itself influences what is evaluated, the 'tail wagging the dog' phenomenon in which attention is focused on demonstrating attainment of the particular criteria or targets that have been laid down. This problematisation of objectivity is not confined to the social sciences. Modelled as they are on natural sciences, approaches to social scientific evaluation which rely on objectivity and atomisation are brought into question by the crisis in the paradigm of modern natural science and the 'new science' that has accompanied the crisis. Heisenberg and Bohr, for example, in quantum physics 'demonstrated that it is not possible to measure or observe our object without interfering with it, without actually changing it in such a way that, after being measured, the object is no longer the same as it was before' (Sousa Santos 1995: 18). Or, as the bio-physician Heinz von Foerster puts the matter: 'objectivity is a subject's false view that observing can take place without him' (1991).

The inherently political nature of evaluation, denied in the depoliticised and technical discourse of managerialism, also problematises objectivity claims. This is the nub of the discussion by Nikolas Rose of what he terms 'political numbers'. He recognises that numbers are 'crucial techniques for modern government . . . [and] have become indispensable to the complex technologies through which government is exercised'. But he does not take them at face value:

Acts of social quantification are politicized not in the sense that the numbers they use are somehow corrupt – although they may be – but because political judgements are implicit in the choice of what to measure, how to measure it, and how to present and interpret the results. . . . [W]hilst numbers are indispensable to politics they also appear to depoliticize whole areas of political judgement. They redraw the boundaries between politics and objectivity by purporting to act as automatic technical mechanisms for making judgements, prioritizing problems and allocating scarce resources. . . . The apparent objectivity of numbers, and of those who fabricate and manipulate them, helps configure the respective boundaries of the political and the technical. Numbers are part of the techniques of objectivity that establish what it is for a decision to be disinterested.

(Rose 1999: 198–199)

Concepts such as 'quality', coming from the business world and now frequently used in the evaluation of children's services, have also come under critical scrutiny. For example, in the early childhood field, an increasing number of writers on 'quality' have understood quality to be a subjective, value-based, relative and dynamic concept, with the possibility of multiple perspectives or understandings of quality. Some have gone further, arguing that the very concept of quality is constructed within modernist values and assumptions, presuming as it does the possibility of identifying stable, objective and rational criteria which can be applied irrespective of time, place or values (for a fuller discussion and critique of the concept of quality, see Dahlberg *et al.* 1999). Readings has similarly problematised the concept of 'excellence', much beloved in and applied to the university sector: 'Measures of excellence raise questions that are philosophical in that they are fundamentally incapable of producing cognitive certainty or definitive answers. Such questions will necessarily give rise to further debate for they are radically at odds with the logic of quantification' (1996: 24).

These and other critical evaluators have problematised an approach to evaluation that is situated within the modernist project with its epistemology of logical positivism, its belief in stable criteria, its assumption of the objective social scientist and its distaste for philosophy and moral issues. Linked to the increasing dominance of economism and the logic of markets in all spheres of life, with the conversion of ethical and political issues into managerial and technical issues, 'what can't be measured and has no easily auditable outcome ceases to exist within certain influential frames of policy making' (Rustin 1999: 256). In this context, evaluation becomes focused on methodological concerns, overwhelming ethics.

Why children's services?

What rationalities and forces produce the constructions of childhood and public provisions for children we have just described? It seems to us that three of the themes discussed in the previous chapter contribute to this assemblage of ideas about children and children's services, and to the taken for granted quality that indicates a dominant discursive regime: modernity and its understanding of the world; the values and needs of a resurgent neo-liberal or free market capitalism; and advanced liberalism. However, we do not claim a comprehensive account. We seek to start, not complete, the exploration of possible linkages between a wider philosophical, social, economic and political frame, and the ways in which we think, talk and act towards children.

The idea of the child as poor and needy, because immature, dependent and incomplete, is part of an Enlightenment narrative which envisaged a state of pure reason as maturity, represented by the autonomous, independent and self-sufficient adult. The child is in a state of nature that must be ordered, indeed 'to arrive at reason is to destroy nature, to reach maturity is to forget childhood' (Readings 1996: 63). Central to this narrative, and its belief that knowledge would make mankind free and rational, is the role of education, which involves a process of transmission to an empty vessel, to fill or mould the child into the adult ideal: 'education, that is, transforms children, who are by definition dependent upon adults, into independent beings, free citizens' (ibid.: 158). Here we have many elements of the dominant construction: children valued primarily for what they will become, children as wanting, needy and poor, education as the producer of predetermined outcomes.

This narrative is not only about a happy ending, it is also about the way of getting there. For within modernity there is a belief in the possibility of and right to seek dominance and control – be it of nature or nurture. Through control, progress can be achieved, order imposed and the future assured. The child viewed as futurity is the vehicle for progress, order and living happily ever after.

What we have just outlined is an idea with a long historical pedigree. But it retains currency in contemporary British public policy. We can take two examples. The first concerns the high policy priority given by the Labour Government (voted into office in 1997, and re-elected in 2001) to developing provisions and programmes for young children and their families. This has included an expansion of 'early education and childcare', and a large-scale intervention – Sure Start – aimed at children under 4 years of age and their families in areas of disadvantage. The emphasis is, however, very much on the future, of working through young children as the means to long-term goals.

This investment [Sure Start] will make a difference to families in the short and medium term but above all it is an *investment* in higher school standards and greater social cohesion in *ten or fifteen years time*. It is a crucial step towards breaking the cycle of deprivation. . . . Children's experience in the early years of their life are critical to their *subsequent development*. They have a significant impact on their *future performance* at school and the extent to which they are able to take advantage of opportunities *later in life*. That is why we have invested heavily in early years education.

(Department of Education and Employment, 2001: paras 1.13, 2.1: emphases added)

For the second example, we turn to the pledge made by the same Labour Government to eradicate child poverty. While welcoming this new concern by government with child poverty, Prout points out that the Government's stated rationale for tackling child poverty is mainly concerned with ideas of investment in the future and the reduction of adverse adult outcomes.

The central focus is on the better lives that will, it is predicted, emerge from reducing child poverty. It is not on the better lives that children will lead as children. In pointing this out I do not question the government's sincerity in its attack on child poverty. Nor do I doubt the need to make a collective investment in children. . . . My point is that on its own a focus on futurity is unbalanced and needs to be accompanied by a concern for the present wellbeing of children, for their participation in social life and for their opportunities for human self-realisation. In trying to understand why such a strong emphasis is placed on the futurity of children it is important to remember that, despite the different local and national shapes that modernity takes, a powerful common dynamic can be seen in the attempt to take control of both society and nature through rational knowledge and planning. It is this project of control, I would suggest, that is rather one-sidedly expressed in the concentration that current UK policy has on children as a means of shaping the societal future.

(Prout 2000: 305–306)

Prout argues that 'modernity's project of rational control', in particular via children and through the 'quintessentially modernist idea of prevention', appears to have become more intensive at a time when that project seems to have met its limits (as we also discussed in Chapter 2). There is a sort of vicious circle in operation. As society becomes more complex and uncertain, and as prevention becomes more difficult to engineer, 'the failure of such interventions summons up a renewed commitment to prevention . . . [and] children as a primary target of prevention seem caught in a system that can only respond to its failure through ratcheting up control' (ibid.: 306). In the last five years, Britain has witnessed a flood of social strategies, programmes, plans, targets, indicators and other initiatives, many involving new or reformed 'children's services', intended to address the social ills that have piled up over the preceding twenty years and to prevent fresh outbreaks. The consequence is, as Prout observes, public policy and practice that are marked by 'an intensification of control, regulation and surveillance around children'.

Burman (2001) points to a similar contrast between 'the manifest failure of the project of modernity' and persisting hopes of effecting change through children and their development. Children have been one of the main subjects of modernity's project of social improvement, providing a perceived means to fulfil broader economic and political agendas. We (that is adults) place on children great expectations, to achieve what we could not, and to put right what we made wrong. The result, as Burman poignantly observes, is that 'onto the child we heap the thwarted longings of decaying societies and try to figure something better. It's a hard burden for children to carry. Surely they should be their own future, not ours' (ibid.: 11).

Over and above a response to increasing complexity and uncertainty, why might this project of rational control become more intensive at this time? Why is the instrumental and controlling construction of 'children's services' becoming more dominant in public discourse, in Britain at least? Linked economic and social factors play a part. Changes in the economy and employment, within the context of increasing global competitiveness, bring business and government to the point of needing both more 'services' and services that are more efficient in the production of desired outputs. The need for more women workers and the increasing concentration of employment on women and men in their so-called 'prime working years' (i.e. between 25 and 50 years of age, coinciding with parenthood) (Deven *et al.* 1996) leads to an increasing institutionalisation of childhood, to ensure safe and secure care for children while parents are working. At the same time, there is a growing belief in the importance of early education for later performance both in school and at work. The 'business case' and *raison d'état* coincide:

> As the global economy takes hold, politicians and business leaders – heretofore largely uninterested in young children – are voicing concern and demonstrating readiness for action. Facing an increasingly competitive global economic market, they are worried about economic productivity. . . . Given this climate, quality early care and education services have been advocated as a cost-effective approach to maintaining a stable, well-prepared workforce today – and preparing such a workforce for the future.
>
> (Kagan *et al.* 1996: 12)

But economic change also generates other demands for children's services, not just more of them but services guaranteed to produce more effective outputs – including better control. For the economic values espoused by neo-liberal or free market capitalism – flexibility, competition, inequality, individualism – and the practices they produce are a recipe for social dislocation, serving up a long menu of attendant problems which threaten in due course to impede the efficient operation of the market economy. The social consequences of this particular form of capitalism are beginning to be defined and discussed.

Richard Sennett (1998) identifies 'new capitalism' with short-termism, linked to 'flexibility'. He argues that the corrosion of long-term commitment in the workplace – and the trust, loyalty and mutuality that it fosters – is dysfunctional for personal and family life:

> It is the time dimension of the new capitalism, rather than hi-tech data transmission, global stock markets or free trade that most affects people's emotional lives outside the workplace. Transposed to the family realm, 'no long term' means keep moving, don't commit yourself and don't sacrifice. . . . This conflict between family and work poses some questions about adult experience itself. How can long-term purposes be pursued in a short-term society? How can durable social relations be sustained? How can a human being develop a narrative of identity and life history in a society composed of episodes and fragments?
>
> (Sennett 1998: 27)

Bauman similarly traces a connection between the economic values of 'new' or 'neo-liberal' capitalism and their social consequences. Transparency and flexibility are key concepts for this economic order:

> the pressures which they simultaneously reflect and reinforce turn increasingly into the major factors of a new inter-societal and intra-societal polarization. Scope and speed of movement make all the difference between being in control and being controlled; between shaping the conditions of interaction and being shaped by them; between acting 'in order to' and behaving 'because of'; between pursuing goals with near certainty of success or defensive actions undertaken in a situation composed entirely of unknown variables that change without warning. . . . The deepest socio-psychological impact of flexibility consists in making precarious the situation of those affected and keeping it precarious.
>
> (Bauman 1999: 27–28)

Furthermore, Bauman argues, a prime victim of neo-liberal theory and practice has been solidarity, defined by him as 'the dense network of solidarities, overlapping and criss-crossing, observed in all societies as (however imperfect) a shelter and guarantee of certainty, and thus of trust, self-confidence and the courage without which the exercise of freedom and the willingness to experiment are unthinkable' (Bauman 1999: 30). Gray also notes a clear connection between free market (neo-liberal) capitalism and a serious weakening of social cohesion:

> It is odd that there are still those who find the association of free markets with social disorder anomalous. Even if it could itself be rendered stable the free market is bound to be destructive of other institutions through which social cohesion is achieved. . . . By privileging individual choice over any common good it tends to make relationships revocable and provisional.
>
> (Gray 1999: 37)

Neo-liberalism may extort a high social price, but it appears to deliver the goods economically. It also appears difficult, if not impossible, to control, since capital can seek more congenial surroundings at the first hint of serious trouble. It seems more feasible to adapt society to capital, than expect capital to be responsive to social needs. The consequence of economic deregulation, to create a world fit for the practice of neo-liberal capitalism, has been increased social regulation, a search for more effective methods of control and surveillance. As the nation state loses economic power, the shaping of children as the future labour force becomes an increasingly important role (Prout 2000), an important contribution to supply side economics, the proper role of the nation state as development agency. The dual aim is to produce a subject suited to new conditions, who embodies the values and assumptions of neo-liberalism (including what Fendler (2001) refers to as the 'flexible soul'), and to deal with the disconcerting consequences of that practice. Neo-liberalism assumes winners and losers in the great game of continuous competition, and a role for services in containing the discontent and repairing the failures of the losers. There remain the same belief and hope as was current in the nineteenth century: 'if we can somehow intervene in the lives of children, then poverty, racism, crime, drug abuse and any number of social ills can be erased'.

Thus, 'children's services' as producers of outcomes have received a double and linked boost from economic and social rationales. More services are wanted – but they must be efficient producers, they must offer 'best value', their outcomes must be economically calculable, they must 'deliver' the goods that have been advertised. The instrumental rationality, with its concern to guarantee and maximise predetermined returns on investment, which Bauman refers to as 'business values', is in the driving seat. Under the bonnet, there is a new engine. What are wanted are services that deliver their predetermined outcomes – and what is available, what gives new promise of achievement, is new or revamped technologies which claim to deliver improved performance.

What those technologies are we shall come to shortly. But before that we need to consider the role of advanced liberalism in the construction of provisions for children as 'children's services'. The theory of liberalism speaks of autonomy, freedom and choice, and the limitation of government. John O'Neill writes of 'Liberal atomism . . . [requiring] individuals be considered absolutely independent of their institutional contexts . . . [so that] the liberal political subject is constituted in total isolation' (1994: 39). Because liberalism assigns the dependent child to the private sphere, and as the private responsibility of her parents, liberal theory has great difficulty in finding a place for the child in its political discourse, except perhaps as 'potential human capital from whom a dividend may be expected' (O'Neill 1994: 46). Indeed O'Neill goes so far as to speak of 'the *missing* child in liberal theory'.

But in practice liberalism does control, it does attempt to govern in the interests of morality and order. The state seeks to govern without governing society, by acting on the choices and self-steering properties of individuals, an example of the governmentality we discussed in Chapter 2. It does this by working through families, and other institutions such as schools, to create individuals who do not need to be governed by others but will govern themselves. The family has always been understood to be far too important to be actually left to its own devices, and to address this dilemma (the public importance of the private family), 'a whole range of technologies were invented that would enable the family to do its public duty without destroying its private authority' (Rose 1999: 74; see also Donzelot 1979). The trick has been to govern through the family without appearing to do so. The account by Rose of the development in Britain of public interventions involving the family and the child provides a critical analysis of this process:

> The modern private family remains intensively governed, it is linked in so many ways with social, economic and political objectives. But government here acts not through mechanisms of social control and social subordination of the will, but through the promotion of subject-ivities, the construction of pleasures and ambitions, and the activation of guilt, anxiety, envy and disappointment. . . . The autonomous responsible family stands as the emblem of a new form of government of the soul.
>
> (Rose 1990: 208)

Yet a continuing problem is that some, even many families, remain unwilling or unable to embody and enact the desired aspirations, objectives and norms, and have had to be the subject of more overt interventions (for a fuller discussion of this history, see Rose 1990, 1999).

[The family of the labouring classes was] to be shaped, educated and solicited into a relation with the state if it was to fulfil the role of producing healthy, responsible, adjusted social citizens. The political task was to devise mechanisms that would support the family [of the labouring classes] in its 'normal' functioning and enable it to fulfil its social obligations most effectively without destroying its identity and responsibility. The technical details of the internal regime of the working-class family would become the object of new forms of pedagogy, for example through medical inspection of schoolchildren and the invention of health visitors, to instil norms of personal hygiene and standards of child care. While the mothers of the wealthier classes had been solicited into alliances with medics in the nineteenth century . . . one sees a new specification of the role of the working-class mother as one who was to be educated by educationalists, health visitors and doctors into the skills of responsible government of domestic relations.

(Rose 1999: 128–129)

This description of developments at the turn of the last century resonates with later interventions. Taking a historical perspective, the Sure Start programme started in Britain in 1998 (referred to in Chapter 2) becomes the latest in a long line of interventions, aimed at instilling norms and skills into a marginalised underclass, so they may be included in liberal society, and at eradicating poverty – which remains stubbornly persistent across the years.

But with the emergence of advanced liberalism has come new confidence in the possibilities of intervention: 'neo-liberalism does not abandon the "will to govern"': it maintains the view that the failure of government to achieve its objectives is to be overcome by inventing new strategies of government that will succeed' (Rose 1996: 53). Cometh the hour, cometh the technology! Central to the aspirations of the Labour Government in Britain has been the application of the procedures and techniques of new managerialism. Linked to the application of selected knowledge and research, mostly situated within a positivistic, empirical–analytic paradigm, managerialism promises human technologies able to produce more certain outcomes. It offers rationalism, neutral and objective knowledge and 'calculative technologies . . . [that] provide a foundation for enacting the new logics of rationing, targeting and priority setting' (Clarke 1998: 177). Critical of the *ancien régime* of control – professional, bureaucratic and political forms of rule, all relics of the social state – managerialism 'proclaims itself the universally applicable solution to problems of inefficiency, incompetence and chaos' (ibid.: 174). It promises rationalised order and certainty, removing politics and ethics and replacing them with techniques of control:

[Managerialism promises to cope] with the complexities and uncertainties of the modern world – 'the chaos of the new' – through the quasi-scientific techniques of strategic management and the delivery of fast-paced change and innovation. . . . The problems which the managerial state is intended to resolve derive from contradictions and conflicts in the political, economic and social realms. But what we have seen is the managerialisation of these contradictions: they are redefined as 'problems to be managed'. Terms such as 'efficiency' and 'effectiveness', 'performance' and 'quality' depoliticise a series of social issues (Whose efficiency? Effectiveness for whom?) And thus displace real political and policy choices into a series of managerial imperatives.

(Ibid.: 178, 179)

Parton has described this process in social work with children, how new managerial strategies, consisting of systems, procedures and organisational frameworks, have emerged concerned with 'risk management'. Replacing notions of 'artistic, situated judgement' for intrinsically complex, ambiguous and uncertain situations, these strategies for risk management 'operate as if issues were resolvable in any kind of realist, scientific or calculative/probabilistic sense' (1998: 23).

Managerialism is not the only technology underpinning advanced liberalism's new found belief in the processing qualities of 'children's services'. For example, there are what Rose refers to as the 'psy sciences', which he claims 'play a key role in rationalities and techniques of government, with legitimacy claimed by "engineers of the soul" on the basis they can deal truthfully with the real problems of human existence in the light of a knowledge of the individuals who make it up' (Rose 1999: xxii). The role of developmental psychology, one of these sciences, has been the subject of extensive critique (cf. Walkerdine 1984; Burman 1994, 2000; Morss 1996; Dahlberg *et al.* 1999), most recently by Fendler who talks about 'developmentality': 'normalisation operates through the discourse of developmentality when the generalizations that stipulate normal development are held to be defined and desirable . . . (and serve) as the norm and the lives of individual children are evaluated with reference to that norm' (2001: 128).

What managerialism offers, however, is the means to more effectively control, coordinate, deliver and monitor other technologies, some of recent origins, others of long standing. It sits in the control centre of the modern state, targeting, guiding and assessing impact. With the computer, it personifies what Gilles Deleuze (1992) called the 'society of control', in the process of succeeding Foucault's 'disciplinary societies' which themselves emerged in the eighteenth century and reached their peak in the early twentieth century. Disciplinary societies created 'vast spaces of enclosure . . . [and the] individual never ceases passing from one closed environment to another, each having its own laws: first the family; then the school; then the barracks; then the factory; from time to time the hospital; possibly the barracks'. But in control society, monitoring is continuous, standards ever changing and the individual is never finished with anything, 'controls are a modulation, like a self-deforming cast that will continuously change from one moment to the other . . . control is of short term and of rapid rates of turnover, but also continuous and without limit, while discipline was of long duration, infinite and discontinuous'. Taking the example of one children's service, the school, Deleuze outlines some consequences of being in a society of control:

> Just as the corporation replaces the factory, perpetual training tends to replace the school and continuous control to replace the examination – which is the surest way of delivering the school over to the corporation. . . . What counts is that we are at the beginning of something. . . . For the school system, continuous forms of control and the effect on the school of perpetual training, the corresponding abandonment of all university research, the introduction of the 'corporation' at all levels of schooling.
>
> (Deleuze 1992: 4, 6)

The joylessness of children's services

The concept of 'children's services' is both more influential now in policy and practice, confronted by economic and social change and uncertainty, yet more open to question as its values, assumptions and aspirations are caught in a growing scepticism about modernity. With an ever-growing emphasis on the technical and economic aspects of children's services, two lines of questioning open up. One is whether they will work in their own terms. Will they produce the desired outcomes? Will they deliver the flexible and autonomous workers, parents and adult citizens who will enable Britain (or any other country) to be winners in the global free market place – or at least not fall off the juggernaut?

The other line of questioning is about the very terms and conditions of 'children's services'. The more atomised, controlling and delivery-driven they become, the more instrumental and technical their approach, the more triumphal and dominant the discourse of economism and performativity – the more we are drawn to ask whether they have lost all connection with ideas of the good life and of what is truly important and worthwhile about being human. As Sennett (1998) puts it, 'operationally, everything is so clear; emotionally so illegible'. Michael Fielding poses this issue in relation to education policy in Britain:

> The discourse of performance and the now regrettably familiar 'delivery' is not only offensive, it is dishonest: offensive because it violates both our interpersonal realities and our intellectual self-

respect; dishonest because one can no more deliver learning than one can, with integrity, reduce the richness and complexity of vibrant professional practice to the 'effective management of performance'. . . . [T]here seems no place for either the language or the experience of joy, of spontaneity, of life lived in ways that are vibrant and fulfilling rather than watchfully earnest, focused and productive of economic activity.

(Fielding 2001: 8–9)

Joy, spontaneity, complexity, desires, richness, wonder, curiosity, care, vibrant, play, fulfilling, thinking for yourself, love, hospitality, welcome, alterity, emotion, ethics, relationships, responsibility – these are part of a vocabulary which speaks about a different idea of public provision for children, one which addresses questions about the good life, including a good childhood, and starts with ethics and politics. Once again, we need not reject all economic or other instrumental roles for these provisions. The issue though is whether this is the primary role or whether 'the vision is one in which economics is the servant of a wider and deeper human flourishing' (ibid.: 10). In Chapters 5 and 6 we explore how pursuing this line of questioning leads to a different understanding of public provision for children – the concept of 'children's spaces'.

In this chapter, we have explored some linked understandings and images of the child and of public provisions for children. We have also argued that these constructions do not appear from nowhere, but are the product of certain forces which we discussed in Chapter 2: particular ways of understanding the world, particular economic forces and particular values and beliefs. Faced by problematic conditions for which they are in part responsible, these forces re-double their efforts to find solutions by governing children: we get more of the same, with ever stronger technologies brought in. One theme that emerges is the very instrumental approach to children and children's services apparent in Britain (and perhaps in other countries too), verging on a mechanistic focus on means and ends, which has led us to talk frequently about technologies, factories, processing plants, and to foreground managerialism as a new technology of control.

Before proceeding we need to make clear what we are and are *not* saying. We are not saying that the ends pursued by 'children's services' are necessarily undesirable; nor that public provision should have no predetermined objectives; nor that managerial technologies have no place. What we are saying is that predetermined objectives, and the instrumental thinking that underlies them, should not be assumed, should not be taken for granted, but should be regarded as contestable propositions and matters of political choice. It is possible to imagine them playing a lesser, even minority, role in a different, less instrumental and controlling understanding of public provision for children, produced from a different understanding of who children are – understandings we explore in more detail in subsequent chapters. In short, we need to problematise the concept of 'children's services' and the understandings of children that produce and sustain this concept. By 'problematise' we do not mean reject these understandings out of hand, but rather recognise that they are perspectival and contestable, not universal and self-evident. They are choices we can make, not givens we are fated to accept without question.

What we are also saying, or at least arguing, is that modernity, neo-liberal capitalism and advanced liberalism share an inability to understand children as a social group within society, and childhood as an important period of life of value in its own right. Such ideas do not sit well with a discourse which values independence, paid work, privatised family life, markets and consumerism. They can only recognise and value children in relation to the adults they will become and childhood as an opportunity for shaping a desired adulthood.

4 A case study: the dominant discourse revealed in four English policy documents

In the last chapter we discussed the discourse surrounding children and children's services in England. In this chapter we look in greater detail at four policy documents as vehicles and instruments of that discourse. Selma Sevenhuijsen, undertaking a feminist analysis of a Dutch Government document as a political and ethical exercise, writes of the process and purpose of this type of deconstructive exercise:

> Policy texts are sites of power. . . . By establishing narrative conventions, authoritative repertoires of interpretation and frameworks of argumentation and communication, they confer power upon preferred modes of speaking and judging, and upon certain ways of expressing moral and political subjectivity. Through examining official documents in this way it becomes possible to trace both the overt and hidden gender load in their vocabulary.
>
> (Sevenhuijsen 1999a: 123)

Like Sevenhuijsen, we want to trace the overt and the hidden load in these documents, although in our case we focus on children rather than gender. One of our intentions is to make more visible understandings about children and children's services embedded in these texts. Uncovering the hidden, yet powerful, meanings in policy documents will allow us to 'develop discursive space', that is we hope to question the givenness of the dominant discourse, to point to its provisionality and to allow alternative constructions to be considered.

The documents we have selected are *Meeting the Childcare Challenge* (Department for Education and Employment (DfEE) 1998a); *Homework: Guidelines for Primary and Secondary Schools* (DfEE 1998b); *Extending Opportunity: A National Framework for Study Support* (DfEE 1999); and *Curriculum Guidance for the Foundation Stage* (Qualifications and Curriculum Authority (QCA) 2000). We chose them because they concern children in general. They are not targeted at children seen as especially vulnerable or at risk (we could have chosen many of these from the welfare sector) – although all of them seem to build on children's weakness rather than their strength. Three of the documents are about non-statutory services: childcare, early years settings and study support. There is no obligation on government to provide them and the use of them by children is not obligatory. The fourth document, on homework, relates to a statutory service – the school – but the guidance it contains does not have the weight of law. Between them, the documents cover the age range from birth to leaving school.

The documents, and the understandings they reveal, come from the first administration of the Labour Government, between 1997 and 2001, and thus are the product of a particular era and a particular political and economic context.[7] As we have already discussed, this context includes neo-liberal capitalism and an advanced liberal regime. Combining economic deregulation with social regulation, increasing emphasis is placed on markets, commodification of provisions, the role of the (for profit) private sector, and parents as consumers. The welfare state has an increasingly targeted and residual role as provider. An important task is to eradicate poverty – but not to reduce inequality, a necessary ingredient for a success-ful market economy. The state's main purpose, however, is to 'enable' indi-viduals to become self-regulating, autonomous citizens, able and willing to manage their own risks and those of their family. For those who cannot or will not govern themselves in this way, programmes are put in place which are intended to shape and educate families in the production of flexible, responsible and adjusted citizens and workers.

Central to this task are education and employment. The policy aim of many initiatives is for adults to be brought into employment and children prepared for it. A main assumption of policy is that national survival in an increasingly competitive world, and the alleviation of individual economic and social difficulties, depend on forming a population that is educated, trained and motivated for employment and so able to form a flexible, com-petitive, hard-working, compliant and resourceful labour force. Education (life-long learning) and employment are seen by government as universal answers to a range of interrelated problems, both of adults and of children, with children's well being viewed as related to parental employment. The 'workless' household (and Britain has the highest proportion of such house-holds in the European Union (Eurostat 2001)) is a recipe for poverty and 'social exclusion', with their variety of accompanying ills, economic, moral and social.

Introducing the case studies

Our analysis of these four documents forms part of a case study approach, with English policy towards children and children's services as one of two main cases. The dominant discourse that we contend informs English policy is not inevitable: it is just one possibility of many. It has, however, much in common with, for example, the USA (Moss *et al.* 1999: 15–26).

In Chapter 8, we shall offer the second case, that of Sweden, as an example of a country that works with an alternative discourse. Without wanting to suggest that it might provide the 'right' discourse for all time and all societies, we must none the less acknowledge that Sweden's values and constructions are closer to our own developing appreciations than is the dominant discourse revealed by the English documents: we prefer the Swedish image of the child to that found in English policy.

The contrasting cases of England and Sweden exemplify how, at the beginning of the twenty-first century, different discourses, formed from different histories and contexts, are productive of particular ways of under-standing and perceiving children and the public provisions made for them. How, as a result, the Swedish child and the English child are not equivalent social beings, but live within a social framework of different meanings, values and policies: using an evolutionary metaphor, they swim in different social waters and adapt to local conditions.

In examining the four English documents, we will consider what is said and what is unsaid, what is included and what is excluded. We will look at how much attention is given to the child, in her or his own right, and at what image of the child is presented. For example, we will examine whether the child is seen as situated in the present, the child of the here and now, or whether more attention is given to the child as future adult; we will see to what extent the child is portrayed as passive recipient of adult attention or as social agent, as needy or as strong. In passing, we see how the documents throw light on government understandings of parents and the family, and on the people who work with children.

In general, we shall find that the understandings of the child upon which the documents are based are not perceived as in any way problematic – indeed, they do not seem to be perceived at all. Any discussion of who the child is, or how childhood is understood, is virtually absent in the docu-ments we examine, which mainly dwell instead on technical and managerial issues of change, regulation and delivery. In the case of England, policy concerning public provisions for children is based more often on implicit meanings which are not debated – or at any rate, not at policy level. As a result, the political and ethical choices involved in social construction, the values that permeate the process, are hidden behind a false front, a facade that proclaims the application of objective and value-neutral knowledge and evaluation, and which recognises but one question – 'what works?'. Baker's (1998) observation about the US public school, referred to earlier, seems equally applicable to all aspects of contemporary public policy discus-sion in England (indeed, in Britain) concerning children: 'much education work flows around assumptions about children and their development – but what is meant by being a "child" is not debated'.

There is no recognition that there might be choices to be made in relation to who we think the child is or how we understand childhood in modern society. This lack of transparency applies, also, to other complex concepts, such as learning, education and care, that figure frequently in the documents. Again, these are referred to, often, without discussion, leaving meanings implicit, hazy at best and indecipherable at worst, and, therefore, less contestable than if the authors of the documents had attempted to present a clear position.

The case of Sweden will exemplify a more conscious public engagement in the meanings that might be attached to childhood, an engagement that brings the constructions underpinning policy into the open for discussion and negotiation.

Document 1: *Meeting the Childcare Challenge*

Meeting the Childcare Challenge, an 'essential component in our support for families and children' (13) outlines the National Childcare Strategy for England. The Government's intention is 'to ensure good quality, affordable childcare for children aged 0 to 14 in every neighbourhood' (13). It will do so by expanding childcare in the private sector, by means of start-up grants, and by the formation of Early Years and Childcare Development Partnerships, with members drawn from both public and private agencies, to drive the expansion of local provision. The Strategy will also enable parents who could not otherwise afford childcare to purchase it through the Working Families Tax Credit, that is through funding parents rather than provisions. Issues of quality are addressed by proposals to set up centres of excellence, to work towards a framework of recognised training and qualification and to supply training opportunities for people currently unemployed.

An examination of the document's first paragraph brings to light much of the Government's discourse, 'the regime of truth', as it concerns children and their parents, which is the foundation for the whole work. Paragraph 1.1 is descriptive and makes assertions which purport to be based in a commonly held understanding, not open to question. It begins: 'Children are cared for in many ways and almost all children receive a mix of informal care from parents and relatives in the home and more formal care in other settings.' Thus, from the beginning, children, where they are mentioned, are seen as passive: they are the recipients of care.

The meaning of 'care' is in no way explicated. However, reading between the lines, it clearly relates to a state of dependence or neediness. By and large, 'childcare' emerges as something that meets the *needs* of children and of their parents, for example, 'Childminders, nurseries and out of school clubs focus on meeting the needs of children while their parents are at work' (para. 1.3).

The first paragraph goes on to state that there are two forms of care – formal and informal – of which 'almost all' children are the recipients. The validity of this statement is questionable, especially given the age range, from 0 to 14 years, with which the document concerns itself. Most children and young people are not in childcare services – for example, only about 5 per cent of school-age children attend out-of-school services, and the document itself states that 'Only a third of mothers with children under the age of five use professionally registered childcare' (para. 1.9). Nevertheless, the first sentence of the document asserts that a mixture of formal and informal care is normative. In fact, it is probable that the writers had in mind at this point the children of *employed* mothers, rather than children as a whole.

That this misleading statement has slipped through suggests one of the document's purposes. The National Childcare Strategy is, first and foremost, a strategy for increasing parental, more specifically maternal, participation in the workforce and is an important component in the Government's aim to reduce poverty through employment. This is the first time since the Second World War that a government in Britain has had a policy in favour of mothers' employment: earlier governments have either adopted a hostile or a neutral stance. In the light of this history, the inaccurate generalisation of the first sentence may be seen as an attempt at persuading and reassuring parents and other potential critics of the Strategy.

The remaining four sentences of the opening paragraph place the responsibility for children's welfare firmly in the parents' court.

> Good parenting is the key to ensuring that children grow up happy and well prepared for adult life. Parents have the first and often the greatest influence on their children's development and education. They will always have the primary responsibility for the care and well-being of children. This is true whether they look after their children full-time or combine parenting and paid work.

So, although a more public setting is being proposed for children, from the beginning children are construed primarily as a private, rather than as a public, responsibility. Parents are 'centred', rather than understood as part of a network of relationships and influences, private and public. The subsequent assertions are open to question: can it be true that parents have the greatest influence on children's development and education when structural factors such as social class, poverty, gender and ethnicity play such a large part in children's achievements? When the workings of global capitalism so strongly affect employment and poverty? When the influence of public policy is powerful?

It is instructive that the document came from the then Department for Education and *Employment* (which has since become the Department for Education and Skills, with employment removed to a Department for Work and Pensions). The parent placed at the centre of the document is the economic parent, the parent who is attached, or is to be attached, to the labour force and who needs childcare. In this sense, childcare is a commodity to be purchased, which allows responsibility for children to be assumed, in a partial, temporary way by those other than parents. 'Childcare' is an alleviation of parental responsibility, the charge of children is transferred. The immediate interests of the children, here and now, as they live their daily lives, is not the motivating force behind the document.

Children, indeed, play but a small part in the document. Where they are mentioned there are two main emphases. The first is on children as future adults. Accordingly, a developmental perspective is taken: 'evidence shows that good quality childcare provides long-term benefits for the development of all children, of whatever background' (para. 1.4). (Note, in passing, the modernist reference to 'evidence', what works, and the assumption, here and in the rest of the document, that what constitutes quality is self-evident.) The child of *Meeting the Childcare Challenge* is the child who is in developmental progress. A test of the success of the Strategy, as it affects children, is seen as 'better outcomes for children, including readiness to learn by the time they reach school and enjoyable, developmental activities out of school hours' (para. 1.29).

So while their parents fulfil government objectives via employment, pre-school children are being processed to achieve 'readiness to learn' by the time they reach school. Here, there is no discussion of the meanings that might be given to children's 'learning', but the child who is implicit in the statement is the child as yet devoid of learning, the empty vessel waiting to be filled, the slate that remains blank until inscribed with the school curriculum. The statement seems to discount children's earlier learning: their active involvement in the development of language, and the construction of cultural and physical knowledge goes for nothing.

The understanding of learning that is presented is limited to the child's readiness to engage in the school's formal curriculum. This positions the school as the prime site in which learning takes place. There is no sense of the child's own agency – any agency there is is that of government, mediated through mechanisms such as the National Curriculum and testing at Key Stages, and operated by teachers. Outside school hours, too, the emphasis is on 'developmental activities', albeit enjoyable ones. Development within this framework is a process induced by adults, rather than an unfolding event in which children and adults are joint participants.

These are needy, vulnerable children: they require a 'safe and caring environment'; 'children's needs are therefore at the heart of our Strategy' (para. 1.5); 'many older children are indirectly protected by the Children Act requirements' (para. 1.14); 'children need to be happy and emotionally secure and to have ample opportunities for constructive play' (para. 1.4). The use of the adjective 'constructive' is interesting, suggesting as it does purposeful activity that will serve developmental ends and allied to the 'worthwhile activities', referred to above. From whose point of view, or on what basis, activities are seen as 'constructive' or 'worthwhile' is not discussed. Within the dominant discursive regime, the basis for these evaluations seems to be self-evident; no critical thought or ethical deliberation is necessary.

In any case, what constitutes 'worthwhile' seems to some extent to be left to the opinion of parents. The document springs from a childcare system that is commodified, with parents seen as consumers, choosing in the market between different forms of care: 'deciding who should look after their children is a major and very personal decision for parents' (para. 2.3); they are exercising choice between 'a diversity of childcare provision to meet parents' preferences' (p. 14), to meet 'their own requirements in terms of affordability and availability' (para. 4.6) – in other words they will have to cut their coat according to their cloth. The chequered history of childcare and early years education in Britain has produced an equally chequered range of provision: the diversity was not planned but has arisen out of a lack of policy in this field. But here this diversity is being presented, within a consumerist discourse, as a benefit.

The possibility of the child as a social participant is glimpsed but fleetingly in the document. A rare exception appears in paragraph 4.7. Here the child's own preferences are alluded to in the section on developing services that are responsive to parents' needs:

> *what children want*: as children get older, they will increasingly express their own preferences. They may, for example, prefer an out of school club which offers a supportive environment for homework and the chance to play with their school friends.

The statement is vague, inaccurate and tentative. Compared to what might children prefer an out-of-school club? Do not children from birth express preferences, and express them strongly? (Think of a baby eager to feed, or refusing to feed.) Is it that the dominant discourse finds it more acceptable for older children – children who are further along in the process of becoming adult – to express preferences? (See, for example, Petrie 1989; Clark and Moss 2001, for examples of listening to and taking account of the views and feelings of even the youngest children). There is no application of a principle here: that children should be listened to in matters that concern them – although the paragraph may have been drafted in response to this concern. Instead, the document remains descriptive and places children, alongside their parents, as consumers with preferences.

No critical questions are asked about what might constitute a good childhood and how public provision for children might contribute to this. The document, in any case, is not primarily concerned about children or childhood, being focused on enabling parents to work or train. Because it is framed around an atomising and excluding concept – 'childcare for working parents' – it has no way of talking about provisions open to all children. In the main, the document is given over to technical and administrative issues regarding 'quality', regulation, funding and delivery. Such questions as there are consist of 'consultation points' about these issues – and while these are necessary questions, they are not sufficient for a politically and ethically informed debate. Larger questions about policy are not asked – for example, why single out 'childcare' as a particular subject of policy and in need of a 'strategy'? How does 'childcare' relate to other provisions for children, including for children whose parents are not employed? What policy options were considered and why was one possibility chosen? What was the authors' image of the child?

As we said earlier, public policy selects, without any grand master plan, a particular set of characteristics, gives it priority and proceeds to act upon it. Given a different discourse, children's needs, their vulnerability and their preparation for adulthood would not be at the heart of the strategy. A different image of children and childhood might have been presented: children who are vital, strong and creative, themselves social agents and citizens, living their lives in the here and now. But these are not images with which the policy makers are working, nor would they expect them to resonate for many of their readers.

Document 2: *Homework Guidelines*

We now consider two policy documents which concentrate on school-age children – *Homework: Guidelines for Primary and Secondary Schools* (DfEE 1998b) and *Extending Opportunity: A National Framework for Study Support* (DfEE 1999). Like *Meeting the Childcare Challenge*, both are concerned mainly with technical questions: how to set up study support and out-of-school learning activities in one case, and successful homework policy and practice, in the other.

Homework: Guidelines for Primary and Secondary Schools sets out the Government's view on the purposes of homework, on how much and what sort should be set for pupils of different ages and the parts to be played by schools and parents in supporting pupils. This is the first detailed policy statement on the subject. The foreword, by the Secretary of State for Education, shares the same approach to the concept of learning as that to be found in *Meeting the Childcare Challenge*. It opens:

> Learning at home is an essential part of the good education to which all our children are entitled. It is not just about reinforcing learning in the classroom, although that is important. A good, well organised homework programme helps children and young people to develop the skills and attitudes they need for successful, independent lifelong learning.

The child's learning is placed within a narrow and instrumental framework, largely ignoring the ongoing learning of children, in partnership with adults and other children, from birth onwards. The document's future orientation is apparent from the start: children's learning (or perhaps curriculum-related learning would be more accurate) is seen as a preparation for lifelong learning, itself another way of describing the ability and readiness of adults to adapt themselves continuously to a changing labour market by the acquisition of new skills.

This instrumental and future orientation recurs. The purposes of homework are seen as extending and consolidating school learning, involving parents in the management (*sic*) of children's learning, and 'encouraging pupils to develop the skills, confidence and motivation needed to study effectively on their own'. At primary level, as pupils get older, the aim is to 'develop the confidence and self discipline needed to study on their own, and preparing them for the requirements of secondary school'. At secondary level, developing pupils' ability to study on their own 'is vital given the future of life-long learning and adaptability' (43).

We are not arguing that it is illegitimate for schools to prepare children for the future. What we are drawing attention to here, as elsewhere, is the fact that the document sees children's present lives, at home and at school, primarily as they relate to later stages of schooling and, ultimately as a preparation for membership of an adaptable workforce. It is a policy inscribed with the understanding of the child as futurity, promoting anticipation over currency.

The term 'homework' brings together two powerful concepts – home and work; school derived tasks enter the domestic arena. Throughout, the document is concerned with the management and organisation of homework. The guidelines make clear that the responsibility for homework is not limited to the school, but extends to parents: 'policies should give clear guidance on the role of parents and carers in supporting pupils' homework and how the school expects this role to change as children get older' (32). Elsewhere they speak about 'what is expected of them [teachers and parents] . . . on a weekly basis' (14). At secondary school stage parents should 'expect deadlines to be met and check that they are' (51). Also, parents should 'in the Government's view . . . provide a reasonably peaceful, suitable place in which pupils can do their homework or (at secondary school) help pupils attend other places where homework can be done, such as homework clubs and study support centres' (33, 51).

Children's compliance is to be maintained by educational techniques, such as feedback on work and mentioning achievement in school assembly (35). The compliance of parents is to be maintained by praise for their children's completed homework tasks (32, 51). The value basis for these practices is not given; they are presented within the context of 'what works'.

Note that, even at home, the child of the document is seen as 'pupil', a usage that acknowledges the powerful and central position of the school. Moreover, as in the Childcare Strategy, the child as agent hardly features in the *Guidelines*. The child exists within both documents as the object of adult supervision and management.

The document is legitimated, in the Introduction, by appeals to evidence as to 'what works', including a categorical statement that 'research in this and other countries has shown that homework can make an important contribution to pupils' progress at school' (3). This justifies not only homework but, furthermore, its introduction from the start of compulsory schooling, albeit for short periods only. Yet, in spite of this confident opening statement, a recent review of homework research (Hallam and Cowan 1999) is more equivocal in its conclusions: homework has as many perceived disadvantages as advantages; much of the research concerning the effectiveness of homework is inconclusive; and while the case for homework at secondary level is well established, the case at primary level is less clear. In addition, the reference to 'other countries' assumes the existence, elsewhere, of a concept equivalent to what in Britain is known as homework, and research findings that are directly and readily comparable across different cultural contexts.[8] This is misleading. The cultural specificity of 'homework' is well illustrated by the terms used when it is translated into other languages. These range from words in some cultures which include a connotation of duty (such as *los deberes* and *devoir*), to other cultures in which there is no specific term for this work and such words as *assignment* or *task* must do service instead. In addition, the meaning of homework is very different in countries where the school day and the school year are relatively long, compared with those where it is short. It can be useful to examine the practices of other countries, but this examination must not be context free, and research findings cannot simply be applied from one culture to another (for a fuller discussion of the pitfalls and issues involved in international comparisons in education, see Alexander 2000).

Like 'lifelong learning', 'homework' as presented in this document can be seen as a manifestation of Deleuze's 'society of control' (see Chapter 3), in which monitoring and control is continuous, and the individual is never finished with anything. The child never loses her schooling identity as 'pupil', and is constantly preparing for what is to follow. At the same time, boundaries between 'school' and 'family' are blurred and parents are recruited into management practices emanating from the school.

Document 3: *A National Framework for Study Support*

Extending Opportunity: A National Framework for Study Support sets its sights on raising standards in schools and, again, on the importance of 'lifelong learning'. To this end, the Secretary of State writes that the Government is allocating New Opportunities (national lottery) funding and seeking partnerships from the voluntary and business sectors to help expand 'study support' outside school.

As we have already noted, in all the documents we are examining, the key concepts: 'care', 'education', 'learning', the 'child' all lack transparency. The policy makers treat the meaning of such concepts as self-evident and unproblematic. The concept 'study support' has perhaps a lesser importance than these more overarching concepts, nevertheless its meaning is unclear and needs more explanation. The document uses the term to cover a wide range of activities: sports, mentoring, revision support, summer literacy classes, homework clubs, arts and crafts, 'learning about learning', residential courses and family learning – and more, but all are seen as 'learning activities'. The proposed providers range over schools, faith-based groups, voluntary organisations, youth services, businesses, museums and Training and Enterprise Councils.

'Study support' is a term that describes and tries to impose some coherence on this wide range of activities, all outside formal education but all, potentially, instrumental to the Government's aim to increase educational achievement and thereby increase employability. The document's stress is on how to make 'out of school hours learning' succeed, rather than on what might be desirable for children and childhood, over and above educational achievement. As with the *Homework Guidelines*, the *Framework for Study Support* sets its sights on the future and with a developmental emphasis whose status derives from a scientific discourse:

> After thirty years of research this is no longer a matter for debate. We know that those who are going to do well in life are marked out by their self-esteem, their motivation and their ability to take responsibility for their own learning. We know too that good learning habits begin to develop at an early age.
>
> (Macbeath 1999: 8)

In this extract, doing 'well in life' is predicated on individual attributes. The Secretary of State also is concerned with the individual and her or his success in later life: 'all of us want to be among life's achievers, and to have the opportunity to show what we can do'. Although neither the Secretary of State nor the author of the introduction to the document explain what they mean by doing 'well in life' or being 'among life's achievers', both seem to suggest a successful life measured in economic and employment terms.

None the less, the child emerges as a rather less shadowy figure in this than in other documents. The Secretary of State speaks of children 'experiencing the thrill of learning and succeeding' and, later, the document acknowledges that children are themselves active in choosing to participate: 'two of the greatest strengths of study support are its diversity and that children choose take part' (para. 1.4). There is also encouragement for the active involvement of children, or rather 'young people', in study support activities: 'consulting young people on what is best for them and involving them in their own learning and decision making is crucial to the success of out of school hours learning' (para. 3.9). However participation is not proposed as a positive value in itself, for the next sentence asserts that 'this in turn helps to foster an ethos of learning within the school as a whole and to provide positive role models – those who regard learning as cool – from among the pupils themselves'. The rationale for consultation is, therefore, instrumental: it contributes to the aims of the school, rather than expressing a principle of democratic practice.

'Cool' pupils are to be models for those who are more disaffected – and it is disaffected, vulnerable and needy children whose image emerges predominantly. The child who appears in the document is often the child who needs to re-engage with education, the child whose self-esteem needs to be maintained or recovered. The more fortunate 'gifted and talented child' is to be given opportunities to learn 'more widely or in greater depth'. This is a very different child from the culturally active child, the co-constructor of knowledge, to be met in other discourses. The child implicit within the *Framework* is the client of the adult world and fulfiller of adult wishes, the child defined in terms of what s/he is currently lacking.

Document 4: *Curriculum Guidance for the Foundation Stage*

This document has been produced for all private establishments in receipt of nursery grant funding, to provide early education for 3- and 4-year-olds, and for public sector schools with nursery and reception class children. The 'Foundation Stage' (note the language of building upon early experience) covers children aged 3 to 5 years, a three year period spanning the two years before compulsory schooling, and the first year of compulsory schooling. It prepares children for the National Curriculum proper, and is linked to working with the English Government's *Early Learning Goals* (QCA/DfEE 1999). These goals 'set out what most children are expected to achieve by the end of the reception year' (i.e. by the age of 6 years), and are an example of what has been called a 'central, competency oriented curriculum', prescriptive in tone, with centralised control and quite specific goals, targets or competences that children should achieve (Bennett 2001).

In this case, sixty-eight specific goals are set out in six areas of learning: personal, social and emotional development; language and literacy; mathematical development; knowledge and understanding of the world; physical development; creative development. Examples drawn from each area include:

- Understand what is right and wrong, and why (personal, social and emotional development).
- Read a range of familiar and common words and simple sentences independently (language and literacy).
- Count reliably up to ten everyday objects (mathematical development).
- Investigate objects and materials by using all of their senses as appropriate (knowledge and understanding of the world).
- Move with confidence, imagination and safety (physical development).

- Use their imagination in art and design, music, dance, and role play and stories (creative development).

The Early Learning Goals set out a menu of predetermined outcomes, though the individual items vary widely in level and specificity, from being able to count to making unerringly correct ethical judgements!

The *Guidance* 'reflects and is consistent with Early Learning Goals' and aims to 'help practitioners meet the diverse needs of all children so that most will achieve, and some, where appropriate, will go beyond the early learning goals by the end of the foundation stage'. The *Guidance* is 'on effective *learning and teaching*' (original emphasis) and 'the term curriculum is used to describe everything children do, see, hear, or feel in their setting, both planned and unplanned'.

The *Curriculum Guidance* begins by defining terms: 'throughout this booklet, we use the term setting to mean local authority nurseries, nursery centres, playgroups, pre-schools, accredited child minders in approved child-minding networks, or schools in the independent, private or voluntary sectors, and maintained schools'. What these settings have in common is that they provide for children from the age of 3 to 5 years (although some, such as day nurseries and childminders, may also provide for younger children). Providers and proprietors range from local authorities, to businesses, to community groups, private schools and individual childminders. They are in receipt of at least some public funding, either to a limited extent, in the case of private provision, or totally in the case of public provision. For the purpose of the document, they are all 'settings', however and wherever they are provided, in a church hall, school, purpose-built private day nursery, or in a childminder's home. A setting may contain 300–400 children or only one child.

Those working in a setting are referred to, equally, as practitioners; some are trained teachers or nursery nurses, others have little in the way of training or qualification. So, as practitioners, what is it that they practice?

> The role of the practitioner includes establishing relationships with children and their parents, planning the learning environment and curriculum, supporting and extending children's play, learning and development, and assessing children's achievements and planning their next steps. The word teaching is used to include all these aspects of their role.

The *Guidance* sets out to help practitioners plan and deliver an 'appropriate curriculum', as defined in the *Early Learning Goals* and their six areas of learning. The document identifies 'stepping stones' in each of these areas that 'show the knowledge, skills, understanding and attitudes that children need to learn during the foundations stage in order to achieve the early learning goals'. It may be seen, therefore, as a technical manual, first and foremost. Its intention is to help practitioners as technicians to plan, to assess, and to teach, thereby delivering the prescribed outcomes.

Practitioners are instructed to behave in certain ways, on the basis of assertions. For example:

> Certain ideas captivate many children and steer their learning. Observations of children show that what appears to be random play can often be linked to the development of concepts such as position, connection or order. For example, a child constantly assembling wooden blocks gives the practitioner an insight into that child's learning, so that activities can be planned that will develop the child's understanding of ideas such as shape, space and number.
>
> (QCH/DfEE 1999: 21)

The paragraph lacks clarity. It uses technical terms – 'position', 'connection', 'order' – that in themselves need explanation, and then provides an example that does not refer to any of these. The approach is to identify examples of what children do, 'snapshots', which will help practitioners to identify when 'appropriate' knowledge, skills understanding and attitudes have been achieved, so that they can plan the next steps in children's learning. It also sets out what practitioners need to do, 'showing how practitioners can both support and consolidate learning and help children make good progress towards, and where appropriate beyond, the early learning goals'. Between eleven and twenty-four pages are devoted to each of the six areas of learning, each formatted in the same way. There are some pages of background material, then a series of double-page spreads, with colour-coded footprints showing a progression of age related 'stepping stones' leading to the specific learning goals that are to be achieved at the end of the Foundation Stage.

The very specificity of the *Guidance* (and the *Early Learning Goals*) suggests a lack of confidence in at least some practitioners, as does the colour-coding of what practitioners 'need to do' with the less advanced stages linked to yellow, and progressing, for each subdivision of an area, through blue to green. The *Guidance* and the associated *Early Learning Goals* are prescriptive because the Government cannot allow or trust 'practitioners' to judge for themselves. Instead, they are told in detail what they 'need to do'.

One reason is that professional/vocational formation for many of them has been slight. The document does not prescribe training for 'teaching' – although the identification and meeting of training needs are put forward as desirable. An example is provided of a group of practitioners:

> Most have been on training courses provided by a range of early-years support groups and charities, and to workshops run by individual

settings. Some have gained qualifications, such as an NVQ level 3 or a degree in child development and/or in teaching.

From this example, some training would appear to be normative for practitioners'. But, nevertheless, the form and contents of the *Guidance* implies that whatever training practitioners have received is an insufficient basis for the delivery of a curriculum couched in broader, less prescriptive terms than those contained in the document.

The *Guidance* takes practitioners – some of whom might previously have seen themselves as childcare workers – into the foothills of the formal education system. Its language is very much that of formal education, unsurprisingly, given that the Foundation Stage is linked to Key Stage 1 of the National Curriculum in the primary school. 'Education' – and more specifically, 'effective education' – is the key domain of the document: 'the establishment of a foundation stage is a significant landmark in funded education in England', giving children 'secure foundations on which future learning can build'. In this document, as in those discussed earlier, the focus is again on the child of the future, the developmental child, the child progressing on stepping stones towards school, its Key Stages, and its more advanced curriculum. This preoccupation with what the child will achieve and the adult they will later become is in line with the Department of Education's mission statement 'Investing in our future' on the cover of the document.

Yet despite the emphasis of this document – and *Early Learning Goals* – on 'learning' by young children, there is no discussion of the authors' understandings either of learning or of the child. What both documents share, however, is a section on the 'diverse needs' of children. The implied child is the 'poor' child, who through the application of 'best practice' by practitioner technicians may achieve the specified outcomes.

Looking at the four documents together

We would like to focus on two main issues that the documents, between them, throw into relief. The first is the difficulty over describing, in any coherent way, work in those 'children's services' that lie outside compulsory schooling. The second is the growing centrality and power of the school in the lives of children and indeed their parents.

All four documents relate to services for children either not yet of compulsory school age or attending services outside the formal school system. The concepts that the writers turn to, to describe what these services deliver, are 'care' and 'education'. Both of these concepts are large and complex (for a fuller discussion of care, for example, see Deven *et al.* 1998). 'Care' can signify meanings such as responsibility – for example the responsibility for looking after children while parents work, as in 'childcare' services; it can equally refer to public authorities taking over the responsibilities of parents on a more long-term basis, as in 'taking children into care'. In these senses, care relates to the actions of providers and authorities: it has a structural sense. It can also mean personal assistance – work undertaken on behalf of someone who requires the intervention of another person in daily activities, such as feeding and washing, for their well-being. In this sense, care usually implies the dependence of the person cared for on the person who carries out caring – they cannot get on without them. It would be less usual, for example, to apply 'care' to a person of high status, an emperor say, whose attendants dress, wash and cook for him and where a closer examination might reveal a state of interdependence between servant and master. In English, 'care' also carries emotional meanings, warm meanings as in 'I care for you', and burdensome meanings as in 'all the cares of the world'. As we saw in Chapter 2, 'care' has also been envisaged as an ethic foregrounding the values of responsibility, competence, responsiveness and integrity.

When the term 'care' is used to describe the processes involved in work with children, any of the above meanings may be implied. However, 'care' cannot tell the whole story about work with children, and the writers of the documents occasionally show their unease with 'care' and some uncertainty about it. In *Meeting the Childcare Challenge*, the authors state: 'for young children there is no clear distinction between care and education' (para. 2.11). If this is so, the reader may find herself asking, why then is the redundant term – whether care or education – retained? The meaning is, perhaps, that work with young children aims at – or should aim at – their physical, emotional, social and cognitive well-being. And if this is the case for younger children, then why and in what ways is the situation different for older children? The statement relies on implicit understandings that the educational domain is closely related to schooling and preparation for school. Indeed it goes on to speak about 'Desirable Learning Outcomes' (a policy document superceded by *Early Learning Goals*) and children being properly prepared for learning when they start school.

When we turn to the *Curriculum Guidance for the Foundation Stage*, we find no discussion of, or statement about, the relationship between care and education (although the Childcare Strategy is mentioned briefly in the Minister's Foreword). Nor is the lack of difference between these concepts – asserted in the Childcare Strategy – mentioned in the *Framework*. This is puzzling, given that the document bears the imprint of the Department of Education – the provenance, also, of the Childcare Strategy – alongside that of the Qualifications and Curriculum Authority. Is it that for educationists, care is of lesser importance? Or that educationists are less focused on the whole child? Or that by the time they are 3 years old, children have already passed into the older group, mentioned in the Childcare Strategy, for whom the two processes are now distinct so that the atomised child can receive care and education separately?

The same quandary is apparent when, in the *National Framework for Study Support*, a link is suggested between study support (the domain of education) and childcare. The statement is tantalising in its brevity: 'good quality childcare shares many of the characteristics of study support, although there are important differences of emphasis' (para. 2.10). The document refers to childcare for school-aged children outside school hours. It goes on to state some of the differences between 'childcare' and 'study support', but limits these to organisational matters, rather than to processes. It speaks of the greater involvement of teachers and links with schools in study support provision, compared with childcare provision, and the shorter hours for which study support provision functions, 'one or two hours a week on average'.

But what the *National Framework* does *not* identify is ways in which childcare and study support may, as it asserts, be similar. Yet the document is concerned with older children, those aged from 5 to 16 years or older – not the pre-schoolers for whom there is 'no clear distinction' between education and care. Both the asserted similarity between study support and childcare, and the lack of distinction that is claimed between early education and childcare, seem to indicate not so much a lack of transparency as an extreme vagueness. In what ways are childcare, education and study support similar, in what ways distinct?

The authors would be helped by a term and concept which envisaged and encompassed work with groups of children and young people. We are speaking here of a conceptual field covering both a variety of settings – including 'childcare services' and 'study support' provisions – and a variety of activities including 'care' and 'education', where children interact with one another and with adults. In Chapter 7, we shall go on to propose and describe such a concept, 'pedagogy', meaning, in brief, the principles and processes that inform work with children, and address the whole child. Here it is perhaps sufficient to say that in many European countries provisions for children (in a variety of settings and with a variety of activities, such as childcare, youth work, family support, residential care, play work, study support – and sometimes early years education) have a greater coherence, because they are informed at the level of theory, policy and practice by commonly held understandings and are seen as belonging to the same field: that of pedagogy. This is the missing concept that could usefully have been brought to bear on the English documents we examined in the last chapter. Without this concept it is difficult to find ways to place and 'join up' work in different settings within a common framework, or to counter atomising approaches to work with children.

The second issue that emerges from these documents is the growing power of the school. Not only does the child portrayed in these documents lack agency, but she is increasingly subjected to control by one institution: the school. The texts we have examined reveal a public policy towards children that focuses increasingly on images of the schooled child and a schooled childhood, or alternatively on the disaffected child, the inadequately schooled child. Not only does the state, through schools, seek to shape and control the future adult population – life-long learners, fitted for employment – but it does so by an expanding influence over children's everyday lives.

Since their inception, the institution of the school and of state schooling have been powerful means of controlling younger members of the population. They have controlled children's activities (kept them out of mischief) and prepared them for work:

> For parents, it is employment outside the home and domestic work and child care within the home which provide the main means of social control over their whereabouts, activities and timetable. For young people, the school mirrors the control exercised by paid employment for their parents. Schooling organizes children's time according to the rhythm of the school day and its yearly calendar of term time and school time.
>
> (Petrie *et al.* 2000: 15)

But, over and above the requirement to attend, children are increasingly subject to the gaze and agenda of the school in other ways. Both *the Study Support Framework* and the *Homework Guidance* purposefully extend the school's domain beyond its physical boundaries and timetable. By means of homework, the school extends its remit into children's home life, controlling their use of time and choice of activities; at the same time it seeks to control parents as managers of their children's homework. With 'study support', organised free-time activities, also, set out to link the child's out-of-school time to the school and its goals.

The power of the school is also apparent in policy documents referring to children who have not yet started school. The Childcare Strategy and the Foundation Stage extend the reach of the school into the period before compulsory attendance, the better to prepare the child for formal education. For childcare and early years settings, the aims of the school throw a shadow back over the pre-school years, with 'readiness to learn' on entering school being taken as an important value (as if children only learn when they start school and on the terms offered by the school).

All of the documents we have considered speak, in short, of the growing imperium of the school and of the structures of formal education. This represents the emergence of education

> as a key site for the control of the future through children. . . . Whilst the effect [of the recent intensification of this project] on teachers and parents has been widely discussed, [its] impact on children has

remained relatively muted in public debate. Implicitly, however, the shaping of children is a fundamental drive in educational policy.

(Prout 2000: 306–307)

The construction of children and childhood and social policy

How we think about children and childhood, the value we place upon them, finds its way into how we act towards them. But interestingly, the opposite, also, is true: policy and practice also shape the way we think about children. Our constructions of children and childhood inform our actions towards them and are in a feedback system with them. Images of the passive and 'poor' child, of the child as raw material for schooling all arise from and inform social policy.

However the system is not closed and it does not have to be opaque. We hope that our analysis of these four documents, textual 'sites of power', begins to penetrate some of the opaqueness of the dominant discourse surrounding and constructing children. Especially we hope that we have suggested the inadequacy of our current conceptualisation of work with children as either education or care. The characteristics, the understandings and values, which might underpin work with children, irrespective of setting, have not been part of public debate, nor have they informed departmental reorganisation. In part, the problem is that within social policy, the child has, as we saw in Chapter 3, been atomised, seen as the site of needs that are of interest to distinct government departments. While the individual child is atomised, children as a group are then categorised according to the services that will process them and produce the desired outcomes. For the purposes of administration and service delivery, children may be pre-schoolers, pupils, users of leisure and sports facilities, and of health services. Other administrative categories have been constructed to denote children who need special interventions: children looked after and ceasing to be looked after, children 'in need', disabled children and children with special educational needs, children with emotional and behavioural difficulties, young offenders; children who are non-attenders at school or are excluded from school.

All of these administrative categories shape public perceptions and reflect the fragmentation of social policy towards children. Children's lives may be seen as the interface for a plethora of social, educational and health policies, which may be either permeable or impenetrable to one another. When children pass from one category to another, for example, from pre-schooler to pupil, perhaps in the course of a single day, they often become caught up in a different system of policies and provisions, with different concepts, purposes, theories, values, understandings, practices and practitioners: they may leave behind nursery workers and childminders, to meet teachers and out-of-school staff. In some cases personnel in the different systems can be at loggerheads with one another – for example, social services, health and education may quarrel as to financial responsibility for children (Petrie *et al.* forthcoming): the person of the child is atomised at great cost.

Admittedly, children make complex demands on public policy and are of interest – to some extent – for many government departments. But that is no reason why public policy should not seek better ways to accept responsibility for the whole child, and responsibility for all children, rather than – or in addition to – the sectional responsibility now exercised by different departments. Individual children are more than the sum of administrative categories. Each has a personal history and personal relationships, each is a social agent in her own right. In moving from notions of 'children's services' to ideas about 'children's spaces' and pedagogy we are hoping to open out room for the whole child, unhampered by labels and in a position to engage in relationships with children and non-children on the basis of personhood, rather than category.

5   An alternative discourse

In this chapter, we turn to our main purpose. We want to present our own position within the politics of childhood and to produce an alternative discourse, different from that manifested in the documents analysed in the last chapter, based in different understandings of children and childhood. We will claim that the child is a fellow citizen and social agent, with rights and strengths, and that her here-and-now life is at least as significant as adult agendas for her future. We will see how this different discourse produces an alternative approach and understanding of public provisions for children, what we term 'children's spaces'.

The rich child: another understanding of the child

We argued that the child of the dominant discourse was understood as private and dependent, needy, weak and poor. The child in our alternative discourse is social and inter-dependent, our image of the child 'strong, powerful, competent and, most of all, connected to adults and other children' (Malaguzzi 1993b: 10). Within our alternative discourse, children are understood as citizens, members of a social group, agents of their own lives (although not free agents, the constraints of society, the duties of citizenship all come into play for children as for adults), and as co-constructors of knowledge, identity and culture, constantly making meaning of their lives and the world in which they live. This child has a voice to be listened to, but with an understanding that listening is an interpretive process and children can give voice in many ways (famously expressed in Malaguzzi's 'hundred languages of childhood'), some of which can get lost in the course of 'development'. In short, our construction of the child produces a 'rich' child.

Within this discourse, childhood is related to adulthood, but not hierarchically. Rather childhood is an important stage of the life course in its own right, which leaves traces on later stages. We are concerned not only with the adult whom the child will become, but with the here and now of childhood – the child whom the child is. We are wary of discourses that concentrate on the child's future and are blind to the present if it does not serve an imagined future goal, whether for the child or for the wider society.

Similarly, we wish to avoid the child-as-redemptive-agent motif. This instrumental way of thinking implies that children can carry adult intentions into the future, continuing adult potency, providing immortality – but notice the burden of expectation this places on children. Each time we use expressions such as 'children are our future', we colonise their lives and make them an instrument of our redemption.

Also, at a pragmatic level, rather than at the level of values, the approach is flawed. The future is unpredictable, it will furnish future adults with social, economic, political, environmental and cultural contexts which we cannot foresee. We have to accept that we cannot control the future – although we, as adults, can certainly act here and now to reduce the damage that our current ways of life are inflicting on our environment. In the unpredictable future, today's plans may have unforeseen outcomes; orienting towards the future, at the expense of opportunities for children and society at present, is something of a gamble. So, not only are we sceptical about the possibility of moulding children to be redemptive agents, but this way of understanding children calls into question the agency and responsibility of today's adults.

We believe that childhood is an important part of the lifecourse – just like 'youth' or 'middle age' or whatever other ways we choose to section life. For children the 'now' is important, not only because a longer view may be less pertinent or less accessible for some of them, but because childhood should carry meanings beyond those of waiting, anticipation and preparation. It is salutary to remember that a small minority of children (small at least in the Minority World, large in many countries of the Majority World) will not reach adult life – the supposed light at the end of the tunnel, the future which adults are sometimes blinded by, so that we cannot see, do not appreciate, or will not let ourselves enjoy the here and now.

With an emphasis on the here and now, we must ask ourselves what we want for children today, for those children who are living their lives now – because although individual children pass through childhood, childhood and children are always with us. So we need to look at how society and public policy are affecting today's children, to consider the quality of their lives, to take into account their own understandings, concerns and wishes, to see them as the subject of rights.

We would also place great importance on children's relationships with others: not only parents but other adults and in particular other children, as well as with the wider society through, for example, the media. The dominant social construction of children positions them primarily within the family rather than as members of a wider society. *Parental* responsibility is stressed (e.g. for England and Wales, see Part I of the Children Act 1989), while *societal* responsibility is less clearly defined. Parents are, of course, very important: they provide children with their first and, often, most stable relationships. However, we do question both the centrality of the child–parent relationship and the degree of responsibility that parents are supposed to assume for their children's welfare, leaving them often positioned as consumers of 'children's services'.

Rather than individual consumers of education and other 'commodities within a service industry, within which parents pick and choose' (Wragg 1993: 13), we would choose to see children and parents as members of communities, communities to which they contribute and by which they are supported. Rather than focusing on the child in her family, we would choose to view children as part of a wider network of relationships, including not only parents but many others, adults and children. An educator from Reggio Emilia described this approach when asked at a conference about 'child-centred' work:

> [In Reggio] the child is not seen as an isolated human being, but as always in relationships, in human, social, cultural and historical context. The child's development is a process of individual and group construction. Nothing exists outside relationships. The child is the most important element of the school, but the child is not enough. We put at the centre the relationships between children, parents and teachers. That is the centre, for the child does not exist in isolation.
>
> (Filippini 1998)

In this way we would decentre the family, recognising that childhood is lived in a variety of settings, each with its own set of relationships. As Loris Malaguzzi noted about the experience in Reggio of how children responded to the provision of early childhood centres,

> the children understood sooner than expected that their adventures in life could flow between places. [Through early childhood centres] they could express their previously overlooked desire to be with peers and find in them points of reference, understanding, surprises, affective ties and merriment that could dispel shadows and uneasiness. For the children and their families there now opened up the possibility of a very long and continuous period of [children] living together with each other, 5 or 6 years of reciprocal trust and work.
>
> (Malaguzzi 1993b: 55)

Malaguzzi is referring here to the nursery and its community of children, parents and staff. The same aspirations could also attach to older children, passing through the stages of primary and secondary schooling – also for at least five or six years in each case. In a recent study of provisions for school-age children undertaken by one of us, the importance of children's friendships with their peers was very apparent. Children appreciated the presence of friends and disliked going to provisions where they had no friends (Petrie *et al.* 2000). Two examples may speak for themselves.

Pritty, aged 5 years and of Indian and Scottish parentage, said she preferred her after-school club to going to school because 'we play with the
cushions and we play Cluedo and we eat sandwiches and we have lots of
giggles and we drink milk'. In this short sentence she speaks as one of a
collective 'we' rather than an individual 'I' and sums up the advantages for
her of the club: unorganised playful interaction – playing with cushions
and lots of giggles; taking part in a structured game – 'you have to guess
who the murderer is and which room they done it in and then what they
do it with'; and playing the game with other children – (How many?) –
'Six or four or five.' We should stress, here, that Pritty knew many of the
children who were now at school with her from her time in nursery.

The presence of other children, construed as friends, and the interchanges
of friendship were important for children's feeling of well-being in the club
Pritty attended. By contrast, at an employer-provided playscheme, children
came from homes situated up to sixty or more miles apart. For them, there
was no common background or history; the only connection was that their
parents were employed at the same workplace, an extreme case of 'childcare
for working parents'. Stephen, aged 12 years, said: 'I know my other friends
a lot better than the people I know at the play scheme, and I still get a kind
of alienated feel there sometimes . . . which I don't get with other friends'.

Children's friendships are relationships, chosen and developed by
children themselves for their own purposes and with greater equality than
is to be found in child–adult relationships. They represent one way in
which children enter and become active in the wider community, outside
the family, co-constructing with other children their own cultural forms (a
subject developed in the next chapter) and increasing their sphere of social
agency.

Children, in our alternative discourse, are also subjects of rights.
Discourse about rights develops from the eighteenth century, from
Rousseau, Tom Paine, the American and French Revolutions, with notions
of inalienable rights that adhere to human beings and of duties which
accompany rights and which together form the 'social contract'. This philosophical and moral discourse is connected to ideas about freedom, self-
determination, equality and citizenship. With the UN Convention on the
Rights of the Child, children have been singled out as a distinct group,
their rights considered separately from those of human beings generally.
This distinction renders their position as 'other', separate from adults,
more transparent; it reveals them as, politically, a minority group capable
of oppression and exploitation by adults, the political majority. It signals
that both abusive public policy and the individual abuse of children by
adults can be seen as actions of the oppressive majority. By recognising
them as a minority, children can be placed in emancipatory frameworks,
similar to those used to promote the rights of other minority groups – such
as those based on gender or race.

Elements of what we have called the dominant discourse concentrate on children's immaturity, their need for protection and acting in the child's best interest, all of which could be placed within a children's rights discourse. Our own position is of children's rights within a model of citizenship and democracy – that social rights and duties cannot be alienated from social membership. Children and adults have a right to be heard, as individuals and as collectives, on matters that affect them and they have the right for their concerns to be taken into account. The reverse of this coin is that adults and children – individually and collectively – listen to the concerns of others and take each other's concerns into account. In citizenship, speaking out and listening attentively are both implicated. Such democratic dialogues can be fostered and modelled in a number of arenas, including children's services – or children's spaces as we would prefer to construct them. In our discussion, we shall not position the rights and needs of children in opposition to the needs and rights of adults: they are different, if connected, parts of social policy and both must be taken into account.

We are aware that for some readers, the discourse of 'rights' may be unpalatable, because they prefer to position human beings within the arena of personal relationships, personal feelings and personal morality, rather than within a more legal and individualistic framework. We also recognise arguments about the limitations of rights, and the danger of pinning too much faith in their efficacy. Viewing rights as the domain of a particular social system, the law, King argues that

> all that appears possible for law is self-regulation, i.e. controlling the environment that law has itself constructed. This is in itself unlikely to affect the operations of other systems. . . . Autopoietic theory would predict that, given the normatively closed nature of social systems and the impossibility of input–output relations, the effective regulation of harmful behaviour to children through [rights] is unlikely to succeed. . . . The very most that children's rights activists have the rights to expect is for their communications to discourage the most blatantly child-harming operations of market and political forces by attributing a negative role to these operations within the system's programmes, such as loss-making, power-losing etc.
>
> (King 1997: 176, 184)

For us, too, the personal has its attraction. Nor do we think rights are a panacea for eradicating injustice and oppression, not least because they need interpretation and enforcement. Nevertheless the discourse of rights is, we believe, necessary for several reasons. It places children and their personal relationships within a wider societal framework of agreed understandings of what is owed to and by human beings towards each other. While the idea of any person relating to others solely on the basis of rights and duties may seem distasteful, legalistic and self-centred, this is not what we are proposing. Our preferred discourse, and the model of children's provision which arises out of it, also values the personal. But to disregard the notion of rights is to disregard the current political position of children as minorities; children's rights must be acknowledged and promoted if we are to reconstruct how we think about them and behave towards them in an emancipatory way. To leave rights out of the equation leaves children as the objects of adult behaviour – whether in private or in the sphere of public policy – and notions of purely personal morality are a hazardous default position, lacking as it does accountability to the wider society. The discourse of rights, coupled to citizenship, allows children to be social participants, while allowing adults who act on behalf of children, to be seen as protecting *children's rights*, rather than protecting *children*. The child as subject of citizenship rights is, socially speaking, in a stronger position than the victim to whom things happen, and who is, potentially, at the mercy of those adults who equate might with right.

Children's spaces

Our construction of children as competent social agents and the subject of rights requires a different construction of public provisions for children: as 'children's spaces' rather than 'children's services'. Before explaining this construction, we should make it clear what public provisions we are talking about. Broadly speaking, 'children's spaces' can encompass a wide range of out-of-home settings where groups of children and young people come together, from schooling on the one hand, to lightly structured spaces for children's outdoor unsupervised play on the other. They include nurseries, 'home zones',[9] various playgrounds, schools, out-of-school clubs, youth clubs, residential homes for looked-after children and many other possibilities, either already existing or waiting to be developed.

We see them as spaces – physical environments certainly, but also social, cultural and discursive – provided through public agency, places for civic life rather than commercial transactions, where children meet one another, and adults. They foreground the present, rather than the future: they are part of life, not just preparation for it. They are spaces for children's own agendas, although not precluding adult agendas, where children are understood as fellow citizens with rights, participating members of the social groups in which they find themselves, agents of their own lives but also interdependent with others, co-constructors of knowledge, identity and culture, children who co-exist with others in society on the basis of who they are, rather than who they will become. Children's spaces are for all children, on a democratic footing across different social groups. They make space for the whole child, not the sectional child of many children's services.

They are spaces of many possibilities, some predetermined but many others not, and for realising many potentials. They are spaces for processes and relationships, not primarily for the production of prespecified outcomes. They are places where children are allowed to manage risk and escape from adult anxieties, where, if they wish, free from the adult gaze, they can lead their own cultural lives.

'Children's spaces', as we understand them, are characterised by particular ethics, relationships and practices. In the next two chapters we shall offer some ideas of what these might be if 'children's spaces' are to avoid the instrumentality and totalising tendencies of modernist 'children's services'. For example, we shall return to the concepts of an ethics of care and an ethics of an encounter, and introduce the concept of pedagogy as a theory and practice for working with collectivities of children.

To say we can understand public provisions for children in this way, rather than another, does not mean that it is just a matter of attaching a new label or that calling public provisions 'children's spaces' automatically makes them different. We use the term 'children's spaces' in part to represent a different way of thinking about children and public provisions for them. But it also means *being* different: 'children's spaces' require different relationships, practices and structures. To understand public provision for children as 'children's services' involves a particular approach – both in theory and practice: to understand that provision as 'children's spaces' requires another approach. So when we say that '"children's spaces" can encompass a wide range of out-of-home settings', the 'can' signifies that all of these settings, from a school to a playground, have the potential to be 'children's spaces': but not all provisions in each type of setting will choose to be or will be able to be.

The concept of 'children's spaces' cannot, however, be applied comprehensively to all aspects of public policy towards children and childhood, nor can it be applied to all settings that are now termed 'children's services'. Public policy towards children covers areas such as the tax and benefit system, family leave entitlements and employment policy: but important as these policies are to the well-being of children, they are clearly not 'spaces'. In addition, the term 'children's services', as currently used, covers services for children as individuals, for example: adoption and fostering services, social services case work and a range of therapies and health services. We think that in all of these there is certainly room to apply the same approach, the same considerations and constructions of childhood that we want to apply to settings where children find themselves as a group. In these situations, too, children should be social agents with the right to a voice, and to contribute to decisions that affect them. Nevertheless, our prime interest is in those settings where children meet each other and spend time together. We see children's spaces as environments provided through the agency of public policy for collectivities of children, sometimes with adult workers present (the nursery) sometimes without (the playground on a housing estate); settings where young people meet each other as individuals and where they form a social group. In these terms, provisions focusing on work with individual children cannot be understood as 'children's spaces'.

We would also restrict 'children's spaces' in other respects. They are public spaces, located in civic life, as opposed to the private space of the family or the consumerist arenas provided by commercial services, and they represent children's introduction to civic life. On these grounds, we rule out spaces that are typified more by consumerism and the market than by notions of civic life. This is in the face of current policy in Britain that often builds on the values of the market place: we cite, as examples, policies that support selective schooling and competition between schools, or those that promote 'childcare' for the children of working parents as, by and large, a matter for the private market or as an occupational benefit provided by individual employers to particular employees. These are values that are not only exclusionary, but cannot help but feed through into practice towards the children (see, for example, the discussion by Gewirtz (2000) of the marketisation of schooling in Britain, with its consequences of the recasting of children as commodities and increased inequalities of access to schooling).

Similarly, we eschew commercial provision as 'children's spaces'. The work of McKendrick, looking at children's play centres attached to, for example, pubs or shops, speaks of the children's loss of control over their own play and of the commodification of the experience:

> These playscapes are primarily being used to address the needs of parents. (Further) loss of control over their own play is a cost that children are bearing as they partake of the exciting new play opportunities which are presented to them by commercial playgrounds.
>
> (McKendrick *et al*. 2000: 312)

This conclusion accords with a study conducted by one of us:

> In some of the playschemes, workers did not place a high value on play. Their concern was rather that the children should not be bored, that they should have enough to do or – as some put it, that they should have fun. . . . [S]taff devised and led activities such as sports, karaoke, arts and crafts, party games, discos and video shows. The children were less active in generating their own activities, creating their own play environments or making use of time in their own way. . . . At Commerce Camps, where parents paid a high fee to have their children looked after, I made the following note: No part of the day was left empty, the children were constantly occupied. Juniors and Seniors chose the activities which they wanted to take part in and moved on from one activity to the next, every 45 minutes to an hour. . . . In the same playscheme, children were often given commercial art kits, with much of the preparation already complete, so that within a short time

they had something 'professional' to show for very little effort and with little opportunity for creativity.

(Petrie 1994b: 99)

We are less interested in these settings where parents buy a 'good time' for children, thus placing them as passive recipients of a service industry. We would not refer to them as children's spaces, seeing them, rather, as commodities traded between providers and parents. At the same time, we know that children may well enjoy visiting them.

As we construct them, children's spaces are products of public policy (although they may be provided by public or private bodies). But this should not blind us to the importance to children of other spaces that they use for their own purposes without any assistance from public policy: while they do not come within our concept of 'children's spaces', they are none the less spaces for children, which we consider to be of the utmost importance. Unfortunately, from our point of view, children's use of public space is increasingly constrained, due to the pressure of adult demands, fears and rules. Frank Furedi quotes a dismal list of evidence, produced in Britain over the last five or so years, of the restriction of children because of adult anxiety: 95 per cent of adults put fears of child abduction at the top of a list of concerns, 70 per cent of parents believe their neighbourhood to be unsafe, and many more do not allow their children to use public spaces, unsupervised. He accounts for these findings in terms of a culture of fear: 'we live in an era of permanent panics, be they about the environment, technology, health, crime or children' (Furedi 2000: 4). For Furedi, children have become the object of adult anxieties and 'paranoia'; what he sees as the professionalisation of parenting means that parents lose confidence and find it 'easier to keep children under guard than to adopt a more "risky", nuanced and differential approach'. He highlights the changing relationships between adults in general, and between parents and those who work with children:

> The relation of trust between parents, teachers, nursery workers and carers has become highly ambiguous. Instead of regarding other adults as a potential source of assistance in the task of child rearing, parents regard them with a degree of suspicion. In particular, adults who are strangers are treated with apprehension. Since most adults are by definition 'strangers', concern for children can often acquire a pathological character.

(Ibid.: 4)

Although the increasing institutionalisation that is a feature of modern childhood cannot be accounted for entirely on the basis of unreasonable adult anxieties, adult anxieties do play their part. They may be seen in the institutionalisation of relationships between adults and children, by which adults become technicians, working to prescribed learning goals and governed by bureaucratic procedures that supersede professional judgements. An extreme example is that, in reaction to concerns about child protection and fuelled by fear of litigation, it may be laid down when and how it is appropriate to touch a child. Societal anxieties may also relate to the insecure position of men within children's work, with the spectre of child sexual abuse contaminating the relationship between workers and employers and parents. They have played their part, too, in the growing limitations on children's play whether in public places or in adventure playgrounds. However, as we shall see, these anxieties and restrictions are not necessarily shared by other European societies.

The issue is whether the increasingly intense adult gaze directed towards children and the technicalisation of work with children can be at all reversed and/or whether it can be reformed. This is at the core of our explorations: the construct 'children's spaces' is an attempt to shift discussion towards claiming social agency for children, within the projects of public policy.

The many possibilities of children's spaces

Our understanding of 'children's spaces' involves moving away from the highly instrumental, controlling and, often, atomising approach that characterises the concept of 'children's services', which links institutions for children in their many forms to narrow policy agendas (e.g learning goals, readiness for school, childcare) and their concern to find ever more effective technologies for governing children. Rather than being for *a* particular purpose, a service established to produce a specified and countable product, 'children's spaces' provide a potential for many possibilities – pedagogical, emotional, cultural, social, moral, economic, political, physical and aesthetic. They can be seen as providing a forum where children, and often adults, can come together to explore and realise this potential. They are places where things *happen*, defined by their ethos and by the approach to children and childhood which they hold in common.

We shall explore some of these possibilities in the next chapter. What we want to emphasise here is that children's spaces are places for provocation and confrontation, dissensus and 'indocility', complexity and diversity, uncertainty and ambivalence. For adults and children, they are places where meanings are kept open, where there is space for critical thinking, wonder and amazement, curiosity and fun, learning by adults as well as children, where questions may be asked to which answers are not known. Some of the sense is captured in these comments on Reggio Emilia:

> The Reggio practice is rich in paradox and irony. . . . Reggio Emilia has turned away from the modernist idea of organic unity and encouraged multiple languages, confrontation and ambivalence and ambiguity.

Therefore, people favouring a strong modernist idea of organic unity often find their practice too noisy and containing too much 'dirt and pollution'. . . . Bachtin was aware of the enormous forces which insist on system, structure, centralization, hierarchy and unity when he proposed a form of intercontextuality characterized by differences, variety, alterity, plurality, otherness, randomness . . . [and created by] combining carnival and public square games, feasts, masks, theatre, philosophies and cosmologies. . . . You get a similar feeling when you visit Reggio Emilia and its pre-schools. . . . The whole milieu speaks of a collective adventure.

(Dahlberg 1995: 16, 17)

In our construction of 'children's spaces' we are trying to suggest the importance we attach to: providing opportunities for excitement, wonder and the unexpected; children living childhoods not entirely ordered and determined for them by adults and their preoccupations; relationships and experiences that are not defined or legitimated only in terms of work and outcomes; the value of play and playfulness in its own right, and not just as means to other ends; a childhood where children's questions and questioning are taken seriously and respected by adults who themselves are open to learning from children. We also want 'children's spaces' to offer the possibility of being places for emancipation – understood not as liberating some 'true self', but as enabling people (children and adults) to be governed less by power, to care for the self, to be critical thinkers – and to do so in interaction with others: civic values claim a high place on the agenda. Finally, our hope would be that 'children's spaces' offer places where children can have some privacy and get away from the adult gaze – in some cases, indeed, children's spaces may be without adults altogether: we believe that environments where children can be adult-free are to be welcomed.

Working in children's spaces

Our construction of public provision for children as children's spaces also produces a reconceptualisation of the role of workers with children and their methods of working. If children are not to be processed and normalised to a limited set of predetermined ends, then the worker-as-technician will not do. We need to think differently of the person working with children.

In 'children's spaces' staff would be viewed as reflective practitioners, as thinkers, as researchers, as co-constructors of knowledge – sustaining children's relationships and culture, creating challenging environments and situations, constantly questioning their own images of the child and their understanding of children's learning and other activities, supporting the learning of each child but also learning from children. This requires methods of working which emphasise and enable constant critical analysis of what is going on and of how workers see and understand the child. Rather than applying technology to normalise and categorise both children and knowledge, workers need to be able to use documentation, dialogue and reflection to deepen their understanding, to recognise themselves as meaning makers rather than 'truth' finders and appliers.

We return to these issues in Chapter 7, when we consider the pedagogue as a type of worker who might be able to work in children's spaces.

6 Children's culture and some other possibilities

We have argued that an understanding of public provision for children as 'children's spaces' implies seeing these provisions having potential for many possibilities, the results of which are not wholly, or indeed mainly, predetermined. In this chapter we want to give some indication of what some of these possibilities might be, and look into two – learning and children's culture – in more detail. However as the use of 'indication' and 'might' suggests, we are cautious: to be too specific runs the risk of closing down imagination and limiting possibilities, leading us back to the apparent safety of predetermination and narrow instrumentality and away from the risks of not knowing and not being in complete control.

Similarly when we say that results are 'not entirely predetermined' we are indicating some tension. Some of the possibilities that 'children's spaces' will develop will be predetermined by adults, with disciplines and technologies applied by adults for these predetermined purposes (for example, a teacher may make use of professional understandings as to how children best learn to write). It is not as simple as 'either/or' – either instrumental 'children's services' or entirely non-instrumental 'children's spaces'. However, the extent and nature of adult determination has to be a contestable issue in 'children's spaces', part of that 'politics of childhood' to which we frequently refer.

Moreover, the concept of 'children's spaces' implies that some, indeed many, of the possibilities that are realised come about through and from the collectivity of children who will exert their own agency, and make use of the opportunities and resources the space provides; we want to recognise and value the use of 'children's spaces' for children's own purposes. If there is no possibility for children's agency, if everything is predetermined, then we have to confront the reality that provision is purely an enclosure – to use the Foucauldian language of the 'disciplinary society' – where adults exercise authority and power, through the application of disciplines and technologies.

Furthermore, we would see 'children's spaces' as predominantly sites for civic participation, with technologies at the service of those who frequent them, rather than a conduit through which such technologies are applied to local populations on behalf of the state. From our perspective, children's spaces require local rather than centralised control: they are the public provision of civic space for children and adults, as members of local society, community contexts for active democratic citizenship. We shall return to this theme of local responsibility in the last chapter, as well as in Chapter 8 where we will see how, in the case of Sweden, the pre-school and school curricula are decided, within broad state guidelines, by the municipality and by the pre-school and school.

Public provision, however understood, needs to offer some justification for itself. It needs to convince the citizenry, including children, that it is in some sense worthwhile, contributing to the good life and to other valued purposes – though what counts as worthwhile and what constitutes the good life are clearly ethical and political issues. So, we end the chapter by considering what evaluation might entail in such cases.

Introducing possibilities

Many possibilities for 'children's spaces' are already written and spoken about, though often in disparate places, reinforcing a tendency to take a rather narrow view of the potential of public provisions for children. Before focusing on two examples, we shall introduce a range of examples here, whilst recognising that we are scratching the surface of what might be envisaged and practised.

Some possibilities are very familiar from the dominant discourse, providing us with an opportunity to re-iterate that it is not our intention to reject all that is in that discourse. Rather, we seek to insert some of the purposes of 'children's services' into a different understanding of children and public provisions for children, in the process reframing these purposes. So, for example, we recognise that it is necessary to address child protection and related issues – but we do so without using the language of the 'child in need' or the image of the 'poor' child that this language creates. Similarly, we recognise the need to provide what is now termed 'childcare for working parents', but would drop this language as being too narrow in concept (e.g. its implication that 'care' means keeping children somewhere safe while their parents are out at work) and too excluding in coverage (i.e. its focus on a group of children defined in terms of their parents' labour market status). Instead we would subsume both purposes within the concept of pedagogy (discussed in the next chapter) which provides a broad theory and practice of work which encompasses the whole child and all children, not just those 'in need' or with working parents. One overarching possibility for 'children's spaces', therefore, is to offer a pedagogical approach to all children.

We also want to rescue 'care' from its association with the banal term 'childcare', which has come to be spoken of as what economists would call a supply-side factor in the economy, one of a number of structural conditions needed to ensure a flexible, competitive labour force. Clearly, in a society where most parents are employed, public provision for children needs to take account of this fact in many respects, including its hours of opening. But 'care', as we suggested in Chapter 2, is a much more important and complex concept, involving in Tronto's words 'particular acts of caring and a "general habit of mind" to care that should inform all aspects of moral life' (Tronto 1993: 127).

We would therefore want to use the term 'care' to refer to an ethic, applicable to all practices and relationships within a children's space, and to *all* children irrespective of their parents' employment status. To recap on Chapter 2, the care ethic, so applied, would foreground responsibility, competence, integrity, and responsiveness to the Other, an important part of which is the art of listening. It would also provide a basis for evaluation, which would be regarded as an ethical judgement, located within a concrete and specific context and set of conditions.

Other possibilities are less widely recognised. Children's spaces can be seen as means for *children's social inclusion*, 'enabling children to participate in an essential world of relationships and activities in the local community and wider society beyond those available in the family' – to become part of that wider network of relationships we referred to in the previous chapter. Carlina Rinaldi speaks about the early childhood centres as places for the *creation of common values* (for example, reciprocity), *rights* (for example, of children) and *culture* (more broadly than the 'children's culture' we shall discuss later).

'Children's spaces' also have the possibility of being '*loci of ethical practices*' (Readings 1997: 155). This implies a consciousness that the relationships and practices that arise from being in a collective setting are not just technical, but also ethical and, as such, are guided by an ethical approach. We have just outlined one such approach, an ethics of care with which another approach, the ethics of an encounter (also discussed in Chapter 2), has much in common. Influenced by the thinking of Levinas, Dahlberg (2001) argues that 'to think an other whom I cannot grasp is an important shift and it challenges the whole scene of pedagogy' (8). The challenge includes: hearing the ungraspable call of the child, having the capacity to relate to absolute otherness, interrupting totalising practices, opening up for the unexpected. She goes on:

> How to open up for radical difference and to 'hear' what children are saying and doing? We need spaces where children can speak and be heard, where we as adults can become surprised and able to see the possibilities in uncertainty and doubt. This possibility could be seen as (in Derrida's words) 'the impossibility of controlling, deciding or determining the limit, the impossibility of situating by means of criteria, norms or rules'.
>
> (Ibid.: 8)

Dahlberg suggests that the pedagogical work in Reggio Emilia, in particular the idea of a 'pedagogy of listening' (Rinaldi 2001), provides an example of this shift in thinking which seeks to respect otherness and singularity:

> When we talk about listening we talk about an active as opposed to a passive listening, and about receiving and welcoming. Listening is a welcoming of the other and an openness to the difference of the other. . . . To listen means being open to the Other, recognising the Other as different and trying to listen to the Other from its own position and experience, and not treating the other as the same. Hence, in a pedagogy of listening the child becomes an absolute stranger for whom I have responsibility as a teacher.
>
> (Dahlberg 2001: 10)

More specifically, the possibility of a 'children's space' being a locus for ethical practice means explicitly recognising that work with children constantly raises many issues requiring an ethical choice, that is choices determined (in the words of Cherryholmes from Chapter 2) by 'judgements about good and bad, beautiful and ugly and truth and falsity'.

A related project can be promoting *local politics*, including a politics of childhood. Children's spaces can provide sites for new forms of democratic practice such as those referred to in Chapter 2, for example Rose's discussion of 'minor politics' and 'ethico-politics' (with their minor engagements in cramped spaces, their concern with the here and now, their pragmatism and modesty) and Beck's discussion of cosmopolitan republicanism (with the importance it attaches to the local and an active civil society). Whitty (1997) also seeks new places and forms for democratic practice, in relation to education:

> Neither the state nor civil society is currently much of a context for active democratic citizenship through which social justice can be pursued. Reassertion of citizenship rights in education would seem to require the development of a new public sphere somehow between the state and a marketized civil society, in which new forms of collective association can be developed. Foucault . . . pointed out that what he called new forms of association, such as trade unions and political parties, arose in the 19th century as a counterbalance to the prerogative of the state, and that they acted as the seedbed for new ideas (Foucault 1988). We need to consider what might be the contemporary versions of these collectivist forms of association to counterbalance not only the prerogative of the state, but also the prerogative of the market. Part of the challenge must be to move away from atomized decision-making to the reassertion of collective responsibility. . . .
>
> (Whitty 1997: 25–26)

To operate in this way would require the development of new conditions and practices, for example to enable the participation of children (of all ages) and that of parents and other adults. This might involve widening the methods which enable the expression of experience and view, for both children and adults, and developing Beck's concept of 'public work'. If children's spaces, enabled by 'public work', were part of a process of creating (in Beck's words) 'new foci of political action and identity formation', that action would have both an external and internal element. External, in the sense that children's spaces could be forums for action about more general issues of childhood (as well as about parenthood, care and other issues), including discussion of critical questions (what do we want for our children? what is a good childhood? what is our image of the child?); internal, through making the practices and purposes of children's spaces themselves open to critical discussion by children, parents and others.

One means of doing this is 'pedagogical documentation', a process developed in Reggio Emilia (cf. Dahlberg *et al.* 1999: Chapter 7) whereby the pedagogical practice of institutions is made visible and subject to discussion, confrontation and reflection by practitioners, parents, children and an array of other interested parties. Dahlberg and her colleagues, using a Foucauldian analysis, argue that pedagogical documentation can be seen as a means to challenge the way we always exercise power over ourselves, that is how we discipline and govern ourselves in our struggles to find knowledge about ourselves and the world:

> Through documentation we can unmask – identify and visualise – the dominant discourses and regimes which exercise power on and through us and by which we have constructed the child and ourselves as pedagogues. Pedagogical documentation, therefore, can function as a tool for opening up a critical and reflective practice challenging dominant discourses and constructing counter-discourses. . . . Through documentation we can more easily see, and ask questions about, which image of the child and which discourses we have embodied and produced, and what voice, rights and position the child has got in our early childhood institutions. . . . It is above all a question of getting insight into the possibility of seeing, talking and acting in a different way, and hence cross boundaries, in particular to transgress the grandiose project of modernity and its determination to map all human life.
>
> (Dahlberg *et al.* 1999: 152–153)

Hughes and Macnaughton argue, more generally, for 'a politics of parent involvement' based on a postmodern notion of emancipatory dissensus:

> Hope for change lies not in our agreements but in our disagreements, because in our disagreements (dissensus) we argue about what is 'the truth' and we question the dominant norms and values and seek to change them. . . . We must redefine the benefits of parent involvement in early childhood education. Instead of a boost to national economy, the benefit would be a boost to local democracy by informed citizens who create local, collective knowledge about what is in children's best interests. . . . [We can] promote local democracy by challenging the norms underpinning a consensus view of 'the child', revelling in the diverse ideas emerging from uncertainty. Through dissensus, staff and parents could challenge the 'traditional' view that expertise is neutral, independent and 'external' to social relations.
>
> (Hughes and Macnaughton 2000: 255–256)

The children's space as site for ethical and democratic practice offers another possibility, that is to *mitigate certain forms of injustice*, for example associational injustice ('patterns of association amongst individuals and amongst social groups which prevent some people from participating fully in decisions which affect the conditions within which they live and act' (Power and Gewirtz 2000: 41)) and cultural injustice (including cultural domination, non-recognition and disrespect). Some caution is needed, however, in setting our expectations as to how far children's spaces, by themselves, can reduce such injustice – or indeed economic injustice: we must take care not to regard them as a panacea which avoids addressing larger and more intractable political issues.

Possibilities for learning

Learning is one of the possibilities for children's spaces. But what learning? In addressing learning, we confront what Rinaldi (1999b) refers to as fundamental questions. What does it mean to learn? How is knowledge constructed? How do we learn? What is the relationship between teaching and learning? Our view of learning is influenced by the theory and practice of pedagogy, which is the subject of our next chapter.

The practice of the pedagogue, 'pedagogy', as used in continental Europe, relates strongly to on-going social learning – learning about what it is to be a human being living in society, not in a theoretical way but through the activities and relationships of daily life. It also encompasses learning about the world, through the activities of daily life, as a social being in the company of others, discovering and exploring. Because it relates to learning, and social learning in particular, pedagogy cannot be value-free.

What we have called the dominant discourse produces the construction of the young child as a blank sheet of paper upon which the adult writes, so that the child, in turn, may become a reproducer of transmitted social knowledge. It gives rise to an idea of learning as a process of transmitting to, or depositing within, the child a predetermined and unquestionable body of knowledge and values, with a prefabricated meaning. Such knowledge is absolute and unchangeable, with an essential existence 'out there', waiting to be discovered and passed on. As such, it is seen as separate from the child, but contained (at least partially) by the adult, independent of experience and existing in a cultural and historical vacuum. A further difficulty, from our point of view, is a model of individual knowledge acquisition and possession – knowledge here is property, rather than process, with pedagogy as the administration of knowledge, a banking concept in which 'knowledge is a gift bestowed by those who consider themselves knowledgeable on those they consider know nothing' (Freire 1985: 46).

Our alternative discourse arises from a different epistemological understanding in which knowledge is constructed, rather than acquired. Here the child is a partner, a co-constructor of knowledge, with the adult and with other children. In this model, knowledge is perspectival and ambiguous, contextualised and localised, incomplete and paradoxical, and produced in diverse ways: 'there is a change in emphasis from confrontation with nature to a conversation between persons, from correspondence with an objective reality to negotiation of meaning' (Kvale 1993: 51). We can no longer fall back on knowledge as universal, unchanging and absolute, producing the one correct answer. Instead knowledge is seen as socially constructed so that we must take responsibility for our own learning and meaning making:

> education is no longer the one-way transmission of information and knowledge, but the patterns of interaction which allow us to acquire new information, develop the disciplines which can lead to greater understanding, and discover shared meaning through mutual comprehension.
>
> (Bentley 1999: 188)

It involves a different focus, too:

> it contrasts an approach to learning measurable by hard indicators – the culture of numbers – with a culture of meaning. The dominant focus in schools and education policy is on the first of these, despite growing evidence it will fail to develop every child's full potential.
>
> (Scottish Council Foundation 1999: 5)

Adopting a broad historical and disciplinary perspective, Sousa Santos also contrasts two forms of knowledge: as regulation and emancipation. Over the last 200 years, he argues, the former gained primacy over the latter, as the cognitive–instrumental rationality of science and technology, with its atomising approach to understanding and its dichotomising of subject and object, overcame other forms of rationality. But with the paradigm shift currently underway, a postmodern emancipatory knowledge, drawing on a moral–practical and aesthetic–expressive rationality, is emerging:

> All emancipatory knowledge is self-knowledge: it does not discover, rather it creates. Metaphysical presuppositions, systems of belief, value judgements do not come before or after the knowledge of nature or society: they are part and parcel of it. . . . In order to reconstruct emancipatory knowledge as a new form of knowing, we have to start from the unfinished representations of modernity, that is from the principle of the community and from the aesthetic–expressive rationality. Emancipatory knowledge is a local knowledge created and disseminated through argumentative discourse; its two characteristics (localness and argumentativeness) belong together, since argumentative discourse can only take place within interpretive communities.
>
> (Sousa Santos 1995: 29–37)

These ways of understanding knowledge require a series of transitions 'from education to learning, from being taught to becoming active participants, from a culture of numbers driven by what is easily measured to a culture of meaning rooted in a more complex understanding of how learning is nurtured' (Scottish Council Foundation 1999: 14). With this understanding, images of knowledge also change. For the dominant discourse, the image is of ladders or of stepping stones (see Chapter 4), a linear process with a beginning and an end moving towards the top of the ladder, or over to the promised opposite bank of mature adult life. Another perspective allows us to see knowledge in a more organic form, as a rhizome, with no distinct beginning or end, with discontinuities and transformations throughout life. This is an image that points to the salience of ambivalence within human meaning making, to the singular and the paradoxical side of life and knowledge.

In presenting these alternative views of learning based on an alternative epistemology – a different understanding of knowledge – we are arguing that we have to be ambitious for ourselves and for children when thinking about the possibilities for learning offered by children's spaces. Today, members of society have to adjust to a high degree of complexity and diversity, as well as to continuous change; the demands and requirements that the future will hold are difficult to anticipate. 'Globalisation' means that identities and cultures are no longer as predetermined as they once were, but much more open to co-construction; whether at the level of personal relationships or of employment, life increasingly becomes a project you have to construct yourself, albeit in relationship with others. We face political/ethical issues of great complexity and significance, and can no longer rely on foundational laws or old political institutions to tell us the correct answers: we have to think for ourselves.

Both the dominant discourse and the alternative discourse we present may view the child as an active learner, flexible and able to problem solve. In daily practice both may start from the child's everyday understanding and construction of the surrounding world. Nevertheless, different understandings of knowledge distinguish the two positions. Within the dominant discourse, the child as reproducer of knowledge is assumed to exist within a context of standardised, stable and objective concepts. The approach does not give the child space to describe her own theories and explore the world from the position of these theories. If a child's theory is seen by the adult to be untrue, that is, not conforming to what the adult 'knows' to be true, the teacher or pedagogue ignores or corrects it, instead of letting the child test her own ideas and theories against a multiplicity of perspectives and constructions – including those of science. In this model, children's thoughts are categorised and valued as right or wrong according to whether they agree with a predetermined definition of knowledge.

By contrast, a teacher or pedagogue working from a social constructionist perspective, with postmodern understandings of knowledge, would give the child the possibility to produce alternative constructions *before* she was brought to encounter scientifically accepted constructions. When this happens, the child is in a position to view her own constructions in relation to scientific constructions, and make her own choices and meanings. This is understood to be a learning process not only for the child but also for the worker, if she is able to encounter the child's ideas, theories and hypothesis with respect, curiosity and wonder (Dahlberg *et al*. 1999). This process can place increasing requirements on the child to form and shape her own understanding of the world and her knowledge, as well as her identity and her lifestyle. Doing so also requires highly developed capacities for learning, self-reflection, communication, and open and questioning relationships with others, since the social construction of knowledge is a social process: the child needs to trust in her own ability, to make choices and to argue for her standpoints, so gaining an increased responsibility for herself and for realizing her own potentials.

'Learning' and 'knowledge' involve making ethical and political choices, about how we understand these concepts and how we work with children. Those choices are closely bound up with our understandings of the child and the public provision we make for children. The appalling poverty and inequality into which British society has declined has exacted a high price in terms of immediate human misery. But it also exacted another high price in terms of impoverished national educational aims, provision and expectations for young people, whether in the school, in youth and play provision or in childcare. Knowledge, learning and regulation have become inextricably linked, to the expense *inter alia* of the ability to think critically.

But, as we have argued, there are other possibilities for learning, linked to different understandings of knowledge. Out of this emerge additional images of public provision for children, not only as children's space, but as 'an interpretive community', 'an integral living organism, a place of shared lives and relationships' (Malaguzzi 1993b: 56), and a 'context for multiple listening' (Rinaldi 2001). Rather than a reproducer, the child is understood as strong, competent, intelligent, a powerful pedagogue, able to produce interesting and challenging theories, understandings, questions – and from birth, not at some later age when they have been made ready, through schooling and pre-schooling.

This idea of the child constructing knowledge, making meaning, with others is captured in these words of Malaguzzi about a 'pedagogy of relationships':

> Children learn by interacting with their environment and actively trans-
> forming their relationships with the world of adults, things, events and,
> in original ways, their peers. In a sense children participate in construct-
> ing their identity and the identity of others. Interaction among children
> is a fundamental experience during the first years of life. Interaction is
> a need, a desire, a vital necessity that each child carries within. . . . If
> we accept that every problem produces cognitive conflicts, then we
> believe that cognitive conflicts initiate a process of co-construction and
> cooperation.
>
> (Malaguzzi 1993a: 11–12)

We have separated this discussion of learning from a preceding discussion about ethics, yet this is an artificial splitting off. The two are closely linked. A learning relationship embodies an idea of ethics, and in particular of an ethical relationship. The idea of meaning making or co-constructing know-ledge carries a very different relationship to transmitting or reproducing knowledge.

We have outlined above how the idea of a 'pedagogy of listening' is connected with the ethics of an encounter, the idea of an ethical relation-ship inscribed with responsibility for the Other and respect for the Other's absolute alterity. There are many similarities with Bill Readings' view of learning. He questions an idea of learning as 'transmission to an empty vessel of a preconstituted and unquestionable knowledge', and the Enlight-enment narrative of education transforming children into adults, autono-mous beings, self-sufficient and independent of obligation. Instead he sees teaching and learning as 'radical forms of dialogue', as a 'relation', and as a 'site of obligation'. Readings, like the pedagogues of Reggio, argues for an idea of learning that foregrounds the importance of listening to the Other and for that which has not yet made itself heard and in which

> [t]he condition of pedagogical practice is an infinite attention to the
> other. . . . Listening to thought is not the spending of time in the pro-
> duction of an autonomous subject or an autonomous body of know-
> ledge. Rather it is to think besides each other and to explore an open

network of obligation that keeps the question of meaning open as a locus for debate. . . . Doing justice to thought means trying to hear that which cannot be said but which tries to make itself heard – and this is a process incompatible with the production of even relatively stable and exchangeable knowledge.

(Readings 1997: 158, 165)

The case of children's culture as possibility

We will consider one more possibility here, to illustrate how 'children's spaces' might differ from the concept of 'children's services': the possibility of providing opportunities for children's relationships and culture. We discuss it at length not because we believe it to be necessarily the most important possibility, but because it provides an illustration of how the potential of children's spaces can enrich children's lives here and now, recognising the value of childhood as an important life stage in its own right. 'Children's spaces' as sites or forums for children's culture and relationships exemplifies the idea of social spaces *for* childhood, as part of life, not just preparation for life.

We have argued the importance of relationships between children, both in general and for their pedagogical significance. For many this may be a familiar argument. 'Children's culture' may, however, be a less familiar concept (at least in Britain, although it is a familiar idea in Nordic countries). What do we mean by it?

We – children and non-children – live in a cultural world which is complex, and where people participate in different cultural fields, each with its own norms, values and preferred activities. An individual can be multi-, inter- and intra-culturally competent. That is they may understand the forms and values of many cultures and may move within and between them. For example, at different times people (of any age) accommodate to the cultures of work, home, school, leisure and places of worship; they may participate in the culture of a particular ethnic group *and* in that of a more general national collective. They may not consider themselves to be strangers in any of these cultures, although they may feel more at home in some than in others. As well as adhering to different cultural forms, participants take part in the ongoing transformation of culture; culture is not a condition of stasis but continually evolving and adapting.

Distinctive cultures arise when people spend time together as a group that has some inferred demarcation from other groups. For children, this happens either when they bring themselves together, for example in neighbourhood play, or when they are brought together by adults in a school, nursery or out-of-school service – or any other social space. In these settings, they interact with adults within the framework of adult culture, often using adult cultural forms. But they also produce their own social environment within the social and physical constraints of the adult world, sometimes in parallel to adult cultures, but also interfacing and interacting with them. The American sociologist William Corsaro (1999) captures this idea of a separate but interfacing children's culture when he says that 'children produce and participate in their own unique peer cultures by creatively appropriating information from the adult world to address their own concerns'. Moreover, he notes that they do not simply internalise adult culture but 'are also actively contributing to cultural production and change'. He defines children's culture as 'a stable set of activities, routines, artefacts, values and concerns that children produce and share in interaction with their peers' and relates it to children making 'persistent attempts to gain control of their lives and to share that control with each other' (92). It is this sharing that takes children's search for control out of the individual and into the cultural domain.

The Opies (Opie and Opie 1967) drew attention many years ago to the 'language and lore' of children, based on extensive fieldwork in school playgrounds in the UK. Scandinavian colleagues and others have turned to the ways in which children learn to take part in play with other children:

> How they may have to settle for being the 'little ones' when they move up to 'big school' – although they have themselves been expert players as the oldest children in the 'little' school – because children's cultures have their own status systems based on knowledge, skill and sometimes age (Kampman 1997). In their interaction with other children they come to know which children are 'experts', who know jokes, who can make the computer work (Mauritsen 1996). When they first join other children they may be constrained – even forcibly – to take the part of the 'baby' in pretend play with older children. In so doing they have an opportunity to learn more advanced play roles and ways of playing which the dominant group of children sees as appropriate. They come to learn about friendship groups and their relative exclusivity. They learn the accepted ways of gaining entry to a game, how to deflect an insult and the customary way to make suggestions about make-believe play.
>
> (Petrie *et al.* 2000: 108)

Prout argues that we have often overestimated the role of adults (including parents) and consequently underestimated the importance of children's collective life and their interactions with each other, referring to the increasing number of detailed studies of children's peer relationships by researchers such as Corsaro.

> In detailed and careful studies [Corsaro] has shown that children's own collective culture is crucial to growing up. It is the medium through which a great deal of their life circumstance is refracted, experienced,

interpreted and transformed. Echoing this approach Judith Rich Harris suggests that parental behaviours towards a child affect how the child behaves in the presence of the parent (or in closely related contexts) and how the child feels about the parent (maybe over their whole lifetime). However, parental behaviour does not strongly affect children's behaviour outside the home and in the wider world. For an understanding of that, she suggests we must look to and acknowledge the potentially powerful effect of the peer group, in particular to the ways in which children creatively socialise each other. Children are, then, to be seen not as passive objects but, as Khalil Gibran memorably expresses it, as 'living arrows' whose life trajectory is partly self-determined.

(Prout 1999: 2)

We do not wish to idealise children's culture: some children's cultures may, for example, allow bullying and racism. Nor do we wish to exoticise it: children's activities are not to be seen as curiosities which might be displayed in an old fashioned anthropology museum alongside those of other 'primitive' peoples. Nor do we wish to limit children's participation in children's spaces to that of what has been called 'tribal children' (James *et al.* 1998) – children whose distinctive social contribution is seen mainly as belonging to a sphere separate from that of adults. We do, however, want to acknowledge that children *as a group* are notionally 'Other' – that is they are distinct from ourselves as adults and are in some significant ways less powerful; physically, economically and politically speaking, children are a minority, legal minors and without full civic rights.

It is thus open to adult policy makers, providers and practitioners to be oppressive in their interactions with children. They can ignore, or deny, children's rights and competences, pay lip service to their social participation in decision making, and may – perhaps most especially in highly structured institutions like the school – attempt to suppress children's culture. Unlike adults as a social group, children's activities, use of time and space are to some extent prescribed by law. For example, they must attend school between certain ages and follow the National Curriculum; they may, as a group, have curfews imposed upon them. For most adults, the use of time and space is subject to proscription, where they may *not* go, and custom (such as employment) rather than statutory prescription.

That children and young people form a distinct social group in today's society comes about as a result of the actions of adults. Over the course of the twentieth century, they became increasingly segregated from the wider society in institutions such as nurseries, schools, out-of-school services, not to mention further and higher education. This has been to meet a variety of educational and employment needs, as well as, in some cases, for purposes of child protection. Some physical and social segregation of children and young people is not new: it became more general with compulsory education late in the nineteenth century. Before that time working class children were often economically active, and it was acceptable for a child to contribute to the household economy. Many children worked in factories, laboured on farms, were out-workers making gloves and lace and plaiting straw.

Such economic functions are less acceptable for children today, when children are largely segregated from the work place both ideologically and physically. The dangers presented by traffic and the perceived threat of 'dangerous strangers' also contrive to keep children segregated from the wider public community, of other children and of adults, in their own localities. To some extent there is also some segregation of children from adults within the home: modern domestic consumer appliances, such as the micro-wave and freezer, allow different members of the family to prepare and eat their food apart from other members. Similarly, children can retire to their own bedrooms to watch television and play with the computer. This is not just a matter of individual preference, it is to some extent a result of commercial operations: children are targeted as a separate market by the food industry and by the entertainment industry. It is in the interest of commerce to maintain the distinction between children and adults because differentiated market niches can increase consumption and profit.

Segregation both reflects and reinforces difference for those inside and outside the group which is 'Other'. Because children and young people have collective experiences within institutional settings, they also develop their own collective social lives within them – social lives lived alongside, and in the context of, the dominant adult culture, with children often transforming, sometimes subverting, adult cultural forms for their own ends. For example, in children's maps features may be given prominence when they have special significance for the children while appearing inconsequential to adults (Ward 1978). Children use features of school playgrounds intended for other purposes for their own; flights of steps may become jumping apparatuses, castles, alien dens, shops. In a London suburb, a grassed bank, with scrubby trees, runs for a short stretch alongside the pavement, by the side of a main road. For at least seventy years (the thirty years cited in an earlier publication has been revised in the light of correction from an older informant) children have scrambled on to the bank and walked behind the trees for a matter of 20 yards and then clambered down again. They have worn a clear, narrow path. This path has no place in adult culture – for adults, paths are usually taken to reach a destination; yet children endow following the path with their own meanings, it is part of their local culture.

Children do not live their lives solely within their own cultures. They are also, perhaps predominantly, able social players within the dominant culture, at home, in school and in other settings. Nevertheless, they are a minority group and 'Other' *vis-à-vis* adults, both politically and culturally.

At the ethical level, social groups may be judged by the way in which they relate to those who are Other – whether Otherness is defined in terms of culture, age, ethnicity, sexuality, social class or any other distinctive social identity. But, respect for Otherness does not, as we have argued before, necessarily come easily. A sense of personal or collective identity sometimes seems to postulate that Otherness is threatening – and this taps into the anxieties which were discussed earlier; the language of many newspaper articles attest to this. Such anxieties underlie racist and sexist 'humour' – jokes about Others both defuse their power and claim superior status for the teller. The ambivalent feelings of adults towards children are often betrayed by so called humorous remarks about them. For example, a popular museum of childhood has the following notice displayed next to a picture of a stained glass window:

> Proposed memorial window to King Herod. Modern Research suggests that the exact number of 'innocents' could not have been more than 12–15. To a museum curator when distracted by annoying or aggravating children this seems a very disappointing total and one well within our capacity to improve.

In this case, 'humour' seems to make the expression of hostility towards child visitors – not, notice, non-child visitors – acceptable. It addresses, primarily, an adult audience and relies on shared understandings of sameness and Otherness. It also brings to the surface the power relationship that often exists between adults and children: power that has both a social and a physical basis and can be exercised at a personal level and within public provision unless a stand is taken to prevent this. Such a stand calls for an examination of the ambivalence that adults experience towards children and a will to accept difference, not denying that children are Other – as society is currently constructed, at least – but seeking to promote social inclusion for them as a social minority. Children's spaces would be built on these values.

Children's spaces offer the possibility of different ways of understanding childhood and of relating to children as Other. They can permit children's development of their own social and cultural lives so that children are seen as *both* Other than adults *and* are respected equally with adults. Working with children in 'social spaces' positions children as partners with adults in a joint social enterprise – co-learners and co-constructors of knowledge – while at the same time recognising and respecting their distinct cultural position, with the possible tensions that this implies.

Working with paradoxes and tensions is not, universally, foreign to policy makers. In Norway, for example, the Norwegian Ministry of Children and Families states, in its Framework Plan for Day Care Institutions (1996), that

> Childhood as a life phase has a high intrinsic value, and children's own free-time, own culture and play are fundamentally important. . . .

> [T]he need for control and management of the establishment (kinder-garten) must at all times be weighed against the children's need to be children on their own premises and based on their own interests (10).

The phrase 'the need to be children' in this statement, as well as the reference to children's 'own culture', implies an understanding of children as cultural beings and as Other. Although in some ways children in Norway are less restricted than many children in the UK, nevertheless there is a constant awareness of the increasing control of children by adults and the need to try and 'restore children's freedoms' as a necessary part of a good childhood. A UK observer describes a Norwegian mayor congratulating those involved in setting up a new playground on 'restoring children's freedoms' (Coward 2000).

The term 'children's culture' is used widely in Norway and other Nordic countries, not only by researchers but also by policy makers, local managers and practitioners. To take just a few random examples: there is a Nordic Council Committee on Children's Culture; the Norwegian *Framework Plan for Day Care Institutions* refers to children's culture, which is 'passed on and developed by children learning from children'. During a visit by one of us to Norway the head of an out-of-school service described (quite unprompted) his objective as creating a 'living children's culture'; while a research project developed in Finland, in which pre-school children tell stories of their own choosing, is described as collecting

> children's self-made culture in the form of tales, stories, narratives and pictures. Our archive consists of 5,000 Finnish stories (from pre-school children) and 300 stories from the other Nordic countries. . . . The children also get the chance to hear the kinds of things that children think about in different parts of Finland and in other countries. . . . In this project children deliver their own culture to other children in other countries in a manner which excludes the adults' way of trans-forming cultural context.
>
> (Riihelä 1997: 3)

More generally, this idea of children's own space, for their culture and relationships, is to be found in many Nordic 'free-time centres'. The term 'free-time' (*fritids* in Swedish, Norwegian and Danish) is applied to before and after-school services. From the point of view of the adult agenda, they have a clear economic function – one of their projects is to provide care for children while parents work. But from the point of view of children, they have a function expressed in their title – as spaces for children's free-time, that is time when children have no scholastic or domestic duties, time which is their own. In contrast to the school curriculum with its specific adult-derived goals, free-time centres emphasise choice, with adults standing back rather than directing and controlling children's activities.

We have seen this way of working in many free-time centres. In one in Norway, for example, the adults 'provide' no activities on two evenings per week, leaving it to the children to get on with their own lives within their own cultural framework. Allowing children to get on with their own lives may present problems for an adult onlooker, especially if that onlooker has responsibilities for the children in question; child protection values may seek to limit children's autonomy 'for their own good'. However, perceptions of what is 'good' for children relates to how 'the child' is constructed and on this basis, what one construction of childhood sees as protection, another may see as over-protection or control.

In Sweden, free-time pedagogues believe that children should not be over-protected from risk, that it is good for them to meet challenging situations so they learn about their capabilities and about the environment through direct experience, without adults constantly overseeing their safety. In this way children come to understand and assess risk, and adults minimise the extent they control children's lives and culture. For example, one of us visited an integrated school in Gothenberg (that is a school where the free-time centre and school are integrated, a form of provision we shall also discuss in more detail in Chapter 8), at the end of the formal school day and when the free-time centre was in operation. Children were playing in the school grounds and in the local woods, with no boundary between the school and the local environment a commonplace feature of schooling in Sweden. The children were 'doing their own thing'. Some played with a hosepipe in the school yard (the day was hot), others scrambled up a granite outcrop, still others climbed a tree. Two free-time pedagogues were walking around the grounds surrounding the complex of school buildings, which incorporated swings and garden patches among other attractions. The pedagogues could not see all the children, but said they were aware of their whereabouts. They were taking little part in the children's activities, not out of carelessness, but seeing non-intrusion as appropriate in the circumstances. When asked if the children ever had accidents, one of the pedagogues replied that a boy had fractured his arm during the previous year and that occasional accidents were to be expected – but not over-protected against. The understanding was that the cost of a broken arm was to be measured against the child's right to play freely with other children.

On another occasion, in another season, young children, enrolled in a school free-time scheme, took off into snow-covered woods with their toboggans. Again, there was no immediate supervision. While there was some perception of risk, the level of risk was judged acceptable, and the children were seen as better off for their collective (and lightly supervised) experience. We should also point out that these were children who, as a social group, had much experience of the forests and snow around their school, and that any 'new' child entering the group would access – and potentially add to – the cultural wisdom of the group and be protected by it. In these cases, the history and culture of the group knowledge extends beyond that held by individual members.

Elsewhere in Sweden, one of us took a seat in a school playground and remained there for some twenty minutes, without being challenged, waiting to keep an appointment (the building was listed as of historic interest and the surrounding wall had not, therefore, been removed). Children played or tended small gardens all around us. Swedish colleagues were surprised that notions of 'stranger danger' would have caused English teachers to challenge any unknown visitor. The implication was that the English approach was unhealthy and over anxious.

These and other examples from our visits in Norway, Sweden and Denmark, reveal societies where there is less anxiety than in our own. In these countries, there is a readiness to weigh risk against children's freedom, and the chance for them to engage in a rich and exciting children's culture and to come down in favour of freedom. Children's provision seems to us to be moving in the direction of children's spaces, with priority given to childhood and with children participating in setting the agenda.

This is in contrast to Britain. The Children Act 1989 extended the regulation of pre-school day care to most out-of-school services. In some quarters, this is considered to have contributed to an increased restriction of the activities which are seen as safe and suitable for children in their free time. Also, while 'childcare' and 'study support' services for children outside school hours have increased, there has been a decrease in settings intended purely for children's play where, amongst other processes, children have learned to assess risk. Indeed risk, as applied to children's play, is often seen purely in negative terms by workers and providers in Britain. In part, this is for fear of the litigation that might follow a child having an accident, in part because it is thought that inspectors might not register settings which allowed children to confront risk. Yet risk is inherent in human endeavour, and for children not to engage with it is for them to be cut off from an important part of human life in the interests of 'child protection'. People learn to assess and manage risk by encountering it, coming to understand the balance to be achieved between the positive and negative outcomes of their actions. The distinction between the terms 'risk' and 'hazard' is not sufficiently used in looking at children's activities. It is useful to reserve hazard for elements of the environment over which the young person has no control, of which they are not aware and which they do not fully understand. Risk, on the other hand, is not hidden, it is understood and has to be taken into account in undertaking an activity and in judging the benefits of the activity compared with the risks. With hazards children cannot make judgements regarding any negative outcomes entailed by their actions; for example, when they use climbing equipment which is not properly maintained but which may seem, misleadingly, to present a low level of risk.

The protective attitude towards children and young people attending 'care' settings, viewed against their participation in sports, reveals an interesting contrast. In most sports some physical risk is seen as intrinsic to the activity, so much so that there is a branch of medicine devoted to sports injuries. Nevertheless, the benefits produced by sport are seen by participants, teachers and coaches – in fact by society at large – as being commensurate with the risks undertaken. In the face of litigation following a sports injury, staff may successfully demonstrate that their actions and procedures were reasonable, that they took steps to reduce hazard and that their behaviour was professional.

The problem in defending children's play as a site for activities involving worthwhile risk is at least twofold. First, play is not generally valued or understood by adults, except as a means to an end: that is, play is seen as a learning activity, serving the ends of the school curriculum, rather than a worthwhile process in its own right. Second, there is as yet no fully developed profession which can speak for play from within its own ranks, and thus no unified understanding of the value of play or of how it may best be promoted – although in Britain it is now the concern of a National Training Organisation and has a place within a national framework of qualifications for work with children.

Where children set the agenda, play is a central activity. It is what children do, often on the margins of the adult world, making use of the minutes between adult directed activities for their own purposes. One of us has seen children playing in a dark school playground, up and down a flight of steps engrossed, night after night, in their own social world and its meanings. The parents/providers at this after-school scheme wanted the children to do something more worthwhile – educational 'activities' – perhaps, they could have recorder practice? But the children preferred to be outside, and the steps had a particular attraction. Plainly children's spaces could be places for children's own culture, specifically play and the related activities which children themselves refer to as 'messing about' or 'hanging out' (Petrie *et al.* 2000). It is within this culture that children can serve their own agenda, alongside that of adult society.

For children, outdoor play is often given highly valued (e.g. O'Brien *et al.* 2000; Petrie *et al.* 2000). There are a growing number of examples of 'children's spaces' which offer children more opportunities to be out-of-doors, both in urban areas (where there is an issue of reclaiming 'children's spaces' from adult traffic through, for example, the introduction of home zones) and in the countryside. In Denmark, for example, in recent years there has been a rapid expansion of what are known as forest kinder-gartens. Young children, below school age, go most days or every day throughout the year, with their pedagogues, into the local countryside, often with only minimal shelter in case of bad weather. The 'children's space' here is literally open space, woods, fields, beaches, sea and lakes.

In Norway, there is a similar emphasis on using the outside environment. Being outside as much as possible is a high priority in the daily pedagogical practice of kindergartens (*barnehager*) and schools. The Government's

Framework Plan for Day Care Institutions emphasises that the *barnehager* has to contribute to

> familiarising children with plants and animals, landscapes, seasons and weather . . . an objective is to develop children's love of nature, an understanding of the interplay of nature and between man and nature. . . . Nature accommodates a multitude of experiences and activities in all seasons and all weathers (26).

During a visit to Norway, one of us visited a *barnehage* which had access to a huge area of woods and seashore. One part-time group of children had no indoor base, but were always outside using a Sami-style tent for shelter; the children from the indoor-based groups, however, also spend a lot of time outside. Another *barnehage* had increased the number of children it can take by groups of children taking it in turns to spend a week completely outside (this has also served as a means to reduce running costs). In both schools we visited, children from grades 1 to 4 spent a day a week outside, while the free-time centres also emphasised outdoor play (and offer skiing classes in January and February). Nationally, there is a government campaign to encourage children to exercise and be healthy, which is encouraging *barnehager* and schools to promote outdoor activities, active play and exercise.

Denmark and Norway are, of course, less urbanised that much of Britain. However, there are many places in Britain where children are within a reasonable walk or a short drive of countryside, and within larger towns and cities there are often urban open spaces that could be made use of. For example, in the Rising Sun Woodland Preschool Project, children in a nursery class in a school in Newcastle go one day a week by coach to a Countryside Centre, where they have a base in an old quarry area in woodlands.

In the light of research, we believe that listening to children would produce children's spaces that, similarly to the examples given above and in other ways, would produce many such opportunities for being out-of-doors.

Modernisation with tradition

Sometimes people remark that the concept of 'children's spaces' merely restates views put forward over the last two or more centuries by progressive educators, in a tradition that goes back to Rousseau. In some ways this is true – but to the extent that we are restating these views, we are doing so at a particular point in history, with its own characteristic social organisation, which furnishes a new and distinct site for rethinking the relationship between children and society.

Unlike Rousseau and proponents of a more libertarian, individualistic approach, our preferred approach does not focus on the child purely as an individual. We are above all interested in seeing the child as a member of society as a whole, both together with adults and in the company of other children – and to this extent the approach is not 'child-centred'. We do not deny that people who work with children in children's spaces will often, and validly, work with children individually. But such 'individual' work itself should take account of the basis of the child's interconnectedness with the whole group, staff and children. Work that relies solely on the one-to-one relationship – adult–child – is inappropriate for children's spaces as we construe them. Even in services where the administration of physical treatment is the main focus of work with children – for example in the case of physiotherapy – the child needs to be understood in terms of their place in a social network. Friends and family can play a crucial part in the outcome of treatment and contribute to the child's understanding of treatment. Indeed, we see the child's relationships as mediating, for good or ill, the understandings of society at large and its interventions.

We see ourselves closer to the tradition of Dewey, Freire and Malaguzzi, with an emphasis on children's social life. In particular we appreciate what John Dewey wrote more than a century ago in his 'pedagogic creed':

> I believe that education, therefore, is a process of living and not a preparation for future living.

> I believe that the school must represent present life – life as real and vital to the child as that which he carries on in the home, in the neighbourhood, or on the playground.

> I believe that education which does not occur through forms of life, that are worth living for their own sake, is always a poor substitute for the genuine reality and tends to cramp and to deaden.

> I believe that much of present education fails because it neglects this fundamental principle of the school as a form of community life. It conceives the school as a place where certain information is to be given, where certain lessons are to be learned, or where certain habits are to be formed. The value of these is conceived as lying largely in the remote future; the child must do these things for the sake of something else he is to do; they are mere preparation. As a result they do not become a part of the life experience of the child and so are not truly educative.
>
> (Dewey 1897: 77–80)

An alternative approach to evaluation

In Chapter 5, we discussed the evaluation of public provision for children and how it foregrounds the quantification and measurement of predetermined outcomes and the workings of particular aspects of the technology, recoursing often to terms such as indicators, targets, goals and drawing on a managerial discourse. We would like to conclude this chapter on children's spaces by turning to a more appropriate form of evaluation for children's services as an 'alternative' form of provision.

Thomas Schwandt argues that evaluation and ethics are always connected, with different approaches to evaluation reflecting different ethical aims, indeed different ideas of ethics. He describes three ethical aims of evaluation: enlightenment, emancipation and practical wisdom. The enlightenment ethic seeks to generate knowledge to ameliorate social problems: complementing new managerialism, it emphasises depoliticising social policy to produce rational and efficient decisions based on allegedly neutral criteria of economy, efficiency and effectiveness. The emancipation ethic arises from criticisms that an enlightenment ethic lacks critical voice and provides a rationale for elitist science: rejecting the idea of disinterested study, it is concerned with power and reducing exploitation and inequality. What these first two ethical orientations share is an interest in keeping professional social enquiry at or near the centre of social life. The practical wisdom ethic, by contrast, decentres social enquiry and treats it as, at best, 'one source of insight that complements our ordinary struggles to understand ourselves and do good' (Schwandt 1996b: 17).

The practical wisdom approach to evaluation, like postmodern ethics and the ethics of care, makes contextualised judgements, emphasising the particularity of concrete conditions and the inherent complexity and ambivalence of life:

> moral knowledge is something that is enacted and hence guided by understanding of the specific circumstance. Codes, principles and general moral rules are indeed available to us but they are secondary to and sensible only in light of the particulars of concrete cases and concrete cases are marked by ambiguity and finitude of understanding.
>
> (Ibid.: 6–7)

Making judgements in such particular situations requires practical ethical wisdom, and the evaluator's task, working within this ethical framework, is to contribute to the cultivation of such wisdom and the ability to make good judgements:

> We cannot engage in some (relatively simple) process of weighing alternative goals, values, criteria and the like that reduces judgement of what constitutes good practice to calculation. Rather, we must engage in

strong evaluation judging the qualitative worth of different ends or aims of our practices. The task for evaluation here is to help clients cultivate this capacity. . . . [I]t means teaching about what it means to engage in evaluation and moral reasoning.

(Ibid.: 18)

Schwandt concludes that social enquiry, such as evaluation, should be reconceptualised as 'practical philosophy', meaning inquiry *with* rather than *on* human actors and intended primarily to enable practitioners 'to refine the rationality of a particular practice for themselves'. Evaluation means rendering a judgement of worth or value. Good judgement, therefore, must be related to concrete particulars, rather than abstract and allegedly universal rules and criteria, and in relation to ethical judgements of what is good and right.

Others share this perspective. Readings speaks of evaluation as an act of judgement and self-questioning, embedded within a context that must be acknowledged. He argues that evaluation produces a judgement of value, which should not be confused with a statement of fact; furthermore, the judge must take responsibility for that judgement rather than hide behind claims of statistical objectivity. He is at great pains to emphasise the provisionality of evaluation as judgement: in other words, the importance of keeping the issues open and subject to continuing discussion rather than seeking to close and finalise the matter. According to Readings (1997), 'the question of evaluation is finally both unanswerable and essential' (133).

Dahlberg and her colleagues (1999) have proposed the concept of meaning making as *an* approach to evaluation based on fundamentally different assumptions than the concept of quality. The concept of quality seeks to judge the conformity of practice to predetermined norms and outcomes: it is about establishing conformity to predetermined standards. The concept of meaning making, in contrast, is first and foremost about constructing and deepening understanding of, for example, the early childhood institution and its projects, especially its pedagogical work – to make meaning of what is going on. From there, it is possible to go on to make a judgement and to seek agreement with others on that judgement, but neither of these stages can precede working on meaning which can, in any case, be important in its own right. It assumes that the meaning of pedagogical work, and its value, is always open to different interpretations: in short, it is contestable.

What these examples have in common is an idea of evaluation as a process of forming a judgement, in relation to a particular setting and its context. Other features include:

Foregrounding the socially constructed nature of knowledge; the emphasis on constructing and deepening understanding of what is going on (i.e. practice or praxis); doing so by engaging with and being in dialogue with others, in particular practitioners, and through reflective analysis; recognising that the process is value-based and therefore political and moral; and being comfortable with uncertainty and provisionality.

(Dahlberg *et al.* 1999: 113)

One might also emphasise that the approach does not delegate evaluation to some external observer or inspector or fall back on the use of an abstract and universal set of norms. Rather it enables evaluation to 'become a social question, not a device of measurement' (Readings 1997: 124), placing responsibility on all those involved with the place and practice being evaluated, not only to participate but to think for themselves and form their own understandings and judgements. By insisting on local participation in evaluation and by recognising the interpretive and contextualised nature of making judgements, this approach enables each 'children's space' to be considered according to its singularity, its values and priorities, and the possibilities that children and adults are working to realise.

Evaluations as judgements of value mean 'recognizing that there exists no homogeneous standard of value that might unite all poles of the pedagogical scene to produce a single scale of evaluation' (Readings 1997: 165). So, it may well happen that participants will disagree in some respects and that evaluations will change over time. But, in the words of Toulmin 'tolerating the resulting plurality, ambiguity or the lack of certainty is no error . . . but the price we inevitably pay for being human beings and not gods' (1990: 30).

7 Pedagogues and pedagogy

Our reconstruction of children's services as children's spaces entails some reconceptualisation of the work and workers in children's spaces. We have already suggested the image of the worker needs to change: from technician to reflective practitioner, researcher, co-constructor of knowledge, culture and identity. But we need to go further, to find a theory and practice for working with children in children's spaces and a type of worker conversant with this theory and practice. The work and worker need to be suited to working with groups of children of varying ages in many types of setting, to relating to the whole child, and to being able to pursue many possibilities. The worker needs to be comfortable in many fields – from ethics to children's culture – and adopting various identities, including reflective practitioner, researcher and co-constructor.

Two terms that we have used in the preceding chapters, without giving them much discussion, will perhaps help us to find a way forward. They are the theory and practice known as 'pedagogy' and the profession that relates to it: that of the 'pedagogue'. For many people in England, but in other parts of the English-speaking world too, these are rather strange terms, sounding unfamiliar, even alien. So, in this chapter, we will look at them more closely, how they are employed in continental Europe and what their employment may offer to the development of public policy towards children, including public provision understood as 'children's spaces'. We will sketch in the training and education of pedagogues in Europe, look at some workforce issues, at the content of pedagogical work and conclude with some proposals for the development of a pedagogical workforce for children's spaces.

We should say, from the start, that we do not think that these terms are value-free. At the level of both policy and practice, pedagogy is a political and ethical field in which choices are to be made. But we do think that naming the field provides useful ways of thinking about and of developing work with children. 'Pedagogy' could also rescue us, in the English-speaking world, from some of the confusion in which we find ourselves when it comes to providing – and discussing – children's services, alleviating some of the incoherence revealed by the policy documents we reviewed in

Chapter 4, and their struggles to connect aspects of 'care', 'learning' and 'upbringing'.

English confusion about 'pedagogy'

Our work in research and development projects in many European countries has meant that we have often found ourselves grappling with 'pedagogy' and allied terms, in the domains of welfare, social work and education.[10] 'Pedagogy' is strange and difficult for English ears, and, outside certain specialist circles, it is largely unused. In educational theory in Britain it is most often used in the sense of 'the science of teaching and learning' (Mortimore 1999), what many of our European colleagues might refer to as 'didactics' rather than pedagogy: 'in Continental European usage pedagogy is a broad intellectual domain which encompasses the study of education and a variety of forms of human enquiry and endeavour related to it, [while] didactics is much more specifically concerned with methods of teaching, and specifically methods of teaching subjects' (Alexander 2000: 543).

In continental Europe, not only does pedagogy imply a wider intellectual domain, it is a concept commonly applied to work with children and young people across many different settings. While it may be named differently in different countries, a distinct field is generally recognised covering four important and connected areas: the development of *theory*, daily *practice* with children, the formulation of *policy*, and the *training and education* of workers. Most usefully, pedagogy can be used to refer to the whole domain of social responsibility for children, for their well-being, learning and competence. It can encompass many types of provision such as childcare, youth work, family support, youth justice services, residential care, play work and study support – provision that, to English eyes, appears somewhat disparate. Yet pedagogy allows for a discourse that can, provisionally, discount differences based on, for example, the age of those who use provision or its immediate goals, and permits any particular provision to be located in the context of a wider social policy towards children.

To add to the confusion of English-speakers, we should point out that what in northern European countries is referred to as pedagogy, or cognate terms, is in France known as *éducation* – although not in the sense in which we are accustomed to use this word, with its implications of the formal educational system. Thus, in France, *éducation spécialisée* does not refer to special education, in the English sense, but to the social education – upbringing almost – of children experiencing a range of disadvantages. Words similar to 'education' are also sometimes used in other southern European countries, with meanings rather similar to those signified by 'pedagogy' in the north. For our discussion, we prefer 'pedagogy' because, difficult as the term may be to English ears, it is less confusing than the ambiguities involved in using 'education', while 'social education', for

English speakers, smacks something of the classroom and of formal instruction in matters personal and social.

Even more confusion has arisen because the word pedagogy as used in continental Europe has no English equivalent, and may be translated into English – including in official documents – as 'education', while having nothing to do with either schooling or formal learning. The same fate often befalls the French *éducation*, with its broader meaning than the English term. Because of such difficulties with translation, English speakers are probably not sufficiently aware of the important role pedagogy plays in social policy in continental Europe – for Anglophone ears the concept is inaudible. In England (and other English-speaking countries) we rarely avail ourselves of 'pedagogy', nor of the related pedagogue. We ignore these terms, not as a deliberate act of choice, but because we have not seen their potential use, whether for theoretical thinking or for practice, work with children. We, in contrast, have to turn to a range of what might be seen as lower level concepts, applied to different types of provision for children and for different age groups: nursery worker, play worker, residential social worker and so on. Instead of an overarching concept, such as pedagogy, that would present the whole landscape of children's provision, we sectionalise children's policy by turning to concepts such as education, play, residential social work, care, and so on. (We should add that pedagogy may also be transmogrified into 'care' in translation, but that this, also, is misleading.)

What follows attempts a general account of the meanings attached to pedagogy that we have found in the course of many studies in different European countries. In particular, it draws on current work being undertaken on pedagogy and the profession of pedagogue in five continental European countries, both in general and specifically in relation to residential care for children. We shall look at something of its history, at pedagogy as a concept, as a profession and at something of the pedagogic approach as it seems to have evolved.

The concept of pedagogy

Etymologically, the term derives from the Greek. 'Pedagogue' (παιδάγωγός) was first used of the slave who looked after the personal safety of the sons of Athenian households, and accompanied them to lessons away from home. During the Roman Empire, pedagogues themselves took on training functions (*Encyclopaedia Britannica* 1911). According to the *Shorter Oxford English Dictionary*, the term was used in late Middle English to denote a school teacher and its use so continued into the mid-nineteenth century – although it was a pejorative term. 'Pedagogy' – the function of the pedagogue – was in use by the sixteenth century and by the mid-nineteenth century its use was expanded, in English, to include *pedagogics* (1864) – the art or science relating to pedagogy.

By this time, the term was already in use in Germany, to relate to a distinct conceptual field, evidenced by a journal: the *Pädogische Revue*. The term social pedagogy was first defined in 1844 (Mager, quoted in Gabriel, unpublished report, 2001) as the 'theory of all the personal, social and moral education in a given society, including the description of what has happened in practice'. It was a field that, throughout the nineteenth century evolved, often in terms of the development of society and of the individual within society, rather than of the more individual aims suggested by the term 'liberal education'. It was concerned with the provision of popular or universal education, the education of the working classes rather than the education of an elite, and with a range of social interventions, for adults, children and young people. In pedagogy, the aims of education (broadly defined) and social welfare found, and continue to find, a meeting place.

From the nineteenth century, sites for pedagogy have been seen as including social work, youth work, community work, 'settlements' – centres in poor areas offering leisure and education to local people – and adult education. Two points must be made here. First, it is important to notice that the term does not necessarily apply to children. Despite pedagogy's etymological roots, it can be used of work with adults. For example, it can relate to community work, parental support services, adult education, and provision for adults in a wide range of difficult circumstances, ranging from people who have problems with drugs or alcohol, to adults with disabilities. However, in what follows, we shall limit our account of pedagogy to children's provision. Second, provision that is seen as 'pedagogic' can be made within the framework of either residual or of universal welfare – that is it can target 'poor' children or be available for all.

It is also important to be aware that pedagogy is applied at two main levels: the level of theory – sometimes called pedagogics – and the level of training and practice, levels that interconnect, informing and drawing on each other. The principal setting for the development of theory is the university and the faculty or department of pedagogics (which may be brought together with other social studies). Pedagogics is sometimes described as the academic field that deals with the relationship between the individual and society. Disciplines that contribute to this field include sociology, psychology, social history, criminology and cultural studies.

Pedagogy is also a field for vocational training. In European universities and colleges, students prepare for pedagogic work, often over the course of around three or four years, in which they may spend up to a year in practice placements, study relevant bodies of theory, and learn the skills needed for their profession – for example how to work with groups and team work. They also take courses, at their own level, in a range of creative and practical subjects, such as art, drama, woodwork, music, gardening. These are interests and skills that they will bring to their work with children and that will be one of the media through which they relate to children. Pedagogic studies may also be undertaken in the last years of secondary school.

Role of child development?

These, too, lead to face-to-face work with children in a variety of settings and those who qualify in this way may later go on to higher education after some years at work.

Other pedagogic courses are more specialised and longer. For example, in Belgium, while some students follow the training routes described above, others may take an initial five year course, resulting in a qualification that is the equivalent of an English masters degree. This prepares students for further academic work, for research and development posts in government and voluntary organisations, for management jobs, and consultancy and advisory positions connected to a range of provision.

All of the above routes, from secondary school qualifications to masters and doctorates, are seen as qualifications within the field of pedagogies. And, although within any one country job titles may differ according to setting, it seems that there is an overarching understanding of the work of pedagogy: it is to achieve societal aims by means of social provision for children and young people. The values that inform pedagogy, however, can differ from country to country and over time. At its starkest, a totalitarian regime produces an oppressive pedagogy (witness the Hitler youth movements), while the politics of emancipation could produce a pedagogy of equality, citizenship and respect for diversity.

In many European countries, overarching pedagogic theory informs training, children's provision and policy development. Across many different domains key understandings are held, by and large, in common – or are a matter for debate and development. This allows, at a national level, for work with children to have a certain coherence. The newest, as yet unqualified recruit knows that s/he is working in a recognised field. Whatever the contrasts between settings, from nurseries, to family support, to secure units for young offenders, there is some common understanding of what the term pedagogy designates and its dominant values. For governments, matters as seemingly unconnected – to British eyes – as policy towards children involved in criminal activities and policy towards out-of-school playschemes can both be contained within a pedagogic discussion that is informed, implicitly or otherwise, by questions such as 'What do we want for our children?' and 'What is a good childhood?', with which we opened this book. In part, it is those who work in children's provision, the pedagogues, who are responsible for realising society's policy towards children.

The profession of pedagogue

The training and education of pedagogues is of importance. As well as providing access to a common core of understandings and knowledge, work in different settings also requires some specialised training, with optional course and practice placements. This is the basis of the work in much of Europe, although different countries may have somewhat different configurations of pedagogical occupations and associated training.

Our experience in conducting research in Europe, suggests that students have often gained some years' work experience before starting their main studies, that courses are popular, and that the call for qualified pedagogues, in different settings, exceeds supply.

In some countries, pedagogues work across the board, in mainstream and in special services. In Denmark, for example, there is now one profession, trained to work with children from 0 to 18 years across a range of services including early childhood institutions, free-time centres and residential settings. This single profession follows the integration in 1992 of what formerly were three separate trainings: for work in kindergartens (with children aged 3 to 6 years); for work in free-time provision for school-age children; and for work in nurseries (with children under 3 years), in residential settings for looked-after children, or with children and adults with disabilities.

> The reform integrated these three types of training into one . . . and increased the length of the course from 3 to 3.5 years. Training takes place in 32 colleges of social education (pedagogue–seminarium), which each take from 400 to 1,100 students. . . . Demand for training far exceeds supply, reflecting the popularity of the new course and, it has been said, a new enthusiasm among young people for working with people. . . . Many applicants are relatively mature with an average student age of 27. Many start their training in their mid-20s after gaining experienceage of as an untrained worker in early childhood services. . . . Colleges view work experience as an important admission [criterion].
>
> (Moss 2000: 34)

In other countries, there may be a greater focus on one end of the spectrum than the other. In France, the *éducateur/éducatrice de jeunes enfants* works across the board, in mainstream early childhood settings, and in more specialised welfare services for children aged 18 months to 6 years (Jaegar 1997: 113). The work of the *éducateur/éducatrice specialisé(e)* (literally male and female special educators – not special needs teachers, who are *enseignant(e)s spécialisé(e)s* takes place, as the name suggests, more frequently in specialised than in mainstream settings (Dréano 2000). The *éducateur technique spécialisé* (this is a mainly male workforce) also works in special provision, for young people or for adults, with the aim of furthering their entry into employment. The *éducateur technique spécialisé* is trained as an educator but also is qualified and has at least five years' professional experience in a technically based occupation, such as gardening or car mechanics (Jaegar 2000). The work of the *éducateur/éducatrice* is regarded as having much in common with that of the *animateur* (Dréano, personal communication) – whose work is seen as, broadly speaking, that of social education, or pedagogy as we have been using the term. The *animateur* 'valorises creativity, communication, and the development of the person in activities that might seem at first sight to be simply leisure activities' (Jaegar 1997: 29, our translation) The author goes on: 'from this perspective, the function of animation should be present in all the social education professions' – and, indeed, the trainings for both professions have much in common.

What is the work?

What of the contents of the work itself? Again, we draw on understandings gained over many projects conducted in different European countries. Briefly, in children's settings sharing daily life is the stuff of the pedagogic approach: pedagogues and children form a community sharing ideas, activities, learning, meals and outings – depending on the particularities of the setting. Their training aims at producing pedagogues who are reflective practitioners: they think about situations and relationships, bring theories to bear on these, decide how to proceed and review the results of their actions. Their training stresses team work with other pedagogues and with other professionals, as well as with parents and neighbourhood networks.

The pedagogical approach to children is holistic. The pedagogue sets out to address the whole child, the child with body, mind, emotions, creativity, history and social identity. This is not the child only of emotions, the psychotherapeutical approach, nor only of the body, the medical approach, nor only of the mind, the traditional teaching approach.

In Chapter 4 we argued that the British dilemma was how to conceptualise the relationship between what are seen as separate fields in the lives of children, for example 'care' and 'education', and how in practice to bring them into a closer relationship. For the pedagogue, working with the whole child, learning, care and upbringing are closely related (indeed inseparable) activities at the level of daily work. These are not separate fields needing to be joined up, but inter-connected parts of the child's life.

Importantly, the pedagogue does not see him/herself as an isolated worker, working *for* children, carrying out actions *on* children. The approach is relational. The child is not regarded as an autonomous and detached subject, but as living in networks of relationships, involving both children and adults.

The pedagogue has a relationship with the child which is both personal and professional. S/he relates to the child at the level of a person, rather than as a means of attaining adult goals. This interpersonal relationship implies reciprocity and mutuality, and an approach that is individualised but not individualistic – the pedagogue most commonly works with groups of children and the value of the group and the needs of the group are given prominence.

But the relationship is not only personal, it is also professional. Pedagogues do not operate solely on the basis of common-sense understandings: for example the work is not seen as work that most mothers could accomplish successfully, with perhaps a little training, just because they have had experience of bringing up children. Nor are pedagogues technicians, applying detailed and prescriptive curricula, as imposed by government. In much of continental Europe, pedagogy draws on professional skills, understandings and theories and on professional ethics and relationships with other pedagogues.

The contrast could not be greater with the workforce employed to work with children in Britain. Not only is this workforce fragmented into different sectors, each with its own identity, training and focus. In many sectors, a trained and educated workforce has been given low priority and the requirements of qualification have often been set low. This is reflected in poor pay and other employment conditions. Underpinning this is a widespread understanding that work with children, especially young children, is naturally women's work and, in particular, a form of substitute mothering since 'children's services', in particular for young children, are often viewed as a second-best to the 'natural' first choice of the home (cf. Cameron *et al.* 1999).

Despite relatively high levels of initial training, the pedagogue also considers what is to be learned in everyday practice as important. Pedagogy, the practice of the pedagogue, places high value on continuing learning. Learning should be ongoing for the pedagogue as well as for the children with whom s/he works. Together, adults and children learn about – co-constuct – what it is to be a human being living in society, but not just in a theoretical way. Pedagogy encompasses learning about the world, through the activities of daily life, as a social being in the company of others, discovering and exploring.

In their working relationships, the pedagogue and children are in the process of learning, and consciously so. Pedagogy has learning at its heart, with the pedagogue as someone whose role is to accompany children in their learning process and, often, to help children become conscious and reflect on their own learning. This approach applies to any setting in which the pedagogue may work, from a youth club to a residential establishment for children. But, we should stress, the pedagogue does not usually set out to teach in any formal sense; there may be no curriculum, no learning goals, little in the way of a timetable. While the pedagogical model sets the relationship between people largely within the framework of learning, this is not in any didactic sense. Within pedagogy, learning is an ongoing process, encompassing learning about self in relation to others, about one's talents and power, about creativity and about the physical world.

The pedagogical understanding of learning has much in common with our discussion of learning as a possibility in children's spaces. It assumes a particular relationship between pedagogue and child, involving the transformation of consciousness that takes place in the intersection of three agencies – the teacher, the learner and the knowledge they produce together. . . . [P]edagogy refuses to instrumentalize these relations, diminish their interactivity or value one over the other. It, furthermore, denies the teacher as neutral transmitter, the student as passive and knowledge as immutable material to impart. Instead the concept of pedagogy focuses attention on the conditions and means through which knowledge is produced.

(Lusted, quoted in Lather 1991: 15)

Pedagogy claims 'reflective practice' as a core activity. In their training and ongoing professional development, pedagogues evaluate their work and any particular incident – learning point – that may occur. What is to be learned from a particular incident? Is there a body of theory that might help the pedagogue to understand it better? What are the implications for future work? In their face-to-face work with children, too, they model a reflective approach and encourage children to reflect on what is happening, and on the meanings of activities and events, meanings that children and pedagogues arrive at together: the pedagogue makes no claim to be a repository of objects of knowledge that can be duplicated in the children with whom they share time and space.

The approach can put considerable demands on the pedagogue. For the pedagogue, the challenge is to provide a space where new possibilities can be explored and realised. In this space, children and pedagogues engage in reflective and critical ways of knowing and in the construction rather than the reproduction of knowledge. It is a space where children can work creatively with others to realise the possibilities inherent in a situation, to handle any anxiety arising from it and to assess risk realistically. It requires a pedagogy that

can hold open the temporality of questioning so as to resist being characterized as a transaction that can be concluded, either with the giving of grades or the granting of degrees . . . [and] which sees teaching and learning as sites of obligation, loci of ethical practices, not means of transmission of knowledge . . . the scene of teaching understood as a radical form of dialogue.

(Readings 1997: 19, 155)

Pedagogues for children's spaces

In Britain, there is a reluctance to rethink work with children, starting with asking basic questions about what type of worker we need for working with children. We want to 'modernise' children's services, without modernising the workforce, relying instead on incremental change within an unchanged framework. One reason is that, from government's perspective, paid work with children (indeed work with people) is a can of worms, which policy makers are reluctant to open. For decades it has been premissed on the availability of women to do the work, and women who have often been poorly educated, poorly trained and poorly paid. Incremental change avoids addressing questions of gender, the social value of the work and the true costs entailed.

But incremental change is also a sign of not wanting to think about work with children, and our understandings of the provisions in which that work is conducted and the children using those provisions. Our attempt to explore a particular understanding of the child and the provisions made for her has led us to an understanding of the work in those provisions and a proposal for who the worker might be who can undertake that work – the pedagogue. We do not suggest that 'the pedagogue' is necessarily the only type of worker who might be envisaged, nor that the pedagogue is identical in every time and place – there are, for example, important variants between pedagogues in different European countries.

Whatever the type of worker – and for the moment we will keep with pedagogues – we would argue that work with children, especially in provisions understood as 'children's spaces', requires a workforce that is, in general, highly trained and viewed as critical and reflective practitioners (indeed, as in Reggio, as researchers) rather than low level technicians. It also needs to be a diverse workforce, reflecting the diversity of contemporary societies, for example in terms of ethnicity, language, sexual orientation, disability and age. They should also represent both genders. Any review of the workforce for children's spaces should pay attention to the highly gendered nature of most current work in 'children's services', perhaps aiming initially for a target of 20 per cent male workers, a target currently set in Norway for work in early childhood centres. Denmark has worked to recruit men into work with children and 25 per cent of pedagogics students are now male (OECD 2001) (for a fuller discussion of the issue of gender in work with children see Jensen 1996; Owen *et al.* 1998; and Cameron *et al.* 1999).

By revaluing work with children in the way we are proposing, we do not want to exclude potential staff from working with children. Reform would mean offering opportunities for existing members of the workforce to (re-)train in the new role, taking account of previous training and experience. It would also leave a substantial proportion of jobs for less trained workers, leading to further training to become a pedagogue, as for example happens in Denmark.

We recognise, therefore, that people who work in children's spaces may be at different stages of their careers. Some may have recently left school with lower level qualifications, others may have much experience but little in the way of formal education, still others may have qualified through higher education and specialised training. We do not wish to be prescriptive as to the proportion of unqualified or untrained staff that is acceptable in any one setting. Having said all that, we do wish to see the development of a pedagogical profession that can inform the work as a whole.

This would be a profession where practice can be critically examined, where theory can be generated and debated, where, as in many other European countries, research can be undertaken by pedagogues and on the basis of pedagogic perspectives. In short, we see pedagogy as a profession that has a theory base and a practice base, accountable to society, but in charge of its own development and of the dissemination of pedagogic understandings – understandings that are informed by learning about the social world in the company of children, in the library and in debate.

Pedagogues as a professional group can make sure that children are properly represented in the development of public policy, so that its agendas are not simply oriented to the needs of adults. One of the functions of the pedagogue is to be an ombudsman, listening to and promoting the rights and ideas of individual children, and of groups of children. Importantly they should be aware of the different positions that children of different social groups occupy, in public policy and in the wider society. In the spirit of democracy, social justice and respect for diversity pedagogues should work against the mechanisms that value certain young people and devalue others, because of characteristics such as 'race', religion, disability, sexuality and gender.

As such, the practice of pedagogy cannot be other than political. As Lorenz tellingly asks:

> Is social pedagogy essentially the embodiment of dominant societal interests which regard all educational projects, schools, kindergartens or adult education, as a way of taking its values to all sections of the population and of exercising more effective social control; or is social pedagogy the critical conscience of pedagogy, the thorn in the flesh of official agenda, an emancipatory programme for self-directed learning processes inside and outside the education system geared towards the transformation of society?
>
> (Lorenz 1993: 93)

The pedagogy that is appropriate for the children's spaces described in earlier chapters aims at emancipation, not control. It looks to children, of all social groups, as citizens, exercising their citizenship in children's spaces, and beyond, engaged with each other and with adults in the ongoing transformation of society towards emancipatory ends.

8 The case of Sweden

In this chapter, we offer the case of Sweden, as an example of a country which seems to be working with perspectives – discourses and understandings – that have something in common with our own, although we do not claim that they are identical. Providing examples immediately raises questions. What is the point of them? Why one example rather than another?

For us, as we indicated in the first chapter, the point of examples is not to supply 'models' or 'programmes' or 'best practices', to be exported or replicated. Each policy or provision is the product of a unique context. The uniqueness of that context is woven from numerous threads, coloured by a particular time, place and history: the social actors, both children and adults; the social, political, cultural and economic conditions; the understandings, discourses and values; and the political and ethical choices made in answer to particular questions. Carlina Rinaldi states this singularity clearly when she says of the early childhood provision in Reggio Emilia: 'We do not offer a recipe, nor a method, our work is not to be copied because values can only be lived not copied'.

From our perspective, examples are best seen and used as provocations. They should surprise us, make us think, ask critical questions, appreciate the peculiarity of what we have taken for granted, illuminate implicit understandings and values, make our narratives stutter, open us to new possibilities. The process of thinking and questioning may, in the end, lead to dismissal – this example is not something from which we can or want to learn, although it will not leave us as we were and may leave us feeling unsettled, dissatisfied, in search of another direction. Or it may contribute to processes of learning: learning not as transmission or re-production, in which examples serve as 'models' or 'programmes' or 'best practices' to be copied. But learning as co-construction in relation with others, in which the example as 'an Other' becomes part of a process of constructing new knowledges, understandings and practices, an institutional parallel to individual and group pedagogical processes discussed in Chapters 6 and 7.

If they are not models simply to be copied, neither do examples represent 'ideal' scenarios. As we have emphasised, with discourses and understandings it is not a case of 'either/or'. In practice, many can and often will co-exist. What differs is the actual assemblage of different discourses and understandings, the relationship between them and the relative weight given one as against another – which assemblage comes to predominate? What we offer below is not a 'pure' example of the discourse on childhood outlined in Chapter 5, nor of public provision understood as 'children's spaces'. Rather, Sweden is an example where these discourses and understandings seem to us to be more prominent than is usually the case, certainly in the English-speaking world. Sweden provokes us by showing the contestability, in practice, of childhood and public provisions for children.

Sweden – reorganising and rethinking

> The Swedish system of pre-school education is outstanding. . . . The [OECD review] team was profoundly impressed by the omnipresent spirit of respect and trust that characterised Swedish early childhood services. . . . The review team was [also] impressed by the diversity of pedagogical efforts, the diversity of programmatic initiatives and the diversity of pre-school structures. . . . The intellectual probing coupled with the desire to work with new ideas all signal a system that is dynamic, not static. . . . [I]t has been said that the merit of any nation may be judged by how it treats its children – particularly the poor and needy. If that adage is true, then Sweden sits on an international pinnacle. Nothing honours Sweden more than the way it honours and respects its young.
>
> (Organisation for Economic Cooperation and Development (OECD) 1999: paras 127, 131, 136)

Sweden shares a number of broad similarities with other Nordic countries. In Chapter 6, a common interest in 'children's culture' was noted. This can be seen as reflecting some shared perspectives towards children and childhood.

Prout cites the Nordic countries as handling the tension between control and self-realisation in late modernity differently to Britain:

> some societies, notably but not exclusively the Nordic ones, make greater efforts towards representing children's interests. Although still subject to tensions between the control of children and their opportunities for self-realisation, these societies handle them in ways that seem to create more space for children in public discourse. . . . [In contemporary Britain] the tensions of late modernity seem to be played out in ways that, overall, constrain and limit the interests and voice of children in public discourse.
>
> (Prout 2000: 305)

There are also striking similarities in aspects of provision for children in the Nordic countries, for example relatively generous systems of leave for parents to provide care for young children and public provision of nurseries and family day-care for young children and of free-time centres for school-age children. While these similarities have led to the Nordic countries often being considered or classified together (e.g. the Nordic welfare state), in practice there are important differences between them in many respects (for elaboration of some of these differences, see Moss and Deven (2000) for leave entitlements for parents; and the reviews of early childhood education and care policy in Denmark, Finland, Norway and Sweden conducted by the OECD and available on the OECD website (www.oecd.org)).

We have decided to focus on Sweden because it seems to us to be a particularly interesting and important country at the present time in terms of policy, provision and practice. Although visitors to Sweden are always impressed by the generosity of its provisions – be it paid parental leave or the extent and accessibility of pre-school or school-age services – we have been struck on our latest visits by the importance of the structural changes under way and by the very clear linkage of these changes to new thinking about children, childhood and learning. This exemplifies a conclusion that has emerged for us from our work over recent years: that organisation and structure matter, but so too does thinking, and that reorganisation without rethinking is a recipe for, at best, little to change and, at worst, chaos.

The important reforms of provisions for children under way in Sweden not only link reorganisation with rethinking, but also span a wide range of provisions for children, in terms both of age ('pre-school' and 'school-age') and settings (including early childhood centres, family day-care, schools and free-time centres). In particular, Sweden is important for the way it is approaching the integration of early childhood and free-time provisions into the education system. Rather than subordinating these provisions to the school, this process of integration is being used to seek new and more equal relationships between all institutions, including schools. Schools and teachers are being called on to rethink, as much as early childhood and free-time provisions and their workers.

Of course, this is a risky business. Schools and teachers may prove resistant to change: integration of early childhood and free-time provision into education may in the end lead to the imperium of the school rather than a federation of equal partners. Some in other Nordic countries remain very suspicious of attempts to bring early childhood and school systems too close together. But it seems to us a brave and unique attempt to transform both organisation and understandings, a real provocation.

Three features of the Swedish context should be mentioned by way of introduction, the first two of which reflect the strong attachment of Swedish society to values of equality and democracy, the third that Sweden is at the forefront of developments in information technology. First, through social and other policies, Sweden has managed to sustain relatively high levels of social inclusion and equality. Despite a period of economic difficulty in the late 1980s through to the mid-1990s (when unemployment grew from

2 to 8 per cent), and despite the highest level of lone parent families among OECD member states, Sweden has kept levels of child poverty low (defined as the proportion of children living in households with an income 50 per cent below the median household income): just 2.6 per cent of children in 1995, compared with 19.8 per cent in the UK and 22.4 per cent in the USA (in 1997). This is the result of several factors, including relatively few workless households and workers on low wages, and high levels of social expenditure (UNICEF 2000).

These high levels of expenditure certainly require high levels of taxation. In 1997, Swedish tax receipts were equivalent to 52 per cent of GDP, compared to 50 per cent in Denmark, 45 per cent in France, 35 per cent in the UK and 30 per cent in Australia and the USA (OECD 2001: Table A.1). Readers will take differing political and ethical views on the issue of taxation. For now, we will emphasise that in Sweden's case high taxes produce high benefits, including impressive policies on leave, public provisions for children and low levels of child poverty.

The consequences of low child poverty are considerable. Not only do Swedish children live their childhoods in better material conditions, with all the benefits associated with that: but Swedish provisions for children are freer to develop as spaces for childhood, and to explore new thinking about childhood, learning, knowledge and so on. There is less expectation on them to provide cures for poverty and its malignant side-effects, through tightly regulated and controlling procedures. There is simply not the widespread poverty and inequality which blights Britain, dominating policy-making and helping to sustain a centralist and prescriptive approach to implementation.

Second, the UN Convention on the Rights of the Child is a 'burning issue'. A study which compared the implementation of the Convention internationally found that Sweden (and other Nordic countries) adhere closely to the resolutions of the Convention, while countries like the UK and Germany more often disregard them (Bartley 1998). Sweden has a Children's Ombudsman (*Barnombudsmannen*, or BO), one of whose tasks is to be proactive in questions concerning the rights and interests of children and young people, and the obligations of Sweden under the Convention. At a governmental level, the Ministry for Social Affairs is responsible for implementing the Convention (since the transfer of pre-school and free-time provisions to education, this Ministry has been given this responsibility, but otherwise is left with two main areas of responsibility for children: social services and child and family benefits). A fact sheet from the Ministry states:

> The implementation of the Convention in Sweden is an ongoing process which must not be allowed to lose momentum. . . . It is a question of changing attitudes, approaches and methods in various spheres of activity and at different levels of society.

The rights outlined in the Convention are seen as all having equal value – so that, for example, the right of children to a personal identity has equal standing with the right for them to express their views. The Swedish Government has made many proposals in order that the Convention might be more thoroughly implemented. They include:

- implementing the Convention shall be an active policy that permeates all Ministries;
- it shall be incorporated into training and in-service training of pro-fessionals and local authority employees;
- child impact analyses shall be made of all government decisions;
- the role of the Children's Ombudsman should be reviewed and strengthened;
- the child's perspective should be included in the terms of reference of commissions of inquiry and similar bodies;
- the influence and participation of children and young people should be developed in social and traffic planning; and
- statistics about children should be developed.

This approach to the Convention is associated with Sweden's strong democratic tradition. This tradition is also reflected in many developments to increase the influence of children in their schools (Moss *et al.* 1999). It permeates the recent pre-school curriculum (discussed further below) which begins with the statement that 'democracy forms the foundation for the pre-school ... the activities of the pre-school should be carried out democratically and thus provide the foundation for a growing responsibility and interest on the part of children to participate actively in society' (Swedish Ministry of Education and Science 1998: 6).

It is also apparent in a process of decentralisation of power and decision-making from national government to local authorities (municipalities) and individual institutions. This process of decentralisation can be seen in the interpretation and implementation of national curricula; in the loosening of central control in other areas, such as standards; and in the growing diversity of provisions, with increasing scope for working with different approaches. The multinational OECD team that reviewed Swedish early childhood provisions in 1999 was 'impressed' by the diversity they found, observing that 'Swedish pre-schools are not only diverse in their struc-tures and audiences, but in their pedagogical approaches' and that the decentralised approach fosters 'freedom of choice and complexity of options' (OECD 1999: paras 78, 77).

Third, Sweden is a world leader of the new information economy. Indeed, according to a recent report, Sweden is 'the world's number one informa-tion economy', based on an index made up of telephone lines and mobile phones in use, as well as computing and social infrastructure. Sweden took over the top spot on this Information Society Index from the USA in 2000 and continued in 2001 'to skate ahead while the Americans tumbled to fourth behind Norway and Finland' (Schofield 2001: 2). We mention that not to claim that our perspective on provision for children, or Sweden's, will guarantee national economic success – but to suggest that they are, at least, not inimical.

Reorganising

Sweden has long had a reputation for the provisions that, as a society, it has made for its children. Many other countries have cast envious or sceptical eyes over the high levels of publicly funded provision, for example nurseries (called 'pre-schools' in Sweden), family day-care and free-time centres. These high levels of provision, part of a Scandinavian welfare state tradition stressing equality and democracy, are an important facet of Swedish public policy towards children. Indeed, in recent years, this aspect of provision has taken a new and important turn with the introduction in 1993 of legislation (implemented in 1995) which requires local authorities to provide 'without unreasonable delay' an early childhood or free-time centre place for children between 1 and 12 years of age, if their parents work or study or if the child has a particular need for a place (before the age of 12 months, children are assumed to be at home with a parent taking parental leave).[11]

Most local authorities (95 per cent in 1998) can now meet their duty to provide 'without unreasonable delay', defined as within three to four months. Moreover, legislation approved in 2000 extends this duty. Children aged 1 to 5 years now have a right to a place of at least three hours a day if their parents are unemployed or on parental leave. The Government emphasises that children with non-employed parents should go to the same provisions as children with employed parents, so further breaking down the connection between early childhood provision and parents' labour market participation, and further moving admission to these provisions from being a parental to a child right. Under the influence of such measures, and despite a squeeze on public spending for much of the 1990s (which began, however, to ease in 1997), 76 per cent of children aged 1 to 5 years attended publicly funded early childhood provisions in 1999, most (65 per cent) going to centres, the rest (11 per cent) to organised family day-care schemes (Gunnarson *et al.* 1999; Swedish Ministry of Education and Science 2000). The remaining quarter of young children were cared for by parents (unemployed, on parental leave, working shifts or working at home), by relatives or private family day carers

However, the importance of Sweden lies not just in quantity of provision and consequent accessibility. It also lies in the way it is reorganising and rethinking its policy and provisions for children in new and challenging ways. From the beginning of the 1990s, many Swedish local authorities (like those in neighbouring Norway) responded to greater decentralisation and autonomy by reorganising services, to bring responsibility for pre-schools, schools and free-time provisions into one department. These local initiatives were followed in 1996 by central government, which incorporated responsibility for all of these services within the Ministry of Education and Science (which takes charge of policy) and the National Agency for Education (which takes charge of administration); prior to this early years and free-time services were the responsibility of the Ministry of Social Affairs and the National Board of Health and Social Welfare. At around the same time, while compulsory school age remained at 7 years, local authorities were required to make provision in school for those 6-year-olds whose parents wanted them to attend. For 6-year-olds, therefore, there are now free pre-school classes, used by 95 per cent of the age group, available usually for three hours a day, with children attending free-time provision for the rest of the day.

In sum, then, early years provision (both pre-schools and family day care) and free-time provision for school-age children now fall within the education system, alongside schools, and all are viewed as engaged *inter alia* with children's learning. During a visit in 1999, Crister Molande, the manager of the Development Department at Älsvjö, a local authority outside Stockholm, said to us: 'We want to keep the whole child in the picture. So services should have a real life perspective, not an organisational perspective.' Since children and parents do not experience childhood as being broken down into phases, with distinct organisational cut off points, provisions for childhood, also, should be as integrated as possible across childhood. He also believed that treating education as an administrative whole, which catered for children from birth to 18 years, meant that responsibility for the child was always contained within the same system. Any problems which the child might present could not be blamed on an earlier stage which had been the responsibility of another provider and another organisational framework.

This administrative integration is reflected in several parallel developments. First, the administrative integration of different provisions for children has given rise to developing and coordinating their curricula. A new and short national curriculum for schools (grades 1 to 9) has been written which sets two kinds of goals, goals to reach and goals to strive towards:

> Goals to strive towards indicate the direction of the work of the school. . . . Goals to reach express what the pupils at least shall have reached when they leave school. It is the responsibility of the school and the school head that the pupils are given the possibility to reach these goals.
>
> (Swedish Ministry of Education and Science 1994: 10)

The interpretation and realisation of these goals is decentralised to the local authorities who formulate their own plans, and to the schools, who work to achieve the goals of the national curriculum within the framework set by their local authority.

Since 1998 a national curriculum for pre-schools (centres for children aged 1 to 5 years) has been in place, which explicitly recognises that 'the pre-school will now constitute the first step in the education system' (Swedish Ministry of Education and Science 1998: 2). Like the schools curriculum, this curriculum for pre-schools focuses on goals to strive for, is short (nineteen pages in the English-language version) and leaves much room for interpretation to local authorities and individual institutions.

At the same time, the national curriculum for schools has been extended to include pre-school classes (for 6-year-olds) and free-time provisions (for school-age children). 'The pre-school class is a part of the school and the first step towards realizing and fulfilling the goals of the curriculum. Free-time services shall contribute to reaching the goals' (Swedish Ministry of Education and Science 1998: 2).

Integration at the administrative and curriculum levels has also supported the integration of provisions within schools. 'Whole day schools', which integrate school classes (either the first grades of compulsory school on their own or together with pre-school classes), with free-time services are increasingly widespread. In a study of fifty-nine field experiments on co-operation and integration between schools and free-time provisions, Björn Flising (1995) found problems, but also substantial potential benefits. He concluded that both have basic similarities: they aim to support children's development and contribute to the quality of life; they work with children of the same age, often with the same children; and both have staff with educational training and competence. The main work of school is about teaching and learning 'established knowledge', while free-time pedagogy is directed towards supporting development in a broader sense, giving children space and time, and resources for play, creativity, friendships, their own interests and explorations. Together the different approaches allow children a more holistic development. Crucial issues for cooperation and integration are: common management (e.g. an interested and energetic joint head teacher); advance preparation (one year); combined planning, follow up, evaluation and development; premises which function well for both sets of activities; and support and freedom for staff to develop cooperative work; and, he stresses, a central role for children.

In 1999, we visited several examples in one local authority where children aged 6 years (i.e. pre-schoolers), 7 and 8 (i.e. the first two grades of compulsory school) formed a distinct part of the school, organised into groups of twenty-five to thirty children, each group called a *barnskola* and with a staff team of three workers. This staff team was made up of one member of staff from each of three main types of worker in Sweden: the pre-school teacher (*förskollärare*), who up to now has mainly worked in early childhood centres and the free-time pedagogue (*fritidspedagog*), who has mainly worked in free-time centres, each with a three year education at university level; and the school teacher, with a $3\frac{1}{2}$ to $4\frac{1}{2}$ years' education, also at university level. They all belong to the same trade union.

Although the actual school day was 8 a.m. until 1 p.m., the *barnskola* which integrated school classes and free-time activities was open from 6.30 a.m. to 6.30 p.m. The day was integrated and planned as a whole, with the staff group having three hours per week for this planning work. This team work approach has been around in Sweden for some time:

> The idea of team work was evoked as early as the 1970s both in the committee on childcare and in the committee of the inner work of school (SOU 1974: 53). Eventually, the school and childcare grew nearer to each other and the activities began to cooperate and began, more and more to be integrated. . . . Could the future team open the school to the outer world? . . . Is cooperation between pre-school–school-school age childcare the educational model of the future? The existing work within the integrated school makes a way of work possible where more competences are at children's and young people's disposal.
>
> (Rohlin 1997: 90–91)

As already indicated, there are still many problems with team working, but in those cases which we saw where it was working well, then it was leading to new ways of working and a process of mutual debate and rethinking about different professional cultures and images of the child. In one of the *barnskola* we visited, which was recognised as a leader in its municipality, the three staff talked of a difficult but rewarding process of becoming a team working with a group of children. In 1991, the preschool teacher and school teacher had come together when a class for 6-year-olds was added to the school. Then in 1995, they were joined by the free-time pedagogue, as the free-time centre was integrated with the school class to form a *barnskola*. This now consisted of twenty-nine children from 6 to 9 years old and was open from 6.30 in the morning until 6.30 at night, operating in spacious and purpose-built accommodation; within this time, the 'school day' was from 8 a.m. to 1 p.m. However all three members of the staff team worked together with the children, and planned their work together during the three hours per week allocated for this purpose.

The teacher commented that

> in the beginning it was not so easy working together. We had the same words, but they meant different things. We worked differently with parents. I wanted to be alone with the class at the beginning (of the school year), but the free-time pedagogue was quite the opposite – she

wanted the parents in from the beginning. I had always taught alone, done everything for the children, so it was difficult to share the children with others.

All three workers had come to better understand their different traditions – as pre-school teachers, teachers or free-time pedagogues. The *förskollärare* spoke of the importance of play in her tradition, of working from children's own fantasies, thoughts and ideas, and of looking outwards from the institution to the external environment. When she came to work in the school she carried 'ideas of a school from my own childhood – but in reality I felt more at home, even though it was still more structured and time governed than pre-school centres'.

The *fritidspedagog* had previously worked in a *barnskola* where there was little team work. The *förskollärare* had worked with the 6-year-olds, the school teacher with the 7- and 8-year-olds. Then the *fritidspedagog* took over outside the school day, but without knowing what the children had done during this time. Each worker had planned and done their own thing.

The team we met had addressed their differences from the beginning. They had talked and planned a lot (although they were clear that the three hours per week available for this purpose was not enough). The *förskollärare* and *fritidspedagog* came from a similar tradition, and their training had much in common – but the school teacher had no idea of their traditions or training, only stereotypes. So there had been much discussion and exchange, to deepen mutual understanding and to identify what each was good at or needed to know more about (for example, the school teacher wanted to know more about free-time work, the *förskollärare* more about older children). They discovered that they looked at the child differently, but this had changed and now they saw the whole child much more so than before. They had read a lot, and were just beginning to work as a team with pedagogical documentation (discussed in Chapter 6) as a way of looking critically and collectively at their pedagogical work. While recognising they had a long way to go, all felt they had achieved a lot: 'The way we work today is something new. It is influenced by all of our traditions and by research. Teachers find there is more to learning than books, and use other methods.'

Another example of this new approach to the relationship between different provisions and professions was to be found in the management of a range of provisions, all now within the administrative responsibility of local education departments: pre-schools (both centres and family day care), schools and free-time centres. The same local authority has been divided into a number of districts, each with its own administrator, or *rektor*, responsible for this range of children's provisions. Moreover, these rektors could come from a range of backgrounds – school teacher, *förskollärare* or *fritidspedagog* (in practice the split had been roughly 50–50 between school teachers and other professions). One *rektor* who we met was a pre-school teacher (*förskollärare*), and had responsibility for three schools (one of which was for children with disabilities), together with four pre-school centres, family day carers, free-time provisions in each school and *fritidsclub*, provision made for children above the age for attending free-time centres (9- to 12-year-olds) – altogether 800 children and 160 staff.

Elsewhere, we found institutions which were no longer called schools, but *houses*, incorporating as they did several functions and different professional groups working collaboratively. For example, there was *Emmahuset*, in Gothenburg. The name was based on an acronym (MA) meaning the house of masses of activities. It served an area described as disadvantaged, where three-quarters of the population were immigrants. Clusters of three classes, for children of different ages, were grouped together and carried out many different activities with their teachers and their free-time pedagogues, who worked together as a team. The school's principal, whose background was as a free-time pedagogue, always referred to her institution as a House because its function was so much larger than that of a school, and the pedagogic approach to children's learning was different from that of the traditional school.

We also saw *Samverhuset* (the Cooperation House), another school which provided an integrated day for children and combined the work of teachers (pre-school and school) and free-time pedagogues. Again there were clusters of classes and free-time rooms. Serving all the clusters was a core block, which included a dining hall, gymnasium, art and craft room and music room, as well as offices.

Partly because of the reforms and the increasing emphasis placed on close team working by members of the three main staffing groups, there has been increasing discussion in Sweden about the future structure of staffing across the main provisions for children and young people. This has led, via an all-party parliamentary committee commissioned to look into teacher training which reported in July 1999, to a major reform of training – not just of early childhood workers, but of *all* workers in the education system working with children and young people up to 19 years of age. From Autumn 2001 a new integrated system of teacher training has been introduced, to replace eight of the previous eleven qualifications. All teachers, except upper secondary vocational teachers, but including *förskollärare* and *fritidspedagog*, will do a degree course of at least $3\frac{1}{2}$ years, and all graduates will be called 'teachers' (after much discussion, the term 'pedagogue' was rejected). Moreover, $1\frac{1}{2}$ years of the course will involve common studies by all students – whether proposing to work with 18-month-olds or 18-year-olds. This general field of education 'should comprise, on the one hand, areas of knowledge that are central to the teaching profession, such as teaching, special needs education, child and youth development, and on the other hand, interdisciplinary subject studies' (Swedish Ministry of

Education 2000b: 1–2). The remainder of the course will involve more specialised studies, for example in early childhood work.

This reform is driven not just by administrative integration and the need for new working relationships (in particular, more team working), nor by a concern to facilitate movement of workers between settings by making it easier to retrain. It is also intended to support new understandings of learning and knowledge, and what it means to be a teacher. We shall return to these in the next section. For now, however, we want to emphasise a concern to change teaching methods within compulsory schooling, and especially amongst teachers in upper secondary school (taking 16- to 19-year-olds), which have been criticised as inflexible and old-fashioned. Understandings and ways of working drawn from other traditions – such as early childhood and free-time work – are seen as having a contribution to make in this project of reshaping learning and teaching.

The reform has much going for it. It is popular among students and employers. Although there is not parity between the training and working conditions of school teachers on the one hand, and *förskollärare* and *fritidspedagog* on the other hand, the differences are not so great as to provide a major impediment to greater integration. All three groups of workers are represented by the same trade union, an important consideration in a country where union membership is high and unions retain influence. The reform is supported by a broader debate about learning and knowledge, which questions more traditional schooling approaches and proposes the need for change. At the same time, there are barriers that may slow change or make it uneven, both in the teacher training system and in schools themselves, in particular the upper secondary system.

Rethinking

As well as addressing organisational issues, the process of reform in Sweden over the last decade has addressed even more basic issues: understandings of the child and learning. As we have already outlined, there are at least three pedagogical traditions involved: the school teacher, the *förskollärare* and the *fritidspedagog*. There has been a recognition that reform should not involve a 'take-over' by one pedagogical tradition and perspective, the triumph of one professional culture, but should instead be based on a general rethinking across all three groups and the search for new and shared understandings.

This has involved an active relationship between theory and practice. A discussion paper, commissioned by the Government, by two leading pedagogical researchers in Sweden, Gunilla Dahlberg and Hellevi Lenz Taguchi, has been one important influence in this process. Titled *Pre-school and School – Two Different Traditions and the Vision of a Meeting Place*, the paper begins by identifying different pedagogical traditions in pre-school and school, each produced by a different social construction of the child: 'the analysis shows that the view of the child which we call the child as nature is, for the most part, embodied in the pre-school, while the child as producer of culture and knowledge is, for the most part, embodied in the school' (Dahlberg and Lenz Taguchi 1994: 2). These different constructions have had 'direct consequences on the content and working methods of pedagogical activity, and in that way affected the view of the child's learning and knowledge-building'. The paper goes on to suggest an alternative construction of the child – the child as a constructor of culture and knowledge – which could 'create a meeting place where both the pre-school teachers and the primary school teachers are given the possibility to develop their pedagogical practices'.

> We do not wish to present a new pedagogical method or model, but a vision of a possible meeting place. This vision can be seen as a provisional, holistic picture of the educational institutions we need in a quickly changing society. The vision deals with a way of relating and a working process in relation to the child's creation of knowledge and everyday reality which is based upon continual discussions and common values which one wants to permeate the child's upbringing and education. This way of relating starts from the view of the child as a competent and capable child, a rich child, who participates in the creation of themselves and their knowledge – the child as a constructor of culture and knowledge. In this pedagogical approach, this way of relating is characterised by a researching, reflective and analytical approach at different levels.
>
> (Ibid.: 2)

What was interesting during our visit to Sweden was to hear directly from practitioners – such as the team at the *barnskola* and the *rektor* mentioned above – how they had read this work. This analysis and this possible solution were influencing their thinking and practice, leading to recognition that staff from different backgrounds had to work to understand each other's traditions and perspectives, as well as seeking new and shared perspectives.

This response by practitioners reflects an openness to rethinking, and an interest in relating public policy on children to a wider analysis of social change. Sweden is moving from an industrial society into a post-industrial information and knowledge society – a learning society. There is also recognition of a profound change – a paradigmatic shift – in how people understand and create meaning in their lives which has consequences for understandings of children and childhood. While many teachers retain the view of the child as 'the empty box', with question-and-answer as their most important pedagogical method, an alternative view is becoming increasingly common (Flising 1999). This way of viewing the child builds on the notion of the child as an active and creative actor, as a subject and citizen with potentials, rights and responsibility. A child worth listening to and having a dialogue with, and who has the courage to think and act by himself ... the child as an active actor, a constructor, in the construction of his own knowledge and his fellow beings' common culture ... a child with his own inclination and power to learn, investigate and develop as a human being in an active relation to other people ... a child who wants to take an active part in the knowledge-creating process, a child who in interaction with the world around is also active in the construction, in the creation of himself, his personality and his talents. This child is seen as having 'power over his own learning processes' and having the right to interpret the world.

(Dahlberg 1997: 22)

This image of the child, and related ideas about knowledge and learning, draw quite explicitly on social constructionist theories. This view informs both the recent national curriculum and the training and education of staff. The official educational perspective is that children are 'actors', that is active participants in and constructors of their own development, including knowledge and identity.

In the Swedish school, opportunities are being given to children to participate in their own learning processes in various ways. At the level of the individual child, there is their participation in developing their own developmental learning plans. This might be long term, through the yearly review of learning, taking into account the child's developing portfolio of work; this contains examples of the child's work from starting school and forms the basis of a yearly 'developmental conversation', involving the child, teacher, parent and sometimes the free-time pedagogue. Or it might be short term. For example, we saw that from starting compulsory schooling each child might organise their activities for each day, in conjunction with the teacher.

Children could also have an input into the organisation of the school. At *Emmahusset*, the 'school' which we described earlier, the children had put forward a strong view that the older children in the school (age 12 years) should no longer be organised as a separate group, and this view was taken into account and prevailed. At the same school, when a group of classes and staff began a new project (e.g. on the Middle Ages) it was the children who suggested the activities and processes which should be involved. The children, too, had had a major input in solving difficulties surrounding school outings to places of interest. That children should participate strongly within their own education is foreseen within the law in Sweden, and it echoes the decentralisation of education, generally, so that decisions are taken at the most appropriate level, so that, e.g. decisions about how the curriculum should be put into operation are made by the municipality, the schools, parents and children.

How is the teacher viewed in this 'new' way of seeing things? No longer as the repository of knowledge, to be transmitted to pupils, inappropriate if children and young people are understood as active learners finding or constructing knowledge from many places. As part of a book written by researchers, to mark the transfer of responsibility for early childhood services from the National Board of Health and Social Welfare to the National Agency for Education, Dahlberg writes:

> The view of the child as co-constructor implies a view of the teacher as co-constructor of culture and knowledge. This view means a twofold professional responsibility, which partly is about going into a dialogue and communicative action with the child, the group of children and colleagues, partly about a reflecting and researching attitude in which the starting point is the work and learning process of both the children and the teacher. . . . The teacher can have many different roles. Sometimes . . . to direct: to present a problem and initiate work around pre-planned material, or to introduce a new field of knowledge, to progress work further. Sometimes you are reduced to being a prompter and an assistant in a process which the children, by their own power, have initiated and direct by themselves. . . . The work of the teacher is mainly to be able to listen, see and let oneself be inspired by and learn from what the children say and do.
>
> (Dahlberg 1997: 23)

It would be misleading to suggest that the new ways of working and thinking outlined above are universally adopted. There is considerable diversity between local authorities in Sweden, and there are resistances among many practitioners to working in teams. Not everyone would accept a social constructionist analysis, nor these new ideas about learning.

The recent OECD review of Swedish early childhood policies and provisions also notes a number of tensions. One of these tensions is between aspects of different discourses, childhood as a current state and childhood as futurity:

> On the one hand, the early years are regarded as a special time, a time when children's curiosity, their motivation, and their childhood in general are to be fostered. . . . More than in other nations, this ethos is reflected in the comparative absence of the need to account for children's accomplishments. Assessing children's 'readiness' (for school or life), so common in other cultures, is absent from the explicit Swedish agenda. . . . On the other hand, the child's future is recognised and valued. Indeed, there is a concern that what happens in pre-school will be continuous with the values, norms, and events of the school. . . . The tension between pre-school education as a pedagogical experience for the day versus pre-school as the preparation for the future seems to

find expression in a duality of strategies. On the individual child basis, the pedagogy of the pre-school respects the 'todayness' of childhood. On an institutional level, it fully recognises that the early years of care are a first step in the trajectory of life-long learning.

(OECD 1999: paras 74–75)

The same report, however, suggests these tensions (the others are between individuality and collectivity, and a focus on the past and the present) reflect the major shift occurring in the Swedish system. Far from being harmful, they are provoking 'Swedes to think hard and long about how they view children, childhood and the institutions that serve youngsters'. The review team concluded that the resulting 'intellectual dialogue' revealed a strong system 'not afraid to question, to be analytic and to be self critical' (ibid.: para. 79). Indeed, what is impressive about today's Sweden is an openness to new ideas, to new relationships, to new ways of working, and a general sense of optimism amongst practitioners.

9 Unfinished business

Five years on

We started out, five years ago, wanting to transform children's services. But 'transform' carries with it ideas of transcendence and magical powers, images of the alchemist and Cinderella, the search for and revelation of the one and only, the true way, the essence of the matter. There is, too, an implied dualism, as we move from the bad old days to the good new times through the benign sorcery of modernisation and managerialism. Five years on, our discussion has become both more cautious and more ambitious.

Cautious, because we now doubt the desirability and feasibility of writing general prescriptions, which deny context, diversity, and complexity: that way lies the misleading certainty of the technical text. By the same token, we have become warier of focusing on structures, necessary as we recognise these to be. So this final chapter will not be an exercise in authoritative conclusions and recommendations, a summation of what works and how to implement this best practice.

Ambitious, because over time we have found ourselves drawn increasingly into rethinking – thinking differently – about policy, provision and practice for children. Moreover, our thinking has been informed by an ever expanding framework of theories, ideas and examples. We find ourselves now struggling to locate our discussions of children and public provision for children in profound issues concerning ways of thinking, seeing, relating and understanding.

There have been continuities, too, over the five years. Early on we identified as important the connection between understandings of childhood and of public provision for children. We argued then that there are many possible understandings of childhood, and therefore of public provision. What has become clearer for us since then is the distinction between two of the many possible ways of understanding public provision: 'children's services' and 'children's spaces'.

This has led us to question a certain way of understanding childhood, reflected in images of the child, ways of talking about children and a construction of the 'children's services' we provide for them. These foreground:

a child who is weak, needy and poor, dependent and privatised; redemption and futurity; atomisation and compartmentalisation; instrumentality and control; limited and specialised purposes; universal laws and criteria; predetermined goals and predictable outcomes; surveillance and normalisation; and a logical positivist approach to evaluation. Children and their childhoods are brought ever more under the adult gaze for adult purposes. There is a will to know, manage and master children. The rationale is a belief in new and effective technologies, providing buttons to push which will deliver solutions that work – interventions that this time will lead, via our children's futures, to the promised land. All this is the legacy of high modernity, with its particular assumptions and hopes, beliefs and values.

With 'children's spaces' we have offered another way of constructing public provision – constructing not in the sense of bricks and mortar (although built environments are themselves symbolic, both representing and reproducing social constructions of children), but in the sense of thinking differently about provision, with a different purpose and ethos, different relationships and practices. This construction foregrounds: a child who is competent and rich, a co-constructor of knowledge, identity and culture, a social agent and a citizen with rights, and a member of a social group; the childhood that children are living now; a holistic, rather than an atomised, approach towards the child and the provisions made for children; the importance of a rich network of relationships (with other children and adults) and of an ethical concept of relationships which respects the alterity of the Other; and public provision for children being sites for ethical and democratic practice. It is a construction that opens up the prospect of many possibilities and experiences. It values participants, children and adults, who can live at ease with not knowing and not controlling events and each other, and who can be open to what is new, surprising and unsettling.

It may be inevitable that in seeking to set out our thesis we have made the distinctions more clear-cut than they need to be. In practice many provisions for children may have elements of both 'children's services' and 'children's spaces'. However by offering extremes we have, hopefully, suggested that there are different ways of thinking about public provisions for children; and that if there is to be a balance or mix, then what that is should be a contestable issue. Public provision for children is not, and can never be, simply a technical subject whose main concern is efficient delivery of a commodity. Evaluation – judgements of value – is important: but before providing a referential framework for these judgements come critical questions concerning meaning and purpose, the good life, justice, democracy, power and relationships, all of which are inescapably ethical and political.

We have also suggested that these two approaches to, or ways of understanding, public provisions will have implications in terms of ethics, practices, relationships and workers. For example, we have suggested that a broad theory and practice of work with children, with an accompanying professional worker, is called for by the concept of 'children's spaces'. We have put forward one possibility for this theory, practice and worker: pedagogy and the pedagogue.

We said earlier that this book was, for us, work still in progress. In this final chapter, we want to flag up some of the many issues that are unfinished business. However in doing so we do not want to give the impression that we are moving towards closure on the subject of public provisions for children. We do not envisage, nor do we want to see, a consensus or a final solution: for these would mean stagnation of practice and the end of new knowledge. Nor are we putting forward provision that is universally applicable or changes that can be made once and for all, to think so would be to imply that some form of 'perfection' is achievable. Perfection is only available in a hypothetical world (or heaven) where all meanings are fixed, all social players share uniform understandings and values, and the social context never changes. Our alternative discourse proposes a journey of continuing rethinking and provisionality, as new understandings arise in new social circumstances.

The local, the national and the global

We have paid particular attention to one example of public provision for children: the early childhood centres in the Italian city of Reggio Emilia. One reason is that these centres provide examples of 'children's spaces'. Another reason is that this community provides a living example of another theme in our book, the need for a critical approach at all times: sceptical in disposition; eager to cross borders in order to gain different perspectives; searching for critical questions; recognising the importance of exercising judgement and the provisionality of judgements once made; capable of putting a stutter in narratives which are now spoken confidently, as if they were the only account; and ready to ask awkward questions of the clichés that abound. Dominant discourses need to be questioned and challenged, treated respectfully but not reverentially. The workings and effects of power relations, and the truth claims to which they give rise, need making visible, heightening awareness of the politics of knowledge and knowledge construction. For visibility and awareness, if linked to critical thinking, offer a prospect of transgression – thinking differently and being governed less.

The critical approach in Reggio has been described in the following terms:

> [their practice, understanding and perspective] is located in a profound understanding of young children in relation to the world and a philo-sophical perspective which in many respects seems to us postmodern. . . . [S]ome of the elements of that practice, understanding and perspective

[include]: choosing to adopt a social constructionist approach; challenging and deconstructing dominant discourses; realizing the power of these discourses in shaping and governing our thoughts and actions, including the field of early childhood pedagogy; rejecting the prescription of rules, goals, methods and standards, and in so doing risking uncertainty and complexity; having the courage to think for themselves in constructing new discourses and in so doing daring to make the choice of understanding the child as the rich child, a child of infinite capabilities, a child born with a hundred languages; building a new pedagogical project, foregrounding relationships and encounters, dialogue and negotiation, reflection and critical thinking; border-crossing disciplines and perspectives, replacing either/or positions with an and/also openness; and understanding the contextualized and dynamic nature of pedagogical practice, which problematizes the idea of a transferable 'programme'.

(Dahlberg *et al.* 1999: 122)

But Reggio is also important as an example of a local community that has sought, over many years, critical questions about childhood and public provision for children and provisional answers to these questions. Through this continuing political and ethical process, the city has produced local solutions related to local constructions of childhood and embedded in a particular historical, political and social context. The origins of the network of early childhood centres in Reggio lie in the conditions of post-war Italy and a clear appreciation of the political implications of public policy towards children:

We asked what prompted the people of Reggio Emilia to design an early childhood education system founded on the perspective of the child. [Bonacci, Mayor of Reggio in the 1960s] replied that the fascist experience had taught them that people who conformed and obeyed were dangerous, and that in building a new society it was imperative to safeguard and communicate that lesson and nurture and maintain a vision of children who can think and act for themselves.

(Quoted in Dahlberg *et al.* 1999: 12)

Our conceptualisation of 'children's spaces' provides a large framework for thought and practice, within which many possibilities can be defined and configured. It is, we believe, well suited to the idea of developing local solutions, responding not only to local conditions but also to local questions, analyses, values and answers. Nor is Reggio a unique example of local communities seeking to construct public provisions for children that embody local values and ideas: although it may have proceeded further down this road than most other communities.

In the course of preparing this book, we visited a local authority in Scotland that has rethought its organisation and delivery of a range of public provisions for children, and which appeared to be embarked on a process of local evolution: we offer this as yet another example. Stirling covers a large area geographically, although it is the third smallest Scottish authority in terms of population, with 89,000 people. Following local government reorganisation, the new council set up an integrated 'Children's Service', within the education department, to include pre-school, out-of-school and play provisions, and social work for children, young people and families. The team in the current Children's Service is multi-disciplinary, with backgrounds including teaching, social work and sociology, and there is a recognition of the importance of different perspectives. The inclusion of play services was very significant, bringing a very particular perspective and culture into the wider group, and questioning some of the current emphases in public policy. Administrative reorganisations had been related to new thinking across a range of issues, for example, discussion about children had been linked to issues of democracy, citizenship and the desirability of extending a range of provision on the basis of universality.

There was a very strong and explicit engagement with children's participation and rights; despite some gaps there was, it was felt, a 'culture of children's participation' running through the services. In a recent article, the Director of Children's Services emphasises their 'approach based upon children's rights [which] ensures that young people are encouraged to take responsibility for their learning, for their environment and for each other' (Jeyes 1999: 3). Children are viewed as 'active learners and active citizens [whose] views are sought about the quality of services and how they should be delivered' (ibid.: 3).

Two examples were offered to illustrate this 'culture of children's participation'. Local residents had objected to the council about children using a school yard for skateboarding, while in another instance adults said they wanted a 'no ball games' notice installed in a housing estate. Both matters were referred to the play officer in the Children's Service and it was decided that they needed to consult with other people in the community – that is, with children – before coming to a decision. They spoke with children and helped them put their views forward, as a result of which the objecting local residents gave way in both cases. Officers saw this sort of action as moving local discussion on, to enable children to participate and to challenge the perception of them as 'lesser beings'.

A second example concerns outdoor space. The most frequent response of children at a nursery school to being asked what they wanted was more out-of-doors facilities. As a result the council has reallocated budgets to shift resources from indoor to outdoor activities.

The officers involved believe it is important to consult children formally and to keep records of this, rather than listening to children on an informal basis. Children are quite capable of understanding that some of their ideas cannot be put into practice, or certainly not immediately, but have been heard to say that the outcomes of the consultations will be nice for 'the little ones', that is the children who will follow them through their school. The officers also see this formal consultation with children as part of children's education in democracy and citizenship. The work is being further developed in primary schools and in schools councils, but they think it important that children become accustomed to having a voice in matters which affect them from an early age: they need to know how to put their point of view across effectively so it is heard, and how to listen to others. An example was given of a child in a reception class (i.e. the first year of primary schooling) who, when asked to do something which they did not find acceptable, replied 'I'll do a deal with you'. This was a child who had learned, in a nursery school, something about accommodating to other people's wishes, but believed that their own point of view should also inform the situation.

There is also a movement to allow children a much greater say in all sorts of matters within the school. Examples include children who were given a budget for the reordering of school toilets (school toilets can be unpleasant and a place where bullying occurs) and were able to get a much better deal on materials than had been foreseen, they provided carpet in the girls toilets, chose colours that appealed to them and introduced bowls of pot pourri and mirrors. The head teacher believes that they have come a long way in involving the children. Children have grown to expect this and have asked to be involved in the appointment of a new teacher (personal communication, Mairi Breen, Headteacher, Allan's Primary School).

Stirling Children's Service sets out, also, to provide local sites for children's unsupervised play. Play workers have woven willow trees into dens in local parks, which then become a focus for children's play, and therefore spaces for children's culture. Play workers have also transformed local areas into play spaces on a temporary basis. Summer play schemes provide 'loose parts', play materials which children can make use of in their own way. For example, in play schemes based on local estates, play workers provide logs and bales of hay for children to use for their own purposes, and leave them in place when the playscheme is over. A mobile stage makes children's own performances possible on housing estates. The play team likes working with children at night, for example staging night walks; arranging a star laboratory with a planetarium and astronomers; employing story tellers, jugglers and fire-eaters to entertain children gathered around campfires; and they have provided an all night café and held a Halloween procession, including the local graveyard.

All of these examples involve children at a neighbourhood level and transform everyday places into sites for play. They also offer children histories and memories to share in common. They may thus be said to support children's culture, making particular forms of loosely structured children's spaces within their local communities, alongside and interacting with adult culture.

Our whole approach values the idea of a reinvigoration of the local within a global context, part of a process we referred to in Chapter 2 as 'glocalisation'. We can be global – with networks of communication and influence developing between different individuals, groups and communities who share certain interests and values – without being universalistic. Reggio is a very good example of glocalisation through the global network of Reggio-inspired work, in which those who are interested in the theories and practices developed in one locality, Reggio, seek to work with them in their local contexts. So, 'children's spaces' can be linked together not only in a particular community, but also with 'children's spaces' in other communities in other countries and continents.

Where does this leave the relationship between 'children's spaces' and the nation state? This presents more difficulties. A lot depends on the country, its political structure (is it a centralised state or does it have intermediate level regional or state governments?) and the nature of that society's nation state. One reason Reggio has been able to flourish locally is because of a weak Italian nation state and a strong tradition of local political autonomy. Sweden, as we have seen, has moved to increasing decentralisation, opening the way for more diversity and innovation at local level. England, by contrast, has a very centralised national government, which in recent years has increasingly sought to impose control and standardisation over 'children's services'.

Clearly, the local cannot be divorced from a wider national (and, in some cases, state or regional) context. There are also risks attached to reliance on the local, not least diversity slipping into inequality: Italy combines some amazing local experiences with others that are very poor (cf. Putnam 1993 for a study of regional inequalities in Italy). The individual institution and community will remain, for the foreseeable future, part of a larger society, located in a region or state in many cases (for example, in the USA and other federal polities), a nation state in all cases, and increasingly likely to be part of a supra-national entity. The degree of decentralisation will vary but the regional, national and supra-national will all make demands on the local. This requires some conformity to others' demands (made through systems of regulation, inspection, norms and required outputs), although the extent and intensity of the conformity required will vary considerably – and should be an important subject for contestation in any politics of childhood or, indeed, any politics about the future shape of democracy. So 'children's spaces' cannot just exist in isolation: they will need 'to walk on two legs', rather than hop on the leg that represents isolated localism or on the leg of conformity to regional or national requirements.

By the same token, 'children's spaces' cannot be legislated for, since they assume certain ways of thinking, relating and acting. We could say that 'children's services' are prescribable, while 'children's spaces' are not (though just because something is prescribable does not mean that the prescription delivers what it promises: prescriptions may be taken without following the instructions on the label and can produce unanticipated or unavoidable side-effects). Perhaps the state and society can smother the prospect of 'children's spaces': but they cannot will them into being. The best they can offer is to create certain conditions which enable 'children's spaces' to emerge and thrive locally, which we consider further below – and even then, much will be down to local circumstance and initiative. We repeat that 'children's spaces' are a possibility, a way of thinking about provisions with accompanying practices, structures and relationships, that some institutions or some communities, perhaps in a few cases certain societies, may choose to try and realise.

Either way, we are led to conclude that rather than 'children's services' being a vehicle for changing society, it is society that produces and changes provisions for children. Or that, at least, there is a complex interplay between society and its institutions for children which, once again, casts doubt over the redemptive hopes invested by politicians and policy makers in children's services. If we know how to read them, public provisions for children offer narratives about their society, its values and dominant understandings.

A role for national government

One of the problems about advocating or prescribing profound change is that things are the way they are for complex and deep-rooted reasons. Understandings of childhood and constructions of public provisions for children are the product of 'historically constructed ways of reasoning that are the effects of power . . . embodying a range of historically constructed values, priorities, dispositions' (Popkewitz and Brennan 1998: 9). It is one thing to suggest what conditions national government might put in place to promote an understanding of public provision for children as children's spaces, with the ethics, relationships and practices that accompany that understanding. It is quite another thing to suggest why a national government might choose to pursue this goal, if its 'historically constructed ways of reasoning' produce other constructions of childhood and public provisions for children.

But if for the moment we decide to overlook this rather large obstacle, there are a number of conditions that national governments might provide that would favour 'children's spaces'. Many involve structure, some a promotion of reflection, a combination of reorganisation and rethinking that we have argued are complementary.

Some of these measures are explicit in our previous discussion. In particular rethinking and restructuring work with children are of vital importance, along the lines for example of pedagogy and the pedagogue. There are some interesting options here. One is to develop pedagogy as work with children and young people, as well as adults, covering a wide field but excluding teaching and mainstream schooling: pedagogy as parallel to, equal with, but different to, school teaching. This is the direction in which Danish policy might be heading: the training has been described as qualifying graduates to work in many different fields, with people from 0 to 100 (Moss 1999). At issue here is whether the pedagogue might become the main worker with adults as she already is across a wide range of provisions for children and young people.

Another direction, which recent Swedish reforms might point towards, is the development of a single profession for work with children and young people. Such a profession might incorporate school teachers, as well as work with groups of children in other settings. This scenario, of course, presumes considerable specialisation within a single profession.

Another measure for government, also raised by Swedish experience, is the enhancement of entitlements for all children to use public provisions. Sweden indeed is in the process of gradual change – from entitlement to access to many non-school provisions (e.g. pre-schools and free-time centres) being linked to parents' labour market participation (i.e. parents are entitled to a place for their children if they are employed), to access being available to all children, irrespective of their parents' employment. This is clearly at odds with more exclusionary notions of access, for example in Britain, 'childcare for working parents' which embodies ideas about provision being first and foremost for parents rather than their children, or 'day care for children in need', which assumes access to services to be temporary and contingent on parental incapacity.

Considerations of entitlement, as well as taking a holistic approach both to children and the possibilities of provision, have implications for funding. In Britain, increasing government attention to 'children's services' has been matched by an increasing movement towards piecemeal funding, in which provisions for children increasingly depend on a plethora of short-term, targeted and small-scale funds, many of which require applications and some competitive bidding: for example, it has been estimated that in 2001 there were forty-five different sources of funding for 'childcare services' alone (Daycare Trust 2001). This 'contract model of resource allocation' is intended to ensure central control and standardisation of approach (Gewirtz 2000). But it also reflects and reproduces an atomised understanding of children and the public provisions made for them: different funding streams are attached to different predetermined goals and particular agendas. It also makes access for children uncertain and/or selective. Funding should not be seen as a reward to managers who can write successful applications in response to particular items on particular agendas of particular departments, but as a means of fulfilling the needs of the local community on behalf of its children.

Centralised control of 'children's services' is also linked, in practice, to particular approaches to evaluation, such as those outlined in Chapter 3. National government can move away from, or limit, such standardised measuring in favour of encouraging local forms of evaluation, linked to the development of local questions and solutions, more along the lines of evaluation discussed in Chapter 6. It is important, we think, to reconnect citizens to the making of judgements of value about the provisions that they or their children use, rather than offering them abstract and decontextualised measurements which take the purposes, values and practices of provisions for granted.

Another possible measure, for government at regional/state and/or national levels, would be to bring together responsibility for public provisions for children into one governmental department. Such responsibility could cover a wide range of provision, for children from birth upwards, from more formal settings such as schools to more informal spaces such as playgrounds and other play facilities. It might also represent children's interests in social spaces which currently fall under the remit of other departments, spaces often shared by children and adults, such as home zones, museums, libraries, parks and swimming pools. More generally, this department might be given a clear and comprehensive remit for children and childhood, including government responsibility for the implementation of the UN Convention.

Some restructuring has already begun in some countries. Early childhood services and 'free-time' services have been brought together with schools within Departments or Ministries of Education in both England and, as we saw in Chapter 8, Sweden. This represents a major shift of responsibility for policy, provision and practice from welfare to education. It leaves the former with a limited remit, mainly for preventive and protection work with a small proportion of children, and the latter with a much expanded remit diluting (in theory if not necessarily in practice) the previous prominence of schools.

Since devolution in 1998, but building on work undertaken previously, Scotland has gone even further. The Scottish Executive's Education Department has been reorganised to include two main policy groups: the School Group (for compulsory education) and a Children and Young People's Group.[12] This latter group 'has a remit to promote effective co-ordination and integration of policies and resources affecting children and young people . . . this reflects a crucially important principle: that what happens to young people in school and outside school is related and interdependent' (Stewart 1999: 2).

However, administrative reform should not just be a matter of shuffling the pieces around on the board, the end result being the transfer of more responsibilities into an expanded Department for Education. To be worthwhile, such departments need to change in many respects, to reflect and support a rethinking of public policy. Otherwise it may easily become a case of just more of the same, with the accompanying danger of ever increasing dominance by one type of public provision – the school – and one type of tradition and culture – school-based education (for a fuller discussion of the dangers inherent in the centrality of the school as the dominant public institution of childhood, see Moss *et al.* 1999). What is needed, in effect, is a change to a pedagogic perspective which would affect how an expanded and diversified department understood itself and was understood by others, and expressed its broader remit with childhood, including but not only learning.

In suggesting this, we realise that we are raising as many questions as we answer. If there is a department with a remit for childhood, what part of life does 'childhood' cover? Would the responsibility of the department also extend to 'young people'? And if so, what part of life does this cover? Where would this leave learning for adults, indeed the whole concept of 'lifelong learning'? Would a 'Department for Childhood, Youth and (Lifelong) Learning' be too diffuse? Might it turn older people away from learning by its association with childhood and youth?

How far should the responsibilities of this new department spread? As we have just noted, both Sweden and England have retained social work with children and families, as well as responsibility for the UN Convention, within the social welfare system, the responsibility of a Ministry for Social Affairs in Sweden and a Department of Health in England, while, at national level, Scotland has gone even further in the range of provisions it has brought together. In many other European countries, social work with children is already framed within pedagogy, and the principal workers concerned are often pedagogues.

We think there is a case for incorporating other collective provisions for children into a re-formed department, including play, as well as social work with children and families. We believe it would be mutually beneficial to all concerned (children, practitioners, parents, policy makers, politicians) to locate social work within a broader children-oriented setting. We recognise that this move might raise concerns about the group of children currently served by social welfare being neglected and badly served in a department concerned with all children. However, this is a risk wherever responsibility is located. The English Department of Health, for example, recognises that this has happened within the social welfare regime: 'there is ample evidence . . . that standards of delivery and achievement are unreliable and that though many children benefit from social services, too many are let down' (Department of Health 1998: para. 3.2). Above all, it seems to us unacceptable to hive off this minority of children into a separate adult-dominated sphere, on the basis of a rationale which treats these children as 'poor' and deficient and in need of 'social care' along with a large number of adults.

However, even with a reconfigured and renamed department, some policy areas of import for children would be left outside. The Scottish

Executive Education Department, for example, recognises that 'it will need to forge close working links with other parts of the Scottish Executive – with health including community care, housing, criminal justice, social inclusion, sport and the arts' (Stewart 1999: 2). In addition, and most importantly, there are those areas of government concerned with benefits, taxation and labour market rights and regulation that need a powerful player to remind them of children's interests.

We see the establishment of an Ombudsman for Children (which has already occurred in a number of countries) as another part of restructuring government for children and childhood. We support the proposals made by the Gulbenkian Foundation (Hodgkin and Newell 1996) that the four key functions of the Office of Ombudsman should be to:

- influence law, policy and practice, both by responding to others proposals and by actively proposing change;
- review children's access to, and the effectiveness of, all forms of advocacy and complaints systems (including the courts) and where appropriate initiate or support legal actions on behalf of children;
- conduct investigations and undertake or encourage research; and
- promote awareness of rights among children and adults.

One reason for supporting a second national agency focusing on children and childhood (i.e. in addition to a government department) is the need to find strategies that address the power issues discussed earlier. A Children's Rights Commissioner can be an important alternative focus (but not the only one) of critical thinking about childhood, able to question, confront and challenge 'regimes of truth', whether from government, professions, managers or others, as well as raise issues if s/he feels they are not receiving sufficient government interest. A democratic society needs to encourage and nurture such loci of dissensus, able to frame and ask critical questions.

These reforms at national level would need to be paralleled by administrative change locally, with the establishment of local departments concerned with children, young people and learning, covering a similar range of functions as national departments. As we saw in the previous chapter, this process has begun to happen in Sweden, where local authorities preceded national government in bringing together pre-school, school and free-time services. It has also taken place in Norway, where reform at national level is yet to happen. Some Norwegian local authorities have gone further than Sweden, incorporating other services including social work, as too has happened in parts of Britain where 'the search for a seamless service ... has led [some] local authorities to merge social services departments with housing, education and even arts and leisure' (Inman 2000: 108).

Interesting and important as such local examples of reorganisation are, we do not want attention to structure to obscure what, for us, is the main issue: the potential for local and diverse action (at or below the level of a local authority, commune or municipality). Will more integrated local structures provide more fertile soil for the growth of innovative and distinctive ideas and practices, emerging from local questions, analyses, debates, experiments and answers, in short a vibrant local politics of childhood? Will they provide a milieux more likely to provoke new thinking and knowledge and stimulate a critical approach to dominant discourses?

A final measure that national government could lead on, or at least play an important role, is perhaps the hardest to bring off; yet, it is also perhaps the most important, since other conditions are to a considerable extent contingent on this condition. We are talking about the need for a society – government, media, private organisations, academic institutions and so on – to be willing and able to open up childhood to critical enquiry and public discussion, recognising its diversity and contestability. Like the Swedish example mentioned in Chapter 8, the traditions and understandings of different disciplines, professions, departments and policy fields should be subject to analysis and critique, the better to see the values, images, constructions and discourses that permeate them. In this way, childhood could be moved from the vulgar pragmatism of solely technocratic and instrumental discourses to the critical pragmatism which involves epistemological, ethical and aesthetic choices as part of a political discourse. The child and childhood would no longer be so difficult to find in public pronouncements, and questions such as 'what is our image of the child?' might appear alongside, or even precede 'what works?'

But these explorations and discussions of childhood need to be located within a wider analysis of the world and how it is changing. We also need to know about the everyday lives of children, how these may be changing and why, and children's views and understandings about their lives. An interesting example of such work was the BASUN Project undertaken in the late 1980s across the Nordic countries, funded by the Nordic Council. This project was an exploration of 'Modern Childhood in the Nordic Countries'.

> We started to analyse the relationship between early childhood institutions and work in industrial society and what consequences the change from an industrial society to a post-industrial information and knowledge society – a learning society – had for these institutions, both in relation to new risks, but also new possibilities for learning and meaning making, freedom and democracy. The [BASUN] Project began to open up discussion about what these societal changes might mean for the child's possibilities to handle life in a postmodern society and for the child's construction of his or her identity and biography, problematizing the idea of the child's identity as fixed.
>
> (Dahlberg *et al.* 1999: 127)

As this quotation shows, the BASUN Project researchers located Nordic childhood within an understanding that these countries were becoming post-industrial and postmodern societies. Other themes of the study were the increasing institutionalisation of children, how they managed growing up in very different environments (home and institution), and the democratisation of family relations.

Last but not least, the research was undertaken with children, for example with 5-year-olds interviewed about their daily lives, these children being understood as 'experts in their own lives' (Langsted 1994: 35). An increasing body of work, stimulated in part by the emerging field of childhood studies, is building on this research approach, providing children's perspectives on the world in which they live and their experience of childhood, including very young children (cf. Petrie *et al.* 2000; Clark and Moss 2001; Kinney 2001; Poulsgaard 2001). These perspectives call on us, adults, to question the highly instrumental adult perspective of 'children's services', seeing them instead as complex sites of social practices and relationships, and including projects (such as children's culture) that derive from children themselves.

Diversifying 'children's space'

We have discussed the more general aspects of public policy towards children, and suggested a theory and practice of working with children and a 'new' workforce with distinct characteristics, because we think that these would support a children's spaces approach, rather than the children's services approach we have today. We have used 'children's spaces' to convey a richer set of meanings over and above the territorial, designating especially those public social spaces shared by children, and by adults and children, which have been brought into being through the action of public policy. We have indicated that many types of provision have the potential to become 'children's spaces' – from lightly structured spaces for children's outdoor, unsupervised play on the other hand to highly structured institutions of schooling. Particular attention needs paying to both extremes.

Schools are a major challenge to the concept of 'children's spaces'. They are present everywhere, their use is virtually universal, large resources are invested in them, they are culturally important and they have well established traditions which embody particular understandings of the child. Moreover, there are indications that, in some countries at least, schools are becoming more powerful and central, not only because of increased government emphasis on the importance of school-based education, but because of moves to link schools to other public provisions for children, including the incorporation of these provisions into schools.

The USA has seen a new and unprecedented wave of school–community initiatives over the last ten to fifteen years, and there is a widespread development of school-linked health and human services programmes: 'schools have become the location of choice for collaborative programs' (Wang *et al.* 1998: 3). These programmes come with various titles, including school-linked services, community schools, extended-services schools or full-service schools (Moss *et al.* 1999). Britain, too, has examples of similar reorganisation, often involving the bringing together of various services on to one school or other site, sometimes combined with new forms of management (e.g. Scotland's New Community Schools: for further details see the New Community Schools website at www.scotland.gov.uk/education/ newcommunityschools). We have also reported on the whole day school of the *barnskola* in Sweden, which brings together school and free-time centre.

We feel some ambivalence about these developments. One of our initial criticisms of 'children's services' (Moss and Petrie 1997) was that they were too often 'uni-functional', citing in particular the unrealised potential of the school which 'has been too little recognised and even less exploited'. We can still see some force in these arguments, and that schools could provide a wider range of possibilities accessible to all children. But we can also see considerable risks.

The centripetal force of the school may draw other provisions and institutions into its orbit making it the centre of a system of children's services. With schools that operate themselves as 'children's services', this may undermine the possibility of other provisions linked to schools constituting themselves as 'children's spaces'. The end result could then be the ever-growing imperium of the school and of a narrow, highly instrumental concept of education.

To allay these reservations, and reduce these risks, requires a number of challenging measures. As in Sweden, closer links between schools and other provisions should involve a critical assessment of the traditions and culture of all provisions and of all the groups which work in these provisions: rather than a take-over by the strongest partner, closer links should involve all parties rethinking and seeking to create something new. What seems lacking so far, at least in Britain, has been an accompanying rethinking so that reorganisation leads to changed understandings, practices and relationships. Because the public policy role for schools is, at present, to deliver agendas linking mainly to future employment and the related classification of children by test and examination results, the whole child and the interests of children in the here and now cannot find a place. In this situation, other services may readily find themselves adopting the school agenda.

Rethinking requires an envisioning of what a school as 'children's space' might be like. With such a vision available, schools themselves need to be supported to become 'children's spaces'. This raises many difficult issues. How to establish a theory and practice of learning compatible with the idea of 'children's space', such as we discussed in Chapter 6? Can schools become spaces for cooperative learning, children's culture and children's voices? How to define the relationship between school teaching and the

school teacher and pedagogy and the pedagogue? Can schools give prominence to the relationship between child and society? It would be important,
in any case, to maintain a wide range of non-school-based provisions, offering the possibility of different theories and practices, and able to question
dominant discourses and institutions.

What seems to be called for is a decentring of the school, which can
then be viewed as one part of a diverse network of provisions for children,
connected by shared pedagogical frameworks. Because of its history and
universal coverage, the school will always have a particularly important
place: but that does not mean it should have a privileged and dominant
place in relation to other provisions. While not rejecting ideas of more
'multi-functional school-based' provisions, there is a real tension here,
which needs recognition and action but for which we think there is no
ready solution.

As well as exploring ways in which schools and other established
'services' can become 'children's spaces', attention needs to be given to
supporting and promoting other types of space. Some we have already
mentioned, such as adventure playgrounds. But there is scope for many
innovations, in particular making far more use of outdoor environments to
support outdoor play and play provisions. Here we are envisaging more
physical spaces for children, but recognising that physical spaces are also
social spaces – the location of social practices and relationships – and can
be discursive spaces also.

Expanding physical space for children leads into a thorny issue for local
and central government to grasp: policy towards traffic. By default, the
ever increasing use of private transport has played a large part in shaping
childhood. No one has questioned its effects until unaccompanied children
have almost disappeared from public places. Nothing illustrates more
clearly the inferior position of children as a group in our society. We have
arrived at today's childhood without discussion and with an almost un-
questioned obeisance to the car. In England, fear of traffic is put forward
again and again as a reason why unsupervised children should not use
public spaces (e.g. Hillman *et al.* 1990; O'Brien *et al.* 2000; Petrie *et al.*
2000). Recent studies have found, for example, that, over time, there has
been a reduction in the number of children saying that they go to school
unaccompanied by an adult – from 94 per cent of 11-year-olds in 1970, to
54 per cent in 1990 (Hillman *et al.* 1990) to 47 per cent in 1998 (O'Brien
et al. 2000). Also children are more frequently ferried to school by car
than was once the case, thus increasing the perceived danger of the streets.
The car seems to have an ambiguous place in parental understandings.
On the one hand, cars are a source of danger, on the other they are a safe
private place, an extension of home and the private family, insulating
children from the perils of the street – but also from a more public dimension of social life – including a potential setting for children's culture. As it
becomes normative for children to be denied the use of public space, the

more the 'good' parent, internalising these controlling values, is reluctant to allow children to be out and about, unsupervised. While the means of social control over children is fairly evident, here, the control over parents' time and activities should not go without comment. Parents are coming to see being a good parent as being one who manages not only children's schooling, but also – sometimes resentfully – their leisure pursuits (Petrie *et al.* 2000: 159). The car's high status as an item of consumption, relating to privacy and individualism, finds an identifiable place within advanced liberalism and 'political government which will govern without governing "society"' (Rose 1999: xxiii). It does so by appealing to parents' perception of what is involved in caring for their children's safety. At the same time, it limits the possibilities for children to use outdoor space.

The desire to play out-of-doors is a recurring motif in research and consultation with children (O'Brien *et al.* 2000; Petrie *et al.* 2000). There is a growing number of examples of 'children's spaces' which offer children more opportunities to be out-of-doors, both in urban areas (where there is an issue of reclaiming 'children's spaces' from adult traffic through, for example, the introduction of home zones) and in the countryside. Children are entitled to play opportunities and association with people of their own choosing under the United Nations Convention, but it is for adults to promote and support these rights.

The part and the whole

There are a number of tensions, even contradictions, in our discourse which might be said to reflect wider dilemmas emerging at a period of change, in particular the relationship between the individual and others and between singularity and wholeness. We have proposed the need for greater structural coherence and unity, for example through a new 'integrated' profession for working with children. Such greater coherence and unity can bring new benefits and possibilities. But they also carry risks, not least the risk of producing more powerful technologies of control with increasing capacities to regulate and discipline the child – a bigger, better and more comprehensive technology. This sense of tension also underlay our ambivalence about closer links between schools and other provisions for children.

We have talked about pedagogy as offering the possibility of working with the whole child, yet that notion has been the subject of critique. In the context of problematising the 'idea of totality', Dahlberg also questions

> the idea of the whole child, a child which is defined through homogeneous and coherent identities and fixed in time and space. In relation to Levinas' thinking the child must be seen as a decentred child who is changeable and with multiple identities.

(Dahlberg 2001: 7)

Others see the 'whole child' approach, as currently advocated in much early childhood education along with 'developmentally appropriate practice' (itself critiqued as part of a technology of normalisation), as an example of the workings of power which enable the child, and her soul, to be governed more:

> The thrust of whole child education is that the child's entire being – desire, attitudes, wishes – is caught up in the educative process. Educating the whole child means not only the cognitive, affective and behavioural aspects, but the child's innermost desires. . . . No aspect of the child must be left uneducated: education touches the spirit, the soul, motivation, wishes, desires, dispositions and attitudes of the child to be educated.
>
> (Fendler 2001: 121)

Fendler, and also Hultqvist (2001) and Popkewitz and Bloch (2001), further suggest that the 'constructionist' ethos can be read not as emancipatory but as introducing new technologies of governing, to produce a new child suited to the needs of new forms of capitalism, for example the need for flexible workers ready and able to adapt themselves to the ever changing requirements of the market.

> The term 'flexibility' has recently been used to describe desirable traits, not only in education but also in business and politics. Analyses of developments in these fields and others have shown that current social circumstances call for 'flexible' and 'fluid' ways of being. These terms rightly pertain to a shift away from the rigidly defined social roles characteristic of modernity, such as the assembly-line positions in a Fordist factory. . . . Flexibility is vaunted as the cutting-edge solution to the challenges of productivity in a fast-moving global economy and the goals and objectives of education reinscribe flexibility through curricular and pedagogical practices.
>
> (Fendler 2001: 119)

Viewed in this way, social constructionism is just another instance of how the self disciplines the self to be the subject desired by liberal economic and political regimes.

The flexible child, continuously constructing not only knowledge but identity, organising both her inner and outer worlds, may also be the individualistic child, detached from any solidaristic relationships. She is independent and self-sufficient, the autonomous subject able to manage her own risks without depending on others. The fluid state of self-realisation militates against any sustained group commitments: self-achievement supercedes class struggle.

These, and similar critiques, are important. They recognise risks inherent in much of what we have argued. To say there are risks in everything is true, but hardly convincing: 'two wrongs don't make a right'. What they point to is the importance of a continuously critical approach to theories and practices, and the development of children's spaces as explicitly ethical and political sites. The 'co' in 'co-constructing' is also important, speaking as it does of the relationships and inter-dependencies with others in processes of knowledge and identity creation.

Further, these critiques also emphasise the importance of pedagogical work that both works with diversity and otherness, while also striving to develop new forms of solidarity – between children, between adults and between adults and children. Pedagogy should cross borders, relating to work that is under way in other fields which attempts to recast ideas of solidarity so that they may encompass cultural and other differences. Fraser (1997), for example, has been seeking an integrative approach between 'the politics of redistribution', which often attempts to remove group difference in the cause of economic justice, and 'the politics of recognition', which tends to promote group differentiation in the cause of cultural justice. Sevenhuijsen, in her discussion of the ethics of care, also distinguishes between different understandings of solidarity. One is based on rationalistic arguments, which can easily take the form of calculating, monologic forms of solidarity ('I have the right to something from you, you have the right of something from me'). This mode of reasoning presumes a norm of sameness.

> It encourages a solidarity of giving and taking, and points to an ethics dominated by mutual exchange. We provide care not because it is needed, but because one day we can expect to get something in return when we are in the same situation. The feminist ethics of care points to forms of solidarity in which there is room for difference and in which we find out what people in particular situations need in order for them to live with dignity. Solidarity without care leads to an impoverished sense of morality and collective responsibility, because it can only recognise others if they are exactly 'like us' or needy, pathetic, pitiful and worthy of 'our' commiseration. . . . This 'caring solidarity' offers more potential for understanding the diversity of needs and lifestyles than a solidarity which takes for granted the norms of homogeneity and a 'standard' human subject.
>
> (Sevenhuijsen 1999a: 147–148)

Uncertainty, crisis and opportunity

From our viewpoint, Reggio provides living witness to how the creation of a crisis in thinking and a struggle over meaning can produce opportunities, opening up the possibility of viewing children, early childhood institutions and early childhood pedagogy in new ways – the child and the pedagogue as co-constructor of knowledge and identity, the early childhood institution as a forum in civil society and early childhood pedagogy as one of the main projects of that public space with the purpose of enabling children to have the courage to think and act for themselves.

(Dahlberg *et al.* 1999: 123)

We have offered another possible understanding of public provision for children, which is produced from within a particular mindset, which as we said in Chapter 2 comes with different 'post-' labels attached. This mindset doubts the possibility of disengagement and objectivity, recognises many types of reason and struggles against dualism and atomisation; it presumes that complexity, plurality and the need for interpretation are not problems to be ironed out but opportunities to be relished; it recognises that we must learn to live with ambiguity and uncertainty, with the need to make ethical and political judgements, and with the necessity of taking responsibility for those judgements.

For this reason we have felt encouraged to go beyond our own modernist inclinations to end this book with firm conclusions, and instead to admit our own ambiguity and uncertainty. The last five years of work have been a process of moving away from wanting to offer solutions – a transformation manual, universal in application, primarily structural and technical in form – towards wanting to explore possibilities, make connections across many borders, return to finding good questions. This leaves part of us feeling uneasy. Is this not very indulgent, a case of fiddling while Rome burns? All around we see and hear urgent problems: millions of children in poverty, rampant inequalities, widespread educational underachievement, children subjected to abuse and neglect, the list seems endless. Shouldn't we, as researchers in the field of childhood, be devoting our energies to improve the ability of children's services to reduce or eradicate such problems?

To which one answer is that we do. As researchers we have done, and continue to do, our fair share of so-called 'policy-relevant' research (so-called because 'policy-relevant' research has become synonymous with research that supports the implementation of a particular policy, rather than research which contributes to thinking and discussion about different policy possibilities). Moreover, as we have repeatedly said, we do not turn our backs on everything that already exists. There may, for instance, be some predetermined outcomes that 'children's spaces' have to address, there may be a place for some performance indicators.

We believe, too, that there is a continuing important role for public policy. Public provision as 'children's spaces', staffed with well-paid pedagogues, assumes substantial public funding – almost certainly substantially higher than at present – and other forms of government support. Reducing poverty and inequality – both in our view high priority objectives of public policy – require government to adopt strong redistributive and regulatory roles.

But having said that, the discourse of 'children's services' has left both of us over the years feeling increasingly uneasy. Having done years of cross-national work, we have been provided with many lenses for looking at our own country, making the familiar irreversibly strange. Doing 'policy-relevant' research for government while at the same time engaging with other discourses about children, including ideas about the social construction of childhood, has left us feeling fragmented, leading double lives, unable to find connections. After decades of neglect, we have welcomed the high policy priority given since 1997 in Britain to provisions for children, both of school age and below: yet at the same time we feel concerned by the lack of thought, the extreme instrumentality, and the values that have accompanied these changes. We wonder if too much responsibility is being loaded on to children's services to cure social problems, the origins of which are complex and not fully understood; and if too many hopes are pinned on children's services to deliver children to a future which is uncertain and contestable. Despite a rhetoric of diversity and choice, in practice policy and the resultant provisions and practices are, as we have tried to show, very uniform: eggs are being packed into one basket. A concern for delivery and outcomes leaves little time or space for thinking differently – or much thinking of any kind. A concern for standardisation and regulation is not conducive to the exploration of different approaches, both in theory and practice.

At the very least, it seems to us important to widen and diversify – not only thinking, but also practice. We need more Reggios – not copies, but similar examples of dissensus, local communities of children and adults creating new thinking and new practices, local work that explores local narratives, and in so doing provides provocations and creates new knowledge and possibilities.

Such examples can contribute, like Reggio, to a crisis of thinking and a struggle over meaning. The crisis arises because of the struggle: if the meaning of childhood can no longer be taken for granted then this throws everything into question. And behind this particular crisis lies the more general crisis of thinking arising from the condition of modernity and the onset of a period of paradigmatic transition – 'the idea that the paradigm of modernity has exhausted all its possibilities of renovation and that its continuing prevalence as the dominant paradigm is due to historical inertia' (Sousa Santos 1995: ix). Rather than determining 'best practice' or knowing what works, this crisis confronts us with many possibilities of viewing children, institutions for children, work with children and the people who do that work – in short an opportunity to engage with important pedagogical issues. It requires of us thought and deliberation, the making of ethical choices and taking responsibility for those choices.

Because modernity abhors complexity and uncertainty, 'crisis' is a worry-ing word. Crises need to be cleared up quickly. But viewed from another perspective, crisis – as questioning the taken for granted, putting a stutter into powerful narratives, creating confusion and uncertainty, making people think twice – is a hopeful word. It opens up for emancipation from dominant discourse, for new ways of viewing children, early childhood institutions and early childhood pedagogy, for new possibilities. Our hope is that this book contributes something to a 'crisis of thinking' about children, childhood and public provision for children.

Notes

1 Since one of our purposes is to question the concept and term 'children's services' and to offer an alternative concept and term, 'children's spaces', we face a dilemma as authors: how to refer to the field that we want to contest – environments provided through the agency of public policy for groups of children – without using a term which already carries certain meanings and values. We have settled on the term 'public provisions for children', although we recognise that in practice there can be no neutral terminology, and that 'public provisions for children' could be deconstructed in the same way as 'children's services'.

2 Reggio Emilia is a city in northern Italy with a population of about 150,000. Over the last thirty years, the local authority has developed a network of eighteen *nidi* (nurseries for children under 3 years) and twenty-one *scuole dell'infanzia* (nursery schools for 3- to 6-year-olds), providing for 2,700 children, mostly operated by the local authority, but some run by co-operatives and supported by the local authority. Reggio has become world famous for this network of early childhood institutions. Tens of thousands have visited the town, the Reggio exhibition has been seen all over the world, and there are groups working with inspiration from Reggio in many countries. The reason for this impact is the pedagogical work undertaken in these municipal early childhood institutions (for a fuller discussion of Reggio and its pedagogical work, see Edwards *et al.* 1998; and Dahlberg *et al.* 1999).

3 Where we write 'Britain' or 'British' we have done so deliberately, in cases where our discussion refers beyond England, to include also Scotland and Wales.

4 By the term 'Anglo-American' we refer to that part of the world where English is the main language and Britain the initial coloniser: in addition to Britain, this includes Australia, Canada, New Zealand and the USA. There are, of course, considerable differences between these countries, but they also share common perspectives on a range of issues.

5 The term 'governing the soul' refers to 'aspects of humanity that were previously sacrosanct [such as desire, fear and pleasure] but that have recently been constructed as objects of psychological and regulatory apparatuses. The term soul deliberately alludes to what have been the innermost qualities of being human (and has been used) to emphasize the depth to which modern technologies of discipline have extended' (Fendler 2001: 123).

6 Sousa Santos (1995) argues that the model of scientific rationality in modern science is going through a profound and irreversible crisis, due in part to a scientific revolution that began with Einstein and quantum physics.

7 A second Labour administration was returned to power in Britain in June 2001, and in November 2001 it published two documents on children, through a recently established Children and Young Persons Unit (CYPU): 'Core Principles

for the Involvement of Children and Young People' and 'Building a Strategy for Children and Young People'. These documents appeared too late to be considered in this book, the manuscript for which had already gone to the publishers. Readers of this book may find both documents (available on the CYPU website at www.cypu.gov.uk) of interest in relation to our discussion of a dominant discourse about children in Britain; and of how that discourse, as an assemblage of ideas and actions, may take in and use new concepts and practices, without changing its basic rationality.

8 We draw here on research into homework in six European countries (Petrie 2000).

9 Home Zones is a widespread movement in the Netherlands (which has 6,500), Denmark and Germany, where they have been around for twenty-five years (Biddulph 2001). Not only does traffic calming and other measures (for example, siting bollards to restrict car parking and giving priority to pedestrians and cyclists) make the streets safer places for children (and others), but they convert streets into informal social space. In the UK the city of Leeds has pioneered this work and it is promoted by the Children's Play Council: in August 1999, the Government announced a pilot programme of nine Home Zones in England and Wales, while other local authorities have proposals in the pipeline. Home Zones are not seen as only for children, nevertheless they are certainly social spaces for children and for children's culture. They tackle the power of traffic to control children's activity and to withdraw them from the general community.

10 Pat Petrie is currently researching social pedagogy and its part in children's residential establishments in five European countries and many of the understandings on which this chapter draws arise out of this work.

11 Parental leave is available for sixteen months, the first thirteen months of which are paid at 80 per cent of earnings; use of this provision is high, and although most leave is taken by mothers, over 50 per cent of fathers now take some leave, averaging about eight weeks (for further details see Moss and Deven, 2001).

12 The Children and Young People's Group includes three divisions: Early Education and Childcare, covering pre-school education and childcare for children up to 14 years of age; Young People and Looked-after Children, which is responsible for adoption, fostering, residential and secure care, and youth justice; and Children and Families, which covers child protection, family support and ensuring that policies across the Scottish Executive take account of children's views. This new group sits alongside the Schools Group, both coming under a Minister for Education and Young People.

Bibliography

Alexander, R. (2000) *Culture and Pedagogy: International Comparisons in Primary Education*. Oxford: Blackwell.

Atkinson, D. and Elliott, L. (1998) 'Anxious? Insecure? You'll get used to it', *The Guardian*, 6 June.

Baker, B. (1998) ' "Childhood" in the emergence and spread of the US public school', in T. Popkewitz and M. Breenan (eds) *Foucault's Challenge: Discourse, Knowledge and Power in Education*. New York: Teachers' College Press.

Ball, S. (1994) *Education Reform: A Critical and Poststructural Approach*, Buckingham: Open University Press.

Bartley, K. (1998) Barnpolitik och barnets rattigheter Avhandling vid Gotebourgs universitet, Institutionen for sociology.

Bauman, Z. (1991) *Modernity and Ambivalence*. Cambridge: Polity Press.

Bauman, Z. (1993) *Postmodern Ethics*. Oxford: Blackwell.

Bauman, Z. (1995) *Life in Fragments*. Cambridge: Polity Press.

Bauman, Z. (1999) *In Search of Politics*. Cambridge: Polity Press.

Beck, U. (1998) *Democracy Without Enemies*. Cambridge: Polity Press.

Beck, U. (2000) *What Is Globalisation?* Cambridge: Polity Press.

Bennett, J. (2001) 'Goals and curricula in early childhood', in S. Kamerman (ed.) *Early Childhood and Care: International Perspectives*. New York: Institute for Child and Family Welfare, Columbia University.

Bentley, T. (1999) *Learning Beyond the Classroom: Education for a Changing World*. London: Routledge.

Berger, P. and Luckman, T. (1966) *The Social Construction of Reality*. New York: Doubleday.

Biddulph, M. (2001) *Home Zones: A Planning and Design Handbook*. Bristol: Policy Press.

Boyle, D. (2001) *The Tyranny of Numbers: Why Counting Can't Make Us Happy*. London: HarperCollins.

Bradshaw, J. (2001) 'Introduction', in J. Bradshaw (ed.) *Poverty: The Outcome for Children*. London: Economic and Social Research Council/Family Policy Studies Centre.

Bruer, J. (1999) *The Myth of the First Three Years: A New Understanding of Early Brain Development*. New York: The Free Press.

Bunting, M. (2001) 'When voters aren't happy', *The Guardian*, 15 January.

Burman, E. (1994) *Deconstructing Developmental Psychology*. London: Routledge.

Burman, E. (2001) 'Beyond the baby and the bathwater: postdualistic developmental psychologies for diverse childhoods', *European Early Childhood Education Research Journal*, 9(1), 5–22.

Cameron, C., Moss, P. and Owen, C. (1999) *Men in the Nursery: Gender and Caring Work*. London: Paul Chapman Publishing.

Cannella, G. S. (1997) *Deconstructing Early Childhood Education: Social Justice and Revolution*. New York: Peter Lang.

Cherryholmes, C. H. (1988) *Power and Criticism: Post-structural Investigations in Education*. New York: Teachers' College Press.

Clark, A. and Moss, P. (2001) *Listening to Young Children: The Mosaic Approach*. London: National Children's Bureau.

Clarke, J. (1998) 'Thriving on chaos? Managerialisation and the welfare state', in J. Carter (ed.) *Postmodernity and the Fragmentation of Welfare*. London: Routledge.

Corsaro, W. (1999) *The Sociology of Childhood*, California: Pine Forge Press.

Corsaro, W. (1999) Keynote speech given at the Ninth EECERA Conference on Quality in Early Childhood, 1–4 September, Helsinki.

Corsaro, W. (2000) 'Early childhood education, children's peer culture and the future of childhood', *European Early Childhood Education Research Journal* 8(2), 89–102.

Coward, R. (2000) 'Risk and freedom in a Norwegian playspace', in *Reared in Captivity: Papers of the Fourth PLAYLINK/Portsmouth City Council Play Conference*. London: PLAYLINK.

Critchley, S. (1999) *Ethos, Politics, Subjectivity*. London: Verso.

Crouch, C. (2001) *Coping with Post-democracy*. London: Fabian Society.

Dahlberg, G. (1997) 'Barnet och pedagogen som medkonstruktorer av kultur och kunskap' (The child and the pedagogue as co-constructors of culture and knowledge'), in *Roster om den svenska barnomsorgen. SoS-rapport 1997: 23 (Voices about Swedish Childcare. SoS Report 1997: 23)*. Stockholm: Socialstyrelsen (National Board of Health and Social Welfare).

Dahlberg, G. (2000) 'Everything is a beginning and everything is dangerous: some reflections on the Reggio Emilia experience', in H. Penn (ed.) *Early Childhood Services: Theory, Policy and Practice*. Buckingham: Open University Press.

Dahlberg, G. (2001) 'We are responsible for the other: reflections on early childhood pedagogy as an ethical practice', unpublished paper.

Dahlberg, G. and Lenz Taguchi, H. (1994) *Förskola och skola – om två skilda traditioner och om visionem om en mötesplats (Pre-school and School – Two Different Traditions and a Vision of a Meeting Place)*. Stockholm: HLS Förlag.

Dahlberg, G., Moss, P. and Pence, A. (1999) *Beyond Quality in Early Childhood Education and Care: Postmodern Perspectives*. London: Falmer Books.

Daycare Trust (2001) 'Call for children's centres', *Childcare Now*, issue 15 (Summer 2001), 3.

Deacon, A. (2000) 'CAVA and the moral reordering of welfare under "New Labour"', paper presented at Workshop 3, ESRC Research Group on 'Care, Values and the Future of Welfare', University of Leeds, 11 February 2000, available at www.leeds.ac.uk/cava/

Deleuze, G. (1992) 'Postscript on the societies of control', *October*, 59, 3–7.

Department for Education and Employment (1998a) *Meeting the Childcare Challenge*. London: DfEE.

Department for Education and Employment (1998b) *Homework: Guidelines for Primary and Secondary Schools*. London: DfEE.

Department for Education and Employment (1999) *Extending Opportunity: A National Framework for Study Support*. London: DfEE.

Department for Education and Employment (2001) *Schools: Building on Success* (Cm 5050). London: The Stationery Office.

Department of Social Security (2000) *Opportunity for All: One Year On, Making a Difference* (Cmnd 4865). London: Stationery Office.

Derrida, J. (1996) 'Remarks on deconstruction and pragmatism', in C. Mouffe (ed.), *Deconstruction and Pragmatism*. London: Routledge.

Deven, F., Inglis, S., Moss, P. and Petrie, P. (1996) *State of the Art Review on Reconciliation of Work and Family Responsibilities and Quality in Care Services* (DfEE Research Report No. 57). London: DfEE.

Dewey, J. (1897) 'My pedagogic creed', *The School Journal*, LIV(3) (16 January) 77–80.

Donzelot, J. (1979) *The Policing of Families: Welfare versus the State*. London: Hutchinson.

Dréano, G. (2000) *Guide de l'éducation spécialisée*. Paris: Dunod.

Edwards, G., Gandini, L. and Forman, G. (eds) (1998, 2nd edition) *The Hundred Languages of Childhood*. Norwood, NJ: Ablex.

Encyclopaedia Britannica (1911), Vol. 21. Cambridge: Cambridge University Press.

Eurostat (2001) *The Social Situation in the European Union 2001*. Luxembourg: Office for the Official Publications of the European Communities.

Fendler, L. (1998 'What is it impossible to think? A genealogy of the educated subject', in T. Popkewitz and M. Breenan (eds), *Foucault's Challenge: Discourse, Knowledge and Power in Education*. New York: Teachers' College Press.

Fendler, L. (2001) 'Educating flexible souls', in K. Hultqvist and G. Dahlberg (eds), *Governing the Child in the New Millennium*. London: RoutledgeFalmer.

Fielding, M. (2001) 'Taking education really seriously', in M. Fielding (ed.), *Taking Education Really Seriously: Four Years' Hard Labour*. London: RoutledgeFalmer.

Filippini, T. (1998) Answer given at National Children's Bureau Conference. Nottingham, July 1998.

Fink, D. (2001) 'The two solitudes: policy makers and policy implementers', in M. Fielding (ed.), *Taking Education Really Seriously: Four Years' Hard Labour*. London: RoutledgeFalmer.

Foerster, H. von (1991) 'Through the eyes of the other', in F. Steier (ed.), *Research and Reflexivity*. London: Sage.

Flising, B. (1995) *Samverkan skola – skolbarnsomsorg. SoS-rapport 1995: 12* (*Cooperation school – school-age childcare, SoS report 1995: 12*). Stockholm: Socialstyrelsen (National Board of Health and Social Welfare).

Flising, L. (1999) The extended role of the school in Sweden, unpublished report commissioned by Thomas Coram Research Unit, Institute of Education, University of London.

Foucault, M. (1980) *Power/Knowledge: Selected Interviews and Other Writings, 1972–1977* (C. Gordon, ed.). London: Harvester Wheatsheaf.

Foucault, M. (1988) *Politics, Philosophy, Culture: Interviews and Other Writings, 1977–1984* (L. Kritzman, ed.). London: Routledge.

Fraser, N. (1997) *Justice Interruptus*. New York: Routledge.

Freier, P. (1985, English edn) *Pedagogy of the Oppressed*. Harmondsworth: Penguin.

Furedi, F. (2000b) 'Why are we afraid for our children?', in *Reared in Captivity: Papers of the Fourth PLAYLINK/Portsmouth City Council Play Conference.* London: PLAYLINK.

Gabriel, T. (2000) Social Pedagogy and Looked-after Children in Germany, unpublished report commissioned by Thomas Coram Research Institute, Institute of Education, University of London.

Ginsberg, C. (1989) *Lestrådar, Essäer am Konst, förbjuden kunskap och dold historia (Threads, Essays on Art, Fobidden Knowledge and Hidden History).* Stockholm: Häften för Kritiska studier.

Gore, J. (1993) *The Struggle for Pedagogics: Critical and Feminist Discourses as Regimes of Truth.* New York: Routledge.

Gore, J. (1998) 'Disciplinary bodies: on the continuity of power relations in pedagogy', in T. Popkewitz and M. Breenan (eds), *Foucault's Challenge: Discourse, Knowledge and Power in Education.* New York: Teachers' College Press.

Gray, J. (1995) *Enlightenment's Wake: Politics and Culture at the Close of the Modern Age.* London: Routledge.

Gray, J. (1999) *False Dawn: The Delusions of Global Capitalism.* London: Granta Books.

Gray, J. (2000) *Two Faces of Liberalism.* Cambridge: Polity Press.

Gunnarsson, L., Korpi, B. M. and Nordenstam, U. (1999) Early Childhood Education and Care Policy in Sweden: Background report prepared for the OECD Thematic Review. Stockholm: Regeringskansliet (Swedish Ministry for Education and Science).

Hallam, S. and Cowan, R. (1999) *What Do We Know About Homework?* London: Institute of Education, University of London.

Hatch, J. A. (1995) 'Studying children as a cultural invention: a rationale and a framework', in J. A. Hatch (ed.), *Qualitative Research in Early Childhood Settings.* Westport, CT: Praeger.

Hillman, M., Adams, J. and Whitelegg, J. (1990) *One False Move: A Study of Children's Independent Mobility.* London: Policy Studies Institute.

Hodgkin, R. and Newell, P. (1996) *Effective Government Structures for Children.* London: Gulbenkian Foundation.

Hughes, P. and Macnaughton, G. (2000) 'Consensus, dissensus or community: the Politics of parent involvement in early childhood education', *Contemporary Issues in Early Childhood*, 1(3), 241–257.

Hultqvist, K. (2001) 'Bringing the gods and angels back? A modern pedagogical saga about excess in moderation', in K. Hultqvist and G. Dahlberg (eds), *Governing the Child in the New Millennium.* London: RoutledgeFalmer.

Hultqvist, K. and Dahlberg, G. (2001) 'Governing the child in the new millennium', in K. Hultqvist and G. Dahlberg (eds), *Governing the Child in the New Millennium.* London: RoutledgeFalmer.

Hutton, W. (1995) *The State We're In.* London: Jonathan Cape.

Inman, K. (2000) 'What a mesh', *The Guardian*, 27 September, 107–108.

Jaegar, M. (1997) *Guide du secteur social et medic-social.* Paris: Dunod.

James, A. and Prout, A. (eds) (1997) *Constructing and Deconstructing Childhood: Contemporary Issues in the Sociological Study of Childhood* (2nd edn). London: Falmer Books.

James, A., Jenks, C. and Prout, A. (1998) *Theorizing Childhood.* Cambridge: Polity Press.

Jenks, C. (1982) *The Sociology of Childhood – Essential Readings.* London: Batsford Academic.

Jensen, J. J. (1996) *Men as Workers in Services for Children (A discussion paper for the EC Childcare Network).* Brussels: European Commission Equal Opportunities Unit.

Kagan, J. (1998) *Three Seductive Ideas.* London: Harvard University Press.

Kagan, S., Cohen, N. and Neuman, M. (1996) 'Introduction: the changing context of American early care and education', in S. Kagan and N. Cohen (eds), *Reinventing Early Care and Education: A Vision for a Quality System.* San Francisco: Jossey-Bass.

Kampman, J. (1997) Relations between adults and children, unpublished seminar paper, ENSAC 8th International Conference, Municipality of Trondheim, Department of Education and Social Security, Norway.

Katz, L. (1993) 'What can we learn from Reggio-Emilia', in C. Edwards, L. Gandini and G. Forman (eds), *The Hundred Languages of Children.* Norwood, NJ: Ablex.

King, M. (1997) *A Better World for Children: Explorations in Morality and Authority.* London: Routledge.

Kinney, L. (2000) 'Children as partners: a guide to consulting with very young children and empowering them to participate effectively'. Stirling: Stirling Council Children's Services.

Knowles, C. (1999) 'Cultural perspectives and welfare regimes', in P. Chamberlayne, A. Cooper, R. Freeman and M. Rustin (eds), *Welfare and Culture in Europe: Towards a New Paradigm in Social Policy.* London: Jessica Kingsley.

Kvale, S. (1992) 'Postmodern psychology: a contradiction in terms', in S. Kvale (ed.), *Psychology and Postmodernism.* London: Sage.

Langsted, O. (1994) 'Looking at quality from the child's perspective', in P. Moss and A. Pence (eds), *Valuing Quality in Early Childhood Services: New Approaches to Defining Quality.* London: Paul Chapman Publishing.

Lather, P. (1991) *Getting Smart: Feminist Research and Pedagogy with/in the Postmodern.* London: Sage.

Lorenz, W. (1994) *Social Work in a Changing Europe.* London: Routledge.

Macbeath, J. (1999) 'Preface', in *Extending Opportunity: A National Framework for Study Support.* London: DfEE.

Malaguzzi, L. (1993a) 'For an education based on relationships', *Young Children,* 11/93, 9–13.

Malaguzzi, L. (1993b) 'History, ideas and basic philosophy', in C. Edwards, L. Gandini and G. Forman (eds), *The Hundred Languages of Children.* Norwood, NJ: Ablex.

Martin, G. (2000) 'New Labour's "Rationality and Morality Mistakes" – and Some Alternatives', paper given at Workshop 3, ESRC Research Group on 'Care, Values and the Future of Welfare', University of Leeds, February 2000, available at www.leeds.ac.uk/cava/

Martin, G. (2000) 'New social movements, welfare and social policy: a critical assessment', paper given at Workshop 5, ESRC Research Group on 'Care, Values and the Future of Welfare', University of Leeds, available at www.leeds.ac.uk/cava

Maturana, H. (1991) 'Science and daily life: the ontology of scientific explanations', in F. Steier (ed.), *Research and Reflexivity.* London: Sage.

Mauritsen, F. (1996) Children's Culture, unpublished presentation at European Network for School-age Childcare Conference, Barcelona, 1997.

McKendrick, J. H., Bradford, M. G. and Fielder, A. V. (2000) 'Kidcustomer? Commercialisation of playspace and the commodification of childhood', in *Childhood*, 7(3), 312.

McMurray, J. (1935) *Reason and Emotion*. London: Faber.

Miller, P. and Rose, N. (1993) 'Governing economic life', in M. Gane and T. Johnston (eds), *Foucault's New Domains*. London: Routledge.

Morris, E. and Cooper, Y. (2001) 'Foreword by Ministers', in *Making a Difference for Children and Families*. London: Sure Start Unit.

Morss, J. (1996) *Growing Critical*. London: Routledge.

Mortimore, P. (1999) *Understanding Pedagogy and its Impact on Learning*. London: Paul Chapman Publishing.

Moss, P. (2000) 'Training of early childhood education and care staff', *International Journal of Educational Research*, 33(1), 31–53.

Moss, P. and Deven, F. (eds) (2000) *Parental Leave: Progress or Pitfall?* The Hague and Brussels: NIDI and CBGS.

Moss, P., Dillon, J. and Statham, J. (2000) 'The "child in need" and "the rich child": discourses, constructions and practice', *Critical Social Policy*, 20(2), 233–254.

Moss, P. and Petrie, P. (1997) *Children's Services: Time for a New Approach*. London: Institute of Education University of London.

Moss, P., Petrie, P. and Poland, G. (1999) *Rethinking School: Some International Perspectives*. York: Joseph Rowntree Foundation.

Norwegian Ministry of Children and Family Affairs (Barne – Og Familiedepartementet (BFD)) (1996) *Framework Plan for Day Care Institutions: A Brief Presentation* (English Language Version). Oslo: BFD.

Organisation for Economic Cooperation and Development (1998) *OECD in Figures: Statistics on the Member Countries*. Paris: OECD.

Organisation for Economic Cooperation and Development (1999) OECD Country Note: Early Childhood Education and Care Policy in Sweden, online at www.oecd.org

Organisation for Economic Cooperation and Development (2001) *Starting Strong: Early Childhood and Care*. Paris: OECD.

O'Brien, M., Justin, M. and Greenfield, J. (2000) *Childhood Urban Space and Citizenship: Child-sensitive Urban Regeneration*. London: University of North London.

O'Neill, J. (1994) *The Missing Child in Liberal Theory*. Toronto: University of Toronto Press.

Opie, I. and Opie, P. (1967) *The Lore and Language of Schoolchildren*. Oxford: Oxford University Press.

Owen, C., Cameron, C. and Moss, P. (1998) *Men as Workers in Services for Young Children: Issues of a Mixed Gender Workforce*. London: Institute of Education University of London.

Parton, N. (1998) 'Risk, advanced liberalism and child welfare: the need to recover uncertainty and ambiguity', *British Journal of Social Work*, 28, 5–27.

Petrie, P. (1989) *Communicating with Children and Adults: Interpersonal Skills for Those Who Work With Children and Adults*. London: Edward Arnold.

Petrie, P. (1994a) 'Quality in school-age child care services: an enquiry about values', in P. Moss and A. Pence (eds), *Valuing Quality in Early Childhood Services: New Approaches in Defining Quality*. London: Paul Chapman Publishing.

Petrie, P. (1994b) *Play and Care, Out-of-School*, HMSO: London.

Petrie, P. (2000) Homework in Six European Countries, unpublished report to the European Commission.

Petrie, P., Egharevba, I., Oliver, C. and Poland, G. (2000) *Out-of-School Lives, Out-of-School Services*. London: Stationery Office.

Petrie, P., Storey, P., Thompson, D., Candappa, M. (forthcoming) *Children with Disabilities at the Interface: Cooperative Action Between Public Authorities*. London: Institute of Education, University of London.

Popkewitz, T. (1998) *Struggling for the Soul: The Politics of Schooling and the Construction of the Teacher*. New York: Teachers' College Press.

Popkewitz, T. and Bloch, M. (2001) 'Administering freedom: a history of the present – rescuing the parent to rescue the child for society', in K. Hultqvist and G. Dahlberg (eds), *Governing the Child in the New Millennium*. London: RoutledgeFalmer.

Popkewitz, T. and Brennan, M. (eds) (1998) *Foucault's Challenge*. New York: Teachers' College Press.

Poulsgaard, K. (2001) 'Children's self-determination and contributory influence: examples from Denmark', *Children in Europe*, 1, 13–15.

Power, S. and Gewirtz, S. (2001) 'Reading education action zones', *Journal of Education Policy*, 16(1), 39–51.

Prout, A. (1999) 'Living arrows: children's lives and the limits of parenthood', *The Parenting Forum Newsletter*, 15, 1–2.

Prout, A. (2000) 'Children's participation: control and self-realisation in British late modernity', *Children & Society*, 14, 304–315.

Prout, A. and James, A. (1997) 'A new paradigm for the sociology of childhood', in A. James and A. Prout (eds), *Constructing and Deconstructing Childhood: Contemporary Issues in the Sociological Study of Childhood* (2nd edn). London: Falmer Books.

Putnam, R. (1993) *Making Democracy Work: Civic Traditions in Modern Italy*. Princeton, NJ: Princeton University Press.

Qualifications and Curriculum Authority (QCA) (1999) *Early Learning Goals*. London: QCA/Department for Education and Science.

Qualifications and Curriculum Authority (QCA) (2000) *Curriculum Guidance for the Foundation Stage*. London: QCA/Department for Education and Science.

Rajchman, J. (2000) *The Deleuze Connections*. Cambridge, MA: The MIT Press.

Randall, V. (2001) *The Politics of Child Daycare in Britain*. Oxford: Oxford University Press.

Ransom, J. (1997) *Foucault's Discipline*. Durham, DC: Duke University Press.

Readings, B. (1997) *The University in Ruins*. Cambridge, MA: Harvard University Press.

Riihelä, M. (1997) 'The Finnish and the Nordic Storyride', Paper given at Conference *Visible Children – Invisible Quality*, Helsinki, November.

Rinaldi, C. (1999a) Paper given to a British study tour to Reggio Emilia, April.

Rinaldi, C. (1999b) Paper given at the Conference *Visions and Choices*, Royal National Hotel, London, October.

Rinaldi, C. (2001) 'Documentation and assessment: what is the relationship?', in C. Giudici, C. Rinaldi and M. Krechevsky (eds), *Making Children Visible: Children as Individual and Group Learners*. Cambridge, MA: Harvard Graduate School of Education and Reggio Emilia: Reggio Children.

Rohlink, M. (1997) *Arbetslaget – en källa till inspiration (The work team – a source of inspiration)*, in *Roster om den svenska barnomsorgen. SoS-rapport 1997: 23 (Voices about Swedish childcare. SoS report 1997: 23)*. Stockholm: Socialstyrelsen (National Board of Health and Social Welfare).

Rose, N. (1990) *Governing the Soul: The Shaping of the Private Self*. London: Routledge.

Rose, N. (1996) 'Governing "advanced" liberal democracies', in A. Barry, T. Osborne and N. Rose (eds), *Foucault and Political Reason: Liberalism, Neo-liberalism and Rationalities of Government*. London: UCL Press.

Rose, N. (1999) *Powers of Freedom: Reframing Political Thought*. Cambridge: Cambridge University Press.

Rustin, M. (1999) 'Missing dimensions in the culture of welfare', in P. Chamberlayne, A. Cooper, R. Freeman and M. Rustin (eds), *Welfare and Culture in Europe: Towards a New Paradigm in Social Policy*. London: Jessica Kingsley.

Schofield, J. (2001) 'Swedes skate ahead', *The Guardian* (Online section), 22 March.

Schwandt, T. (1996a) 'Farewell to criteriology', *Qualitative Inquiry*, 2(1), 58–72.

Schwandt, T. (1996b) 'The landscape of values in evaluation: charted terrain and unexplored territory', paper presented to the Annual Meeting of the American Evaluation Society, Atlanta, GA, November.

Scottish Council Foundation (1999) *Children, Families and Learning: A New Agenda for Education*. Edinburgh: Children in Scotland and Scottish Council Foundation.

Seidman, S. (1998) *Contested Knowledge* (2nd edn). Oxford: Blackwell.

Sennett, R. (1998) *The Corrosion of Character: The Personal Consequences of Work in the New Capitalism*. London: Norton.

Sevenhuijsen, S. (1999a) *Citizenship and the Ethics of Care: Feminist Considerations on Justice, Morality and Politics*. London: Norton.

Sevenhuijsen, S. (1999b) *Caring in the Third Way* (Working Paper 12). Leeds: Centre for Research on Family Kinship and Childhood.

SOU 1974: SOU (1974: 53) *Skolans arbetsmiljö (The inner work of school)*.

Sousa Santos, B. de (1995) *Towards a New Common Sense: Law, Science and Politics in the Paradigmatic Transition*. London: Routledge.

Stewart, G. (1999) 'New children and young people's group', *Children in Scotland Newsletter*, 37 (July–August), 1–2.

Sure Start Unit (1999) Keynote Speech by Gordon Brown, Chancellor of the Exchequer, Proceedings of Sure Start Trailblazer Conference, London, 7 July.

Swedish Ministry of Education and Science (1994) *Curriculum for Schools (Lpo-94)*. Stockholm: Swedish Ministry of Education and Science.

Swedish Ministry of Education and Science (1998) *Curriculum for Pre-schools* (English translation of *Läroplan för förskolan, Lpfö-98*). Stockholm: Swedish Ministry of Education and Science.

Swedish Ministry of Education and Science (2000a) *Maximum Fees and Universal Pre-school* (UOO.017, May 2000). Stockholm: Swedish Ministry of Education and Science.

Swedish Ministry of Education and Science (2000b) *A New System of Teacher Education* (UOO.023, August 2000). Stockholm: Swedish Ministry of Education and Science.

Tronto, J. (1993) *Moral Boundaries: A Political Argument for the Ethics of Care*. London: Routledge.

Toulmin, S. (1990) *Cosmopolis: The Hidden Agenda of Modernity*. Chicago: University of Chicago Press.

UNICEF (2000) *A League Table of Child Poverty in Rich Countries* (*Innocenti Report Card, Issue No. 1*). Florence: Innocenti Research Centre (UNICEF).

United Nations Development Programme (1999) *Human Development Report 1999*. Oxford: Oxford University Press.

Walkerdine, V. (1984) 'Developmental psychology and the child-centred pedagogy: the insertion of Piaget into early education', in J. Henriques, W. Holloway, C. Urwin, C. Venn and V. Walkerdine, *Changing the Subject: Psychology, Social Regulation and Subjectivity*. London: Methuen.

Wang, M. C., Haertel, G. D. and Walberg, H. J. (1998) *The Effectiveness of Collaborative School-linked Services*. Internet web site: www.temple.edu/LSS: Laboratory for Student Success.

Ward, C. (1978) *The Child in the City*. London: Architectural Press Ltd.

Whitty, G. (1997) *Social Theory and Education Policy: The Legacy of Karl Mannheim, Karl Mannheim Memorial Lecture*. London: Institute of Education, University of London.

Wragg, T. (ed.) (1993) *Education: A Different Version. An Alternative White Paper*. London: Institute for Public Policy Research, p. 13.

Wyness, M. (1999) *Contesting Childhood*. London: Falmer.

Young, R. (1990) *White Mythologies: Writing History and the West*. London: Routledge.

Index